EMERGING 2016

The Eighth International Conference on Emerging Networks and Systems Intelligence

October 9 - 13, 2016

Venice, Italy

EMERGING 2016 Editors

William Hurst, Liverpool John Moores University, UK

Fosso Wamba Samuel, University of Toulouse - Toulouse, France

Huang Jen-Fa, National Cheng Kung University -Tainan, Taiwan

Wen-Piao Lin, Chang Gung University -Taoyuan, Taiwan

Printed from e-media with permission by:

Curran Associates, Inc.
57 Morehouse Lane
Red Hook, NY 12571

Some format issues inherent in the e-media version may also appear in this print version.

Printed by Curran Associates, Inc. (2016)

International Academy, Research, and Industry Association (IARIA)
412 Derby Way
Wilmington, DE 19810

Phone: (408) 893-6407
Fax: (408) 527-6351

petre@iaria.org

Additional copies of this publication are available from:

Curran Associates, Inc.
57 Morehouse Lane
Red Hook, NY 12571 USA
Phone: 845-758-0400
Fax: 845-758-2633
Email: curran@proceedings.com
Web: www.proceedings.com

TABLE OF CONTENTS

EMERGING 1 / ONARP I: OPTICAL NETWORKS ACCESSING, ROUTING, AND POSITIONING

Photonic True Time-Delay Beam Steering for Radars 1
Wen Piao Lin, Yu-Fang Hsu

An Integrated Radio-over-fiber and Passive-optical-network for Bidirectional Photonic Accesses 6
Chiu Wei-Hung, Tsai Wen-Shing, Chen Yi-Lin, Lu Hai-Han

Lightwave Robot Positioning based on Composite Codes Acquisition and Evolutionary Computations 11
Chun-Chieh Liu, Jhe-Ren Cheng, Jen-Fa Huang

EMERGING 2 / BDA-CS: BIG DATA ANALYTICS IN CRITICAL SYSTEMS

Micro-CI: A Critical Systems Testbed for Cyber-Security Research 17
William Hurst, Nathan Shone, Qi Shi, Behnam Bazli

A Cyber-Support System for Distributed Infrastructures 23
Sahar Badri, Paul Fergus, William Hurst

Impact of Topology on Service Availability in a Smart Grid Advanced Metering Infrastructure 29
Bashar Alohali, Kashif Kifayat, Qi Shi, William Hurst

Smart Monitoring: An Intelligent System to Facilitate Health Care across an Ageing Population 34
Carl Chalmers, William Hurst, Michael MacKay, Paul Fergus

EMERGING 3: INTELLIGENT SERVICES

Recommendation Method to Make Combined Video from Video Segments 40
YunKyung Park, KyungDuk Moon, Jungtaek Kim, Seungjin Choi

The Study on Effective Management of Cyber Incidents in Graph Database 42
Seulgi Lee, Hyeisun Cho, Byungik Kim, Taejin Lee

Dynamic QoS on SIP Sessions Using OpenFlow 45
Jérémy Pagé, Charles Hubain, Jean-Michel Dricot

Machine Learning Techniques for Mobile Application Event Analysis 50
Ben Falchuk, Shoshana Loeb, Chris Mesterharm, Euthimios Panagos

EMERGING 4: ENERGY

Development of an Energy Performance Assessment System for Existing Buildings 56
Youn-Kwae Jeong, Jong-Won Kim, Tae-Hyung Kim, Jong-Woo Choi, Hong-Soon Nam, Il-Woo Lee

Economic Impact Analysis of Energy Conservation Measures for Building Remodeling 59
Hong-Soon Nam, Jin-Tae Kim, Tae-Hyung Kim, Youn-Kwae Jeong, Ii-Woo Lee

Development of Distributed Simulation Environment for Security-Critical Technological Objects by Means of Microservices (Case Study for Underground Mine Ventilation) 63
Alexey Cheptsov

EMERGING 5 / BIBA I: BIG DATA AND BUSINESS ANALYTICS

How is Big Data Transforming Operations Models in the Automotive Industry: A Preliminary Investigation 65
Gary Graham, Royston Meriton, Bethany Tew, Patrick Hennelly

Big Data Analytics and Firm Productivity 69
Liang Guo, Mingtao Fu, Ruodan Lu

EMERGING 6 / ONARP II: OPTICAL NETWORKS ACCESSING, ROUTING, AND POSITIONING

Reconfiguring Composite Signature Labels over Optical MPLS Network Codecs to Secure Data Packets Routing 75
Jen-Fa Huang, Kai-Sheng Chen, Ting-Ju Su

Biploar Optical Labeling with Spectral Amplitude Coding Scheme for Packet Switching over GMPLS Network 81
Kai-Sheng Chen,Chao-Ching Yang, Jen-Fa Huang

Design and Development of a Large-scale Network Testbed on a Research and Education Network 85
Chu-Sing Yang, Pang-Wei Tsai, Jen-Fa Huang, Te-Lung Liu

Cooperative Computing for Mobile Platforms 91
Jing Chen, Jian-Hong Liu, Tin-Yen Lin

EMERGING 7 / BIBA II: BIG DATA AND BUSINESS ANALYTICS

Sentiment Analysis using KNIME: A Systematic Literature Review of Big Data Logistics 96
Gary Graham, Royston Meriton

Relative Importance of Key Requirements of Business Analytics 3.0. : An Empirical Study 100
Samuel Fosso Wamba

What is the Feasible Business Model in the Age of Big Data? Case Studies on the Business Models of Two Chinese Mobile Applications 105
Liang Guo, Mingtao Fu, Ruchi Sharma, Lei Yin, Ruodan Lu, Sebastien Tran

Author Index

EMERGING 2016

Forward

The Eighth International Conference on Emerging Networks and Systems Intelligence (EMERGING 2016), held between October 9 and 13, 2016 in Venice, Italy, constituted a stage to present and evaluate the advances in emerging solutions for next-generation architectures, devices, and communications protocols. Particular focus was aimed at optimization, quality, discovery, protection, and user profile requirements supported by special approaches such as network coding, configurable protocols, context-aware optimization, ambient systems, anomaly discovery, and adaptive mechanisms.

Next-generation large distributed networks and systems require substantial reconsideration of exiting 'de facto' approaches and mechanisms to sustain an increasing demand on speed, scale, bandwidth, topology and flow changes, user complex behavior, security threats, and service and user ubiquity. As a result, growing research and industrial forces are focusing on new approaches for advanced communications considering new devices and protocols, advanced discovery mechanisms, and programmability techniques to express, measure and control the service quality, security, environmental and user requirements.

The event was very competitive in its selection process and very well perceived by the international scientific and industrial communities. As such, it has attracted excellent contributions and active participation from all over the world. We were very pleased to receive a large amount of top quality contributions.

The conference had the following tracks:

- Optical Networks Accessing, Routing, and Positioning
- Big Data Analytics in Critical Systems
- Intelligent Services
- Energy
- Big Data and Business Analytics

We take here the opportunity to warmly thank all the members of the EMERGING 2016 technical program committee, as well as the numerous reviewers. The creation of such a high quality conference program would not have been possible without their involvement. We also kindly thank all the authors that dedicated much of their time and effort to contribute to EMERGING 2016. We truly believe that, thanks to all these efforts, the final conference program consisted of top quality contributions.

Also, this event could not have been a reality without the support of many individuals, organizations and sponsors. We also gratefully thank the members of the EMERGING 2016 organizing committee for their help in handling the logistics and for their work that made this professional meeting a success.

We hope EMERGING 2016 was a successful international forum for the exchange of ideas and results between academia and industry and to promote further progress in the field of emerging networks and systems intelligence.

We also hope that Venice, Italy, provided a pleasant environment during the conference and everyone saved some time to enjoy the unique charm of the city.

EMERGING Advisory Committee

Tulin Atmaca, IT/Telecom&Management SudParis, France
Carl James Debono, University of Malta, Malta
Robert Bestak, Czech Technical University in Prague, Czech Republic
Zoubir Mammeri, IRIT - Toulouse, France
Constandinos X. Mavromoustakis, University of Nicosia, Cyprus
Raj Jain, Washington University in St. Louis, USA
Phuoc Tran-Gia, University of Wuerzburg, Germany
António Nogueira, DETI-University of Aveiro/Instituto de Telecomunicações, Portugal
Ioannis Moscholios, University of Peloponnese, Greece
Henrik Karstoft, Aarhus University, Denmark
Jean-Michel Dricot, Université Libre de Bruxelles, Belgium
Anne James, Coventry University, UK
Anna Medve, University of Pannonia, Hungary
Nikolaos Tselikas, University of Peloponnese, Greece
Jelena Zdravkovic, Stockholm University, Sweden
Rolf Drechsler, University of Bremen/DFKI, Germany
Christian Blum, IKERBASQUE - Basque Foundation for Science University of the Basque Country, Spain

EMERGING Industry/Research Chairs

Robert Foster, Edgemount Solutions - Plano, USA
David Carrera, Barcelona Supercomputing Center (BSC) / Universitat Politecnica de Catalunya (UPC), Spain
Preetha Thulasiraman, Naval Postgraduate School - Monterey, USA
Anastasiya Yurchyshyna, University of Geneva, Switzerland
Stephan Hengstler, MeshEye Consulting, USA
Haowei Liu, Intel Corp, USA
Jin Guohua, Advanced Micro Devices - Boxborough, USA
Theodor D. Popescu, National Institute for Research & Development in Informatics - Bucharest, Romania
Patrick Senac, ISAE (Institut Supérieur de l'Aéronautique et de l'Espace) - Toulouse, France
Euthimios (Thimios) Panagos, Applied Communication Sciences, USA

EMERGING Publicity Chairs

Ines Ben Jemaa, INRIA, France
Ken Katsumoto, Osaka University, Japan
Stefan Frey, Hochschule Furtwangen University, Germany
Zhihui Wang, Dalian University of Technology, China
Eric Veith, Wilhelm Büchner Hochschule, Germany

EMERGING 2016

Committee

EMERGING Advisory Committee

Tulin Atmaca, IT/Telecom&Management SudParis, France
Carl James Debono, University of Malta, Malta
Robert Bestak, Czech Technical University in Prague, Czech Republic
Zoubir Mammeri, IRIT - Toulouse, France
Constandinos X. Mavromoustakis, University of Nicosia, Cyprus
Raj Jain, Washington University in St. Louis, USA
Phuoc Tran-Gia, University of Wuerzburg, Germany
António Nogueira, DETI-University of Aveiro/Instituto de Telecomunicações, Portugal
Ioannis Moscholios, University of Peloponnese, Greece
Henrik Karstoft, Aarhus University, Denmark
Jean-Michel Dricot, Université Libre de Bruxelles, Belgium
Anne James, Coventry University, UK
Anna Medve, University of Pannonia, Hungary
Nikolaos Tselikas, University of Peloponnese, Greece
Jelena Zdravkovic, Stockholm University, Sweden
Rolf Drechsler, University of Bremen/DFKI, Germany
Christian Blum, IKERBASQUE - Basque Foundation for Science University of the Basque Country, Spain

EMERGING Industry/Research Chairs

Robert Foster, Edgemount Solutions - Plano, USA
David Carrera, Barcelona Supercomputing Center (BSC) / Universitat Politecnica de Catalunya (UPC), Spain
Preetha Thulasiraman, Naval Postgraduate School - Monterey, USA
Anastasiya Yurchyshyna, University of Geneva, Switzerland
Stephan Hengstler, MeshEye Consulting, USA
Haowei Liu, Intel Corp, USA
Jin Guohua, Advanced Micro Devices - Boxborough, USA
Theodor D. Popescu, National Institute for Research & Development in Informatics - Bucharest, Romania
Patrick Senac, ISAE (Institut Supérieur de l'Aéronautique et de l'Espace) - Toulouse, France
Euthimios (Thimios) Panagos, Applied Communication Sciences, USA

EMERGING Publicity Chairs

Ines Ben Jemaa, INRIA, France
Ken Katsumoto, Osaka University, Japan
Stefan Frey, Hochschule Furtwangen University, Germany
Zhihui Wang, Dalian University of Technology, China
Eric Veith, Wilhelm Büchner Hochschule, Germany

EMERGING 2016 Technical Program Committee

Mohd Helmy Abd Wahab, Universiti Tun Hussein Onn Malaysia, Malaysia
Mouhamed Abdulla, University of Québec, Canada
Rawa Adla, University of Detroit Mercy, USA
Smriti Agrawal, Chaitanya Bharathi Institute of Technology, India
Nizar Al-Holou, University of Detroit Mercy, USA
Adel Al-Jumaily, University of Technology, Australia
Eiman Tamah Al-Shammari, Kuwait University, Kuwait
Cristina Alcaraz, University of Malaga, Spain
Firkhan Ali Bin Hamid Ali, Universiti Tun Hussein Onn Malaysia, Malaysia
Mayada Faris Ghanim Alomary, University of Mosul, Iraq
Mercedes Amor-Pinilla, University of Málaga, Spain
Richard Anthony, University of Greenwich, UK
Eleana Asimakopoulou, University of Derby, UK
Tulin Atmaca, IT/Telecom&Management SudParis, France
M. Ali Aydin, Istanbul University, Turkey
Eduard Babulak, Sungkyunkwan University, South Korea
Susmit Bagchi, Gyeongsang National University, South Korea
Zubair Baig, Edith Cowan University, Australia
Valentina E. Balas, Aurel Vlaicu University of Arad, Romania
Kamel Barkaoui, Cedric-Cnam, France
Nik Bessis, Edgehill University, UK
Robert Bestak, Czech Technical University in Prague, Czech Republic
Christian Blum, IKERBASQUE - Basque Foundation for Science University of the Basque Country, Spain
Indranil Bose, Indian Institute of Management – Calcutta, India
Kechar Bouabdellah, University of Oran 1 Ahmed Benbella, Algeria
Lars Braubach, University *of* Hamburg, Germany
Francesc Burrull i Mestres, Universidad Politecnica de Cartagena (UPCT), Spain
Horia V. Caprita, Continental Automotive Systems, Sibiu, Romania
Chin-Chen Chang, Feng Chia University - Taichung, Taiwan
Chi-Hua Chen, National Chiao Tung University, Taiwan, R.O.C.
Mu-Song Chen, Da-Yeh University, Taiwan
Yuh-Wen Chen (Paul), Da-Yeh University, Taiwan
Dong Ho Cho, Korea Advanced Institute of Science and Technology (KAIST) - Daejeon, Republic of Korea
Deepak Dahiya, Jaypee University of Information Technology, India

Copyright Information

Photonic True Time-Delay Beam Steering for Radars

Wen Piao Lin
Department of Electrical Engineering,
Chang Gung University
Kwei-shan Taoyuan 333, Taiwan, R.O.C.
e-mail: wplin@mail.cgu.edu.tw

Yu-Fang Hsu
Department of Electronic Engineering
Chienkuo Technology University
Changhua 555, Taiwan, R.O.C.
e-mail: yfshi@ctu.edu.tw

Abstract—**In this paper, a photonic true time-delay technique for phased-array beam steering is proposed and analyzed for radar systems. It uses a High-Dispersion Compensation Fiber (HDCF) and a phased array antenna, which can provide a continuous radio-frequency squint-free beam scanning. When the dispersion of the fabricated HDCF is as high as -1020±31 ps/nm/km, the laser wavelength can be tuned from 1549.95 to 1550.2 nm. The experimental results confirmed that the scanning angle of far field radiation patterns for the proposed technique can be tuned from -22^0 to +29^0 at frequencies 5.9, 12.7 and 17 GHz.**

Keywords-optical true time delay;high-dispersive compensation fiber; phased array antenna.

I. INTRODUCTION

Microwave photonics is the research of the mixing between microwave and optical waves for applications, like radars, communications, sensor networks, warfare systems and instrumentation [1]. Optical beam formation for phased array antennas has been intensely studied during the last decade. The development of beam-forming systems with high performance, low weight, high efficiency and low cost is essential. Passive optical devices, such as Photonic Crystal Fibers (PCF) prism, coupled micro-ring resonators, Dispersion Compensating Fibers (DCF) and PCFs, are used in the Optical True Time-Delay (OTTD) techniques [2-5]. Many applications of fiber optics in phased array radars are visualized. Optical control systems [6] allow the use of desirable array functions. The most important of these is true time-delay beam-formation, which is required for wide instantaneous bandwidth and squint-free operation.

The use of optical TTD (True Time –Delay) to control the radiation angle for Phased Array Antennas (PAA) allows frequency independent beam steering, compact size and light weight, large instantaneous bandwidth, low loss and Electro-Magnetic Interference (EMI), which make it a promising choice for broadband PAA [7][8]. PAA's also allow high directional control and rapid beam steering, without the need for physical movement. This antenna allows flexible electronic beam scanning over a wide range of angles, without the need for mechanical rotation of the antenna, and gives convenient spatial characteristics to the beam shaping, by independent control of the transmitting elements.

This study proposes an optical TTD system for a 1×2-element PAA that uses a HDCF module and a wavelength tunable laser. The time delay and the radiation pattern for the proposed system are verified by simulation and experimental measurement.

II. THEORY AND DESIGN

A. Antenna Design

The patch antenna design of microstrip transmission line (W and L) has length of approximately one-half wavelength of the center frequency resonant. The geometry of the 1×2-element array antenna and its size is shown in Fig. 1.

All of the designs are simulated using the software package Ansoft High Frequency Structure Simulator (HFSS), based on a three-dimensional finite element method (3-D FEM). The substrates are a FR4 printed circuit board (PCB) and a RT/duroid 6010 with dielectric constant of 4.4 and 10.2 and height of 1.6 and 0.635 mm, respectively. The length of the single patch antenna is 0.5 λ_g. The distance between the antenna and the antenna is 0.7 λ_{eff}. The λ_{eff} is the effective wavelength, calculated by assuming effective dielectric constant for the substrate of $\varepsilon_{eff} = (\varepsilon_r+1)/2$ [9]. From Fig. 1, it is seen that the sizes of the array antenna are, W_1 = 13.61, 4.43 and 3.2 mm, W_2 = 2.97, 0.59 and 0.59 mm, L_1 = 12.76, 2.48 and 3.46 mm and L_2 = 3.47, 1.26 and 0.84 mm, at 5.9, 12.7 and 17 GHz, respectively.

B. Phase Array Aantenn

An N-element linear array has a uniform amplitude and spacing. In order to operate the overall radiation pattern of the connection elements, we need to control several parameters. These parameters include the N array elements in the array, the distance between two adjacent antenna elements, the orientation of each element for the feed amplitude or phase shift. The array factor is expressed as:

$$AF(\varphi) = \frac{\sin(N_{\varphi}/2)}{N\sin(\varphi/2)} \quad (1)$$

with

$$\varphi = kd\cos\theta + \beta \quad (2)$$

where N is the number of elements, k is the wave number of the radiated signal (k =2π/λ_RF), d is the spacing between two antenna elements, θ is the spatial angle around the axis of orientation of the array and β is the phase shift of the electrical signals that feed the antenna elements.

In order to discard the beam squint and to allow a wide range of frequencies, the beam-forming, with OTTD is used.

Rather than producing a phase shift in the electrical signals that influence the antenna elements, time delay phase shift allows all frequencies to be steered in the same direction [5]. Therefore, the phase shift of the electrical signals must be counted on frequency and can be expressed as:

$$\beta = 2\pi f \Delta t \quad (3)$$

f is the frequency of the electrical signal and Δt is time delay phase shift.

III. EXPERIMENTAL ARCHITECTURE

The chamber is used for antenna pattern measurement. Fig. 2 shows the system level diagram for a TTD beam-former that uses a HDCF (DC-C-N-1020-UW-SC/APC/P) and also shows the major modules of the system. The input radio frequency signal (5.9, 12.7 and 17 GHz) is generated by a Signal Generator (SG) and is proposed to Horn Antenna (HA). The PAA receives signal from the HA and transmit signal through port 2 to the Power Amplifier (PA) and the distance between PAA and HA is from 120 cm to 150 cm. The wavelength of output laser from Tunable Laser Source (TLS) is set from 1549.95 nm to 1550.2 nm. The enhanced signal from the output for PA is injected into the Mach-Zehnder Modulators (MZM) which modulates the output of TLS. The PA is used to ensure enough input RF power to drive MZM in order to overcome the dynamic range and inherently high RF loss in the microwave cables line and receiving RF signal that feed the system.

The modulated optical carrier is then fed into the Erbium-Doped Fiber Amplifier (EDFA), which amplifies the optical signal to avoid optical attenuation through devices. Normally, when the wavelength of TLS increases, the time delay decreases in the HDCF that compensates for the dispersion in the standard Single Mode Fiber (SMF). The optical signals are converted into electrical signals by using 70 GHz pin Photo-Detectors (PD, XPDV3120R). A signal from port 1 of PAA output with -35 dBm to 38 dBm is injected into a power splitter which combine the signal from the PD with -35 dBm to 38 dBm for analysis by a spectrum analyzer and vector network analyzer HP 8510C.

Fig. 3 shows the system level diagram for a comparison between the optical phase group delay and the electrical signals and shows the major modules of the system by using a digital communication analyzer. Fig. 4 shows the PAA system for measurement of main lobe beam forming. Signal from port 1 and port 2 of PAA output with -35 dBm to 38 dBm are injected into a power splitter and measured by a spectrum analyzer and vector network analyzer HP 8510C.

IV. RSULTS AND DISCUSSION

The 1×2-element PAA for simulation and the measurement results for the reflection coefficient characteristic, S11, are shown in Fig. 5. The measured -10 dB return loss bandwidths are from 5.8 to 6, 12.22 to 12.42 and 16.1 to 16.4 GHz (0.2, 0.2 and 0.3 GHz), and there is a 3.4, 1.5 and 1.8 percent bandwidth for the center frequency of 5.9, 12.7 and 17 GHz, respectively. The S-parameter performance is somewhat different to the simulation and measurement results because of the fabrication undercut and improper soldering of connectors. The fabricated antenna was measured in an anechoic chamber and was analyzed using an Agilent E5071C network analyzer.

The simulated and measured radiation patterns for the relative phase are shown in Fig. 6, which shows a main lobe at 0 degrees beam forming at 5.9, 12.7 and 17 GHz. In order to better understand the phase properties of the beam steering, the feed network for the 1× 2-element array is used. The measured phases for the optical turn time delay at 5.9, 12.7 and 17 GHz are shown in Figs. 7(a) and 7(b). The phase from the output of power splitter and the group delay of optical and electric signal are measured as shown in Fig. 7(a). The optical true time delays are approximately 20°, 35° and 40° per 0.1 nm at 5.9, 12.7 and 17 GHz, respectively. As is seen, the optical true time can change from -180° to 180° by purely tuning the wavelength of the TLS to about 0.25 nm as shown in Fig. 7(b). The TLS is the optical carrier with a tunable wavelength of 1549.95 to 1550.02 nm and serves as the optical source for the system.

Fig. 8 shows the simulated and measured array factors for a 1×2-element PAA, using the proposed optical TTD. A comparison of the measured results and the simulation results is shown in Table 1. The range of scanning angles for the far field radiation patterns can be tuned at least from -22° to +29° at fixed frequencies of 5.9, 12.7 and 17 GHz, using proposed OTTD technique. The simulated and measured results are in close agreement. The difference in the measured beam-steering and the simulated angle may be due to optical attenuation through the multiple devices and to RF losses in the microwave cables that feed the array system.

V. CONCLUSIONS AND FUTURE WORKS

The proposed OTTD phased array antenna with wide angle beam-steering is designed for a 1 × 2 array. Without the OTTD system in the feed line, as shown in Fig. 4 , the main lobe is directed along the 0° axis. However, in Fig. 8, when the OTTD system is used in the feed lines, the main lobe will be steering. The beam-peak is steered from 33° to -22°, 30° to -27° and 29° to -25° at PAA frequency of 5.9, 12.7 and 17 GHz, respectively, where the wavelength of TLS is tuned from 1549.95 to 1550.2 nm. It can be seen that the beam-steering angle can be tuned by changing the phase shift of the OTTD.

In the future work, the PAA will be increased the number of elements scaling up 4 in the front-end system. It can be used to reduce the phase adjustment scale and therefore a much more accurate beam steering angle is expected.

ACKNOWLEDGMENT

The authors are grateful for the support of the National Science Council under contract number: NSC 102-2221-E-182-065-MY3, in Taipei, Taiwan. We also take this opportunity to appreciate to High Speed Intelligent Communication (HSIC) Research Center of Chang Gung University, Taoyuan, Taiwan, that provided valuable information and support for the completion of this work.

REFERENCES

[1] J. Yao, J. Yang, and Y. Liu, Continuous true-time delay beam-forming employing a multiwavelength tunable fiber laser source, IEEE Photonics Technol. Lett., vol. 14, pp. 687-689, 2002.

[2] J. Yao, A tutorial on microwave photonics, IEEE Photon. Soc. Newsl., vol. 26, pp. 4-12, 2012.

[3] H. B. Jeon and H. Lee, Photonic true-time delay for phased-array antenna system using dispersion compensating module and a multiwavelength fiber laser, J. of the Opt. Society of Korea, vol. 18, pp. 406-413, 2014.

[4] Y. L. Song, S. Y. Li, X. P. Zheng, H. Y. Zhang, and B. K. Zhou, True time-delay line with high resolution and wide range employing dispersion and optical spectrum processing, Opt. Lett., vol. 38, pp. 3245-3248, 2013.

[5] S. Khan and S. Fathpour, Demonstration of complementary apodized cascaded grating waveguides for tunable optical delay lines, Opt. Lett., vol. 38, pp. 3914-3917, 2013.

[6] K. Takada, H. Aoyagi, and K. Okamoto, Complex-Fourier-transform integrated-optic spatial heterodyne spectrometer using phase shift technique, Electronics Lett., vol. 46, pp. 1620-1621, 2010.

[7] B. M. Jung, J. D. Shin, and B. G. Kim, Optical true time-delay for two-dimensional X-band phased array antennas, IEEE Photon. Technol. Lett., vol. 19, pp. 877-879, 2007.

[8] N. K. Nahar, B. Raines, R. G. Rojas, and B. Strojny, Wideband antenna array beam steering with free-space optical true-time delay engine, IET Microwaves, Antennas & Propag., vol. 5, pp. 740-746, 2011.

[9] C. A. Balanis, Antenna Theory Analysis and Design, Harper & Row, Publishers, 2nd ed., Wiley, New York, 1997.

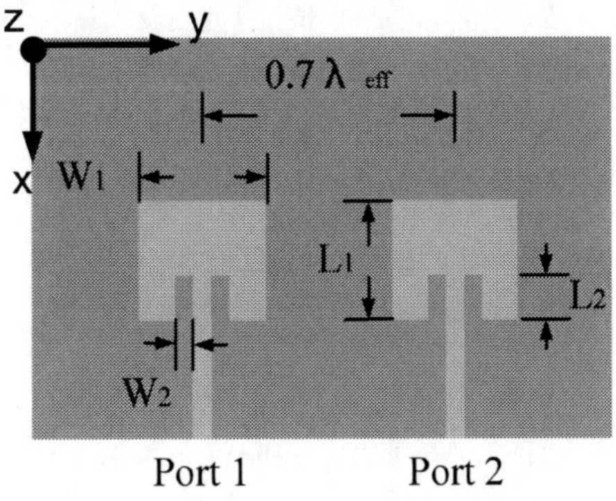

Fig. 1 The geometry of the top view of the planar 1 × 2-element array antenna.

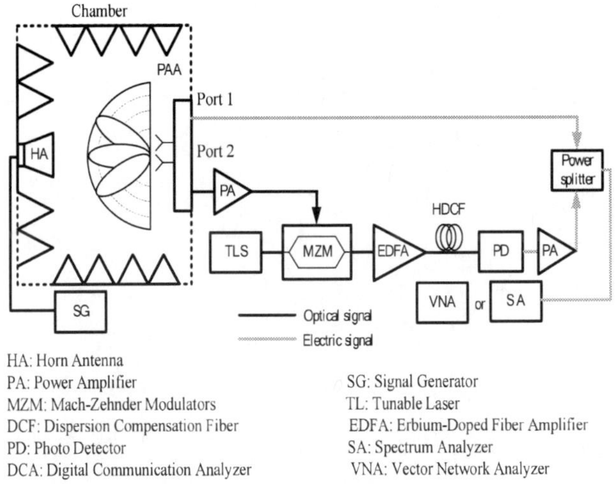

Fig. 2 The proposed OTTD system structure for uniformly spaced 1 × 2-element PAA that use HDCF.

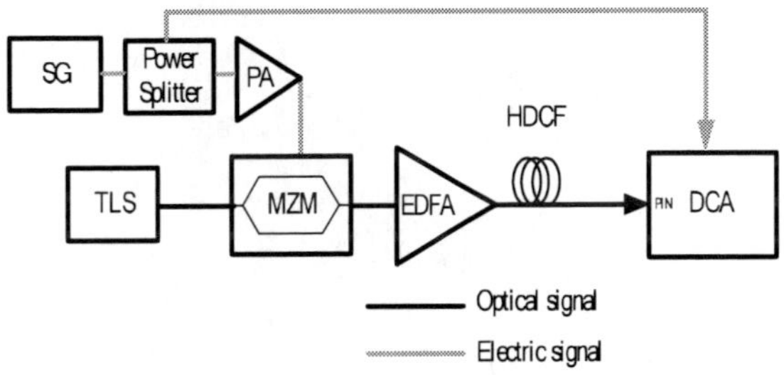

Fig. 3 A comparison of the system level diagrams for the optical phase group delay and the electrical signals.

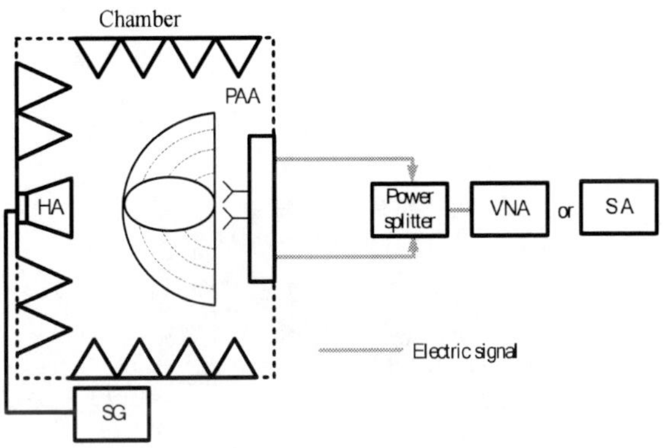

Fig. 4 Measurement of main lobe beam forming.

TABLE I. SIMULATED AND MEASURED RESULTS FOR THE OPTICAL TTD STEERING ARRAYS.

Optical TTD Steered Array	at 5.9 GHz provided 140° and -100°		at 12.7 GHz provided 120° and -90°		at 17 GHz provided 120° and -90°	
	Mea.	Sim.	Mea.	Sim.	Mea.	Sim.
Beam-Steer Angle	33° to -22°	33° to -25°	30° to -27°	32° to -28°	29° to -25°	33° to -29°

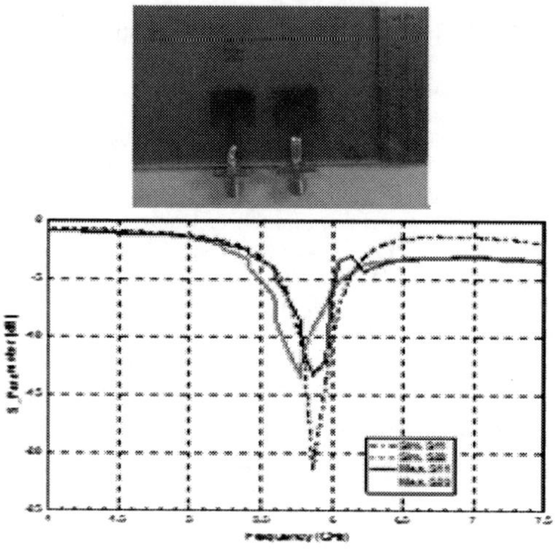

(a)

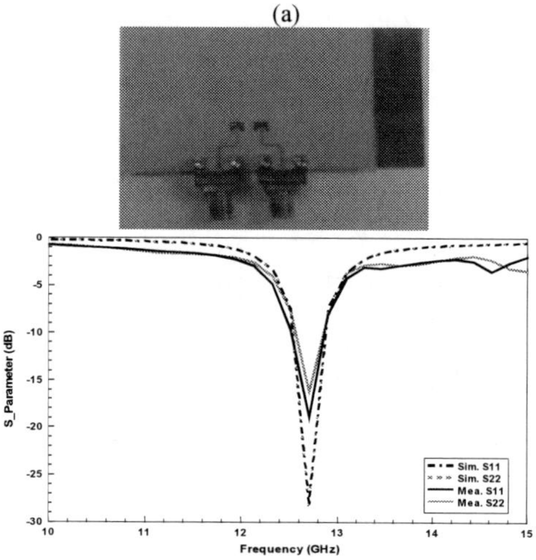

(b)

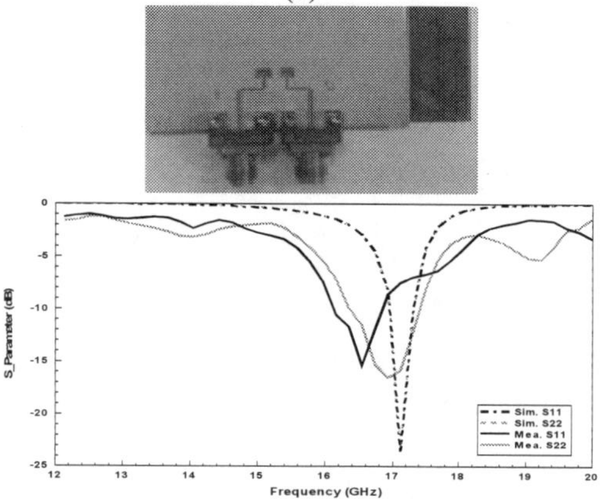

(c)

Fig. 5 A photograph of the fabricated 1 × 2 phased array antenna (Above) and the simulated and measured S-parameters for the antenna (Below) at (a) 5.9, (b) 12.7 and (c) 17 GHz.

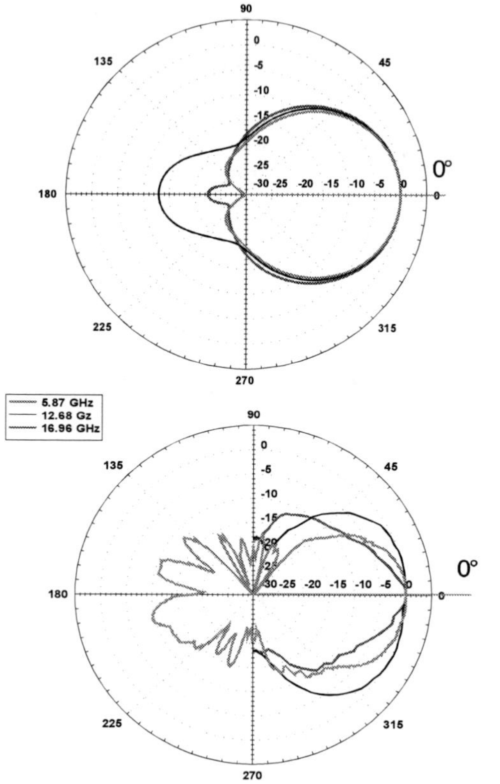

Fig. 6 The normalized gain simulation (Above) and the measured (Below) radiation pattern for the 1×2-element PAA at 5.9, 12.7 and 17 GHz.

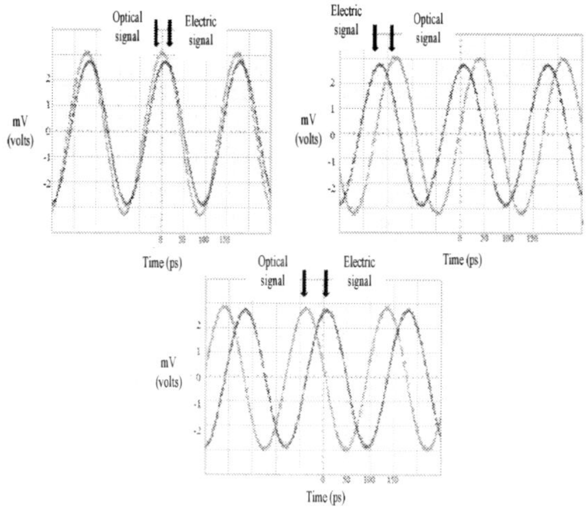

(a)

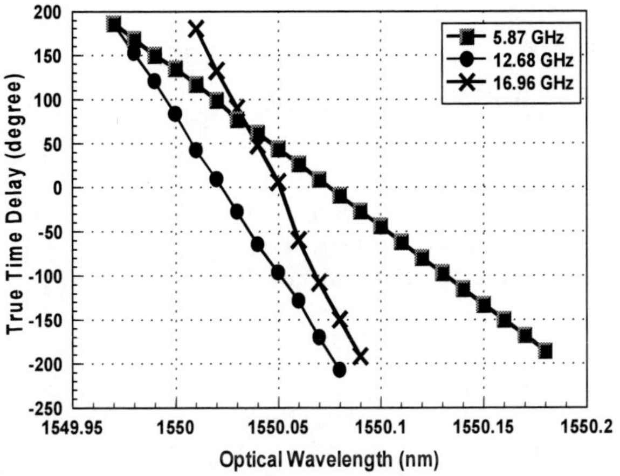

(b)

Fig. 7 The measured phase of the optical true time delay: (a) a comparison of the optical phase group delay and the electrical signals and (b) the optical true time delay per 0.1 nm at 5.9, 12.7 and 17 GHz.

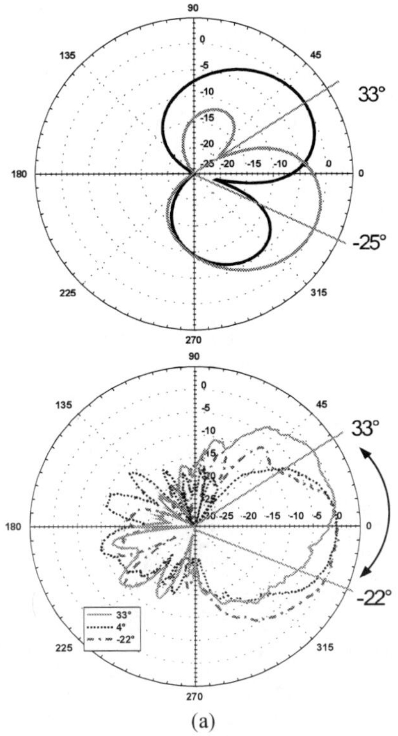

(a)

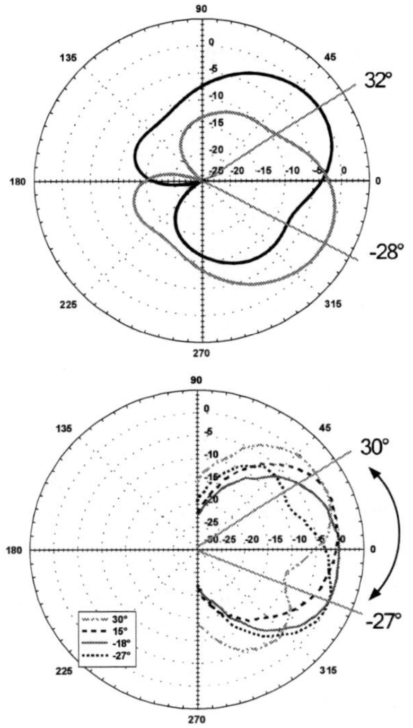

(b)

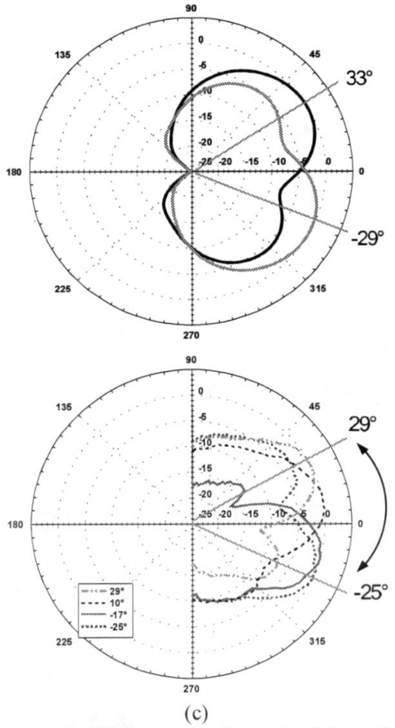

(c)

Fig. 8 The optical TTD normalized gain simulation (Above) and the measured radiation pattern (Below) at (a) 5.9, (b) 12.7 and (c) 17 GHz under a tunable wavelength of TLS from 1549.95 to 1550.02 nm.

An Integrated Radio-over-fiber and Passive-optical-network for Bidirectional Photonic Accesses

Wei-Hung Chiu*[1]
[1]Department of Electrical Engineering
Ming Chi University of Technology
New Taipei City 24301, Taiwan.
*M04128013@mail2.mcut.edu.tw

Wen-Shing Tsai[1]
[1]Department of Electrical Engineering
Ming Chi University of Technology
New Taipei City 24301, Taiwan.
wst@mail.mcut.edu.tw

Yi-Lin Chen[1]
[1]Department of Electrical Engineering
Ming Chi University of Technology
New Taipei City 24301, Taiwan.
M011F8018@mail2.mcut.edu.tw

Hai-Han Lu[2]
[2]Institute of Electro-Optical Engineering
National Taipei University of Technology, Taipei 10608, Taiwan.
hhlu@ntut.edu.tw

***Abstract*—A bidirectional transmission system based on Radio-over-fiber (ROF) and Passive Optical Network (PON) technology is proposed and demonstrated. In this paper, a local oscillator with 15GHz via first Mach-Zehnder modulator (MZM1) and 1.25-Gb/s data via second Mach-Zehnder modulator (MZM2) generate double sideband (DSB) signal. The DSB signal is separated by fiber bragg grating (FBG) into two optical downstream signals. One is the central carrier; the other is the subcarrier, which transports from optical line terminal (OLT) to base station (BS) by 25km single-mode fiber (SMF) transmission. The power penalty of the system is < 0.1 dB(central carrier for downlink and uplink), downlink and uplink transmission of BER values are lower than 10^{-9}.**

Keywords- Double Sideband; Fiber Bragg Grating; Mach-Zehnder modulator; Passive Optical Network; Radio-over Fiber.

I. INTRODUCTION

Radio-over-fiber (ROF) system and Passive-optical-network (PON) have developed rapidly during the past decade. They can be applied to microwave communication systems, such as wavelength division multiplexing (WDM), optical add-drop multiplexing (OADM) and orthogonal frequency-division multiplexing (OFDM) [1]-[3]. The ROF system provides broad bandwidth for users to solve transmission congestion. Optical fiber has lots of advantages in long distance transmission, including high bandwidth, low power loss, and immunity to electromagnetic interference [4]. Rayleigh backscattering (RB) results in power fading, deteriorating system performance and increasing bit error rate because the fiber crystal structure is not uniform in the manufacturing process, shifting the refraction.

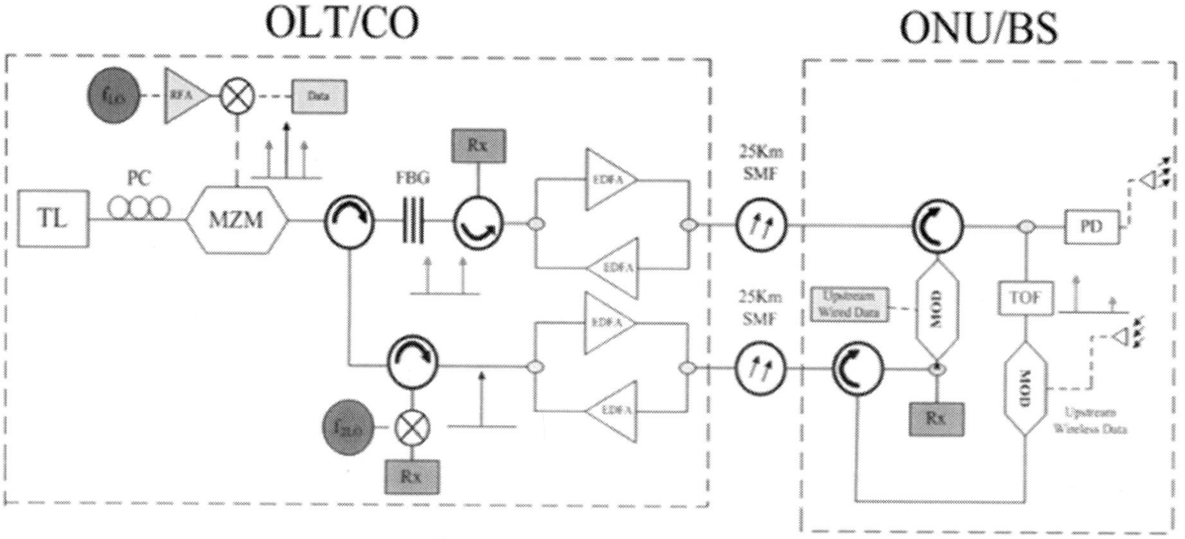

Fig. 1. ROF-PON schematic diagram.

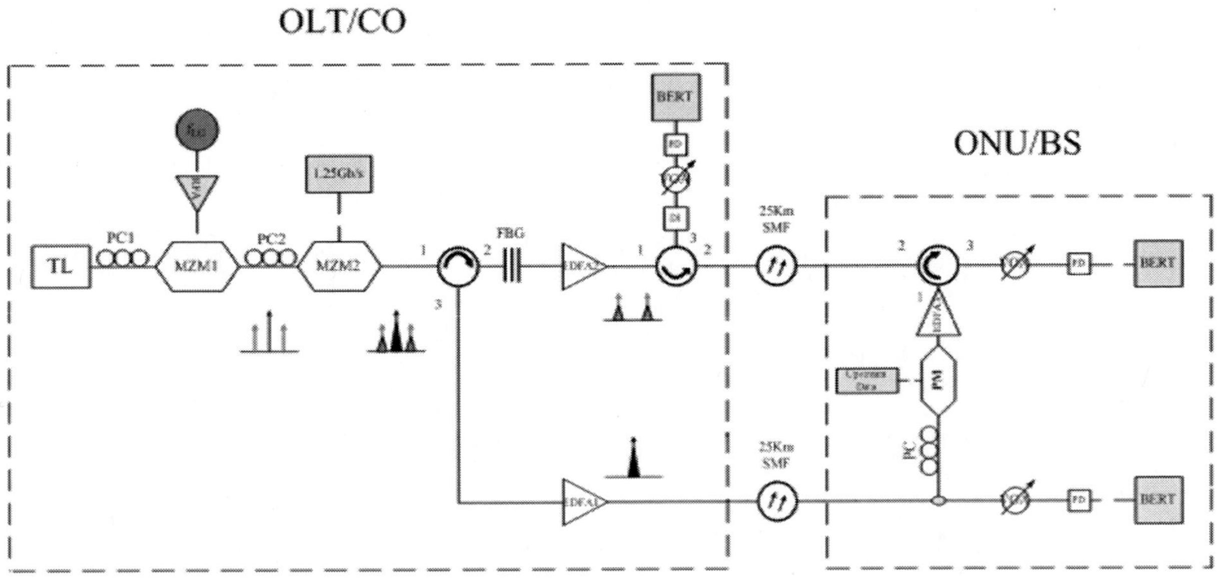

Fig. 2. Experimental setup of bidirectional ROF-PON system.

To solve the RB of power fading, many schemes and demonstrations have been proposed, such as using different path or wavelength between uplink and downlink transmission [5][6]. In this paper, we propose a bidirectional ROF-PON system. The ROF-PON schematic system is shown in Fig. 1, which has only one tunable laser used as an optical source. Part of central carrier is remodulated for upstream transmission, making the structure simple, low cost, and highly flexibility to create different transport structure.

II. EXPERIMENT SETUP

Fig. 2 is the bidirectional ROF-PON system configuration. OLT consists of tunable laser (TL), LO, MZM, polarization controller (PC), FBG, optical circulator (OC), erbium doped fiber amplifier (EDFA), and microwave signal generator. TL is used as an optical source with central wavelength of 1530nm. LO is generated at 15GHz by a microwave signal generator. The MZM1 is driven by an optical source and LO to generate DSB signal. 1.25-Gb/s data and DSB signal are modulated by MZM2 to generate the microwave signal with data.

We use different transmission paths in this system because of the RB. DSB signal is separated by FBG to central carrier and subcarrier as two downstream signals. Each downstream signal is amplified by EDFA via a 25km SMF transmission to base station (BS). BS includes PC, phase modulator, EDFA, OC, variable optical attenuator (VOA), photo-detector (PD), and bit error rate tester (BERT). We use a 10:90 optical coupler to separate the central carrier into two signals. One is used for measuring the BER, the other is reused as upstream light carrier. All of the optical signals are measured by an optical spectrum analyzer (OSA). VOA adjusts the optical signal power. PD transforms the optical signal to an electrical one and measures the BER value. The upstream light carrier uses phase modulator to generate upstream data signal via a 25km SMF transmission. The upstream light signal passes OC and DI to transfer the phase modulated signal into the intensity modulated one. The optical signal goes into receiver to perform O/E convert for BER test.

III. EXPERIMENT RESULT

The wavelength of TL is approximately 1530nm and the optical spectrum is shown in Fig 3. Due to the sensitivity of the MZM affected by polarization, we set a PC before MZM to improve the stability of the MZM. The DSB signal is generated first by MZM, which is presented in Fig. 4. DSB signal with 1.25Gb/s data is generated by the second MZM and the optical spectrum is shown in Fig. 5.

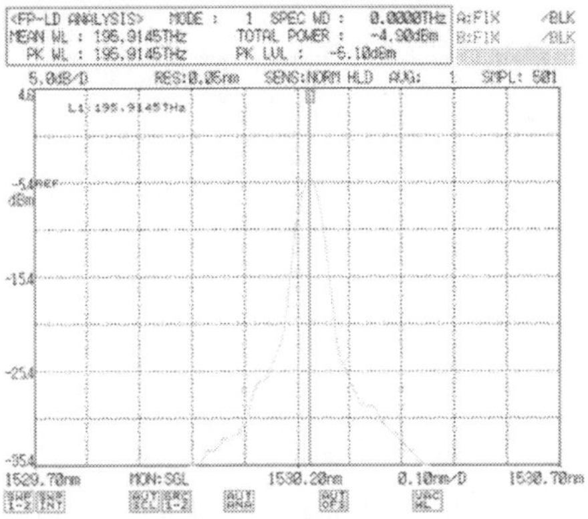
Fig. 3. Optical spectrum of TL in 1530nm.

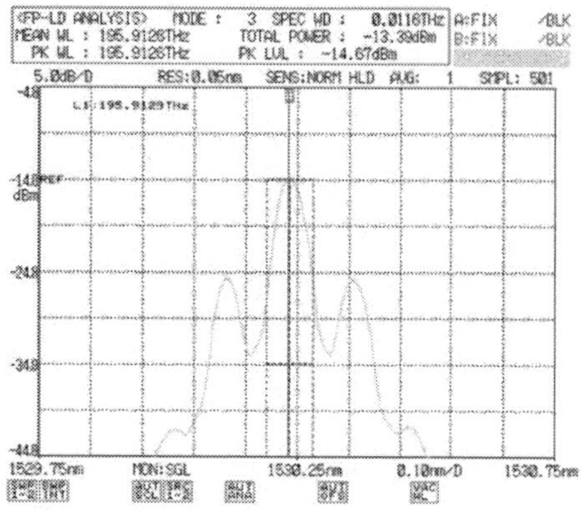

Fig. 4. DSB signal output from the first MZM.

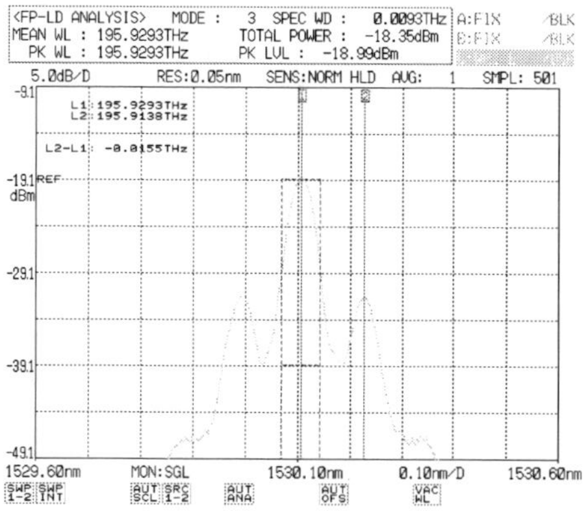

Fig. 5. DSB signal with 1.25Gb/s data output from the second MZM.

After the DSB signal is separated by FBG, the central carrier and subcarrier are used as downstream signals for different paths transmission. The central carrier wavelength is reflected by FBG and the subcarrier passes through FBG. The optical spectrum of central carrier and subcarrier is shown in Fig. 6 and Fig. 7. The downstream signal is amplified by EDFA for avoiding transmission power loss for 25km SMF transport.

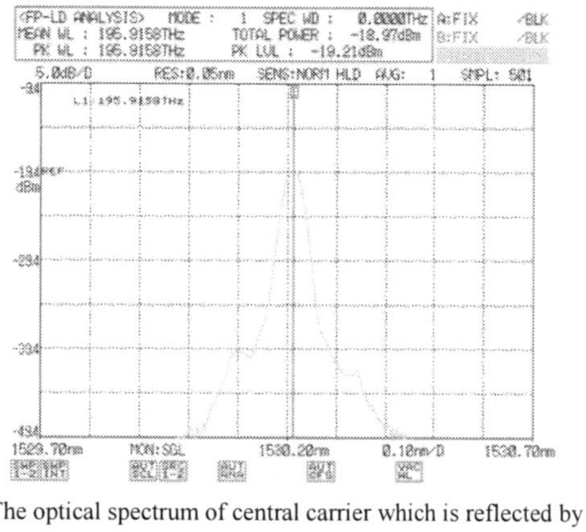

Fig. 6. The optical spectrum of central carrier which is reflected by FBG.

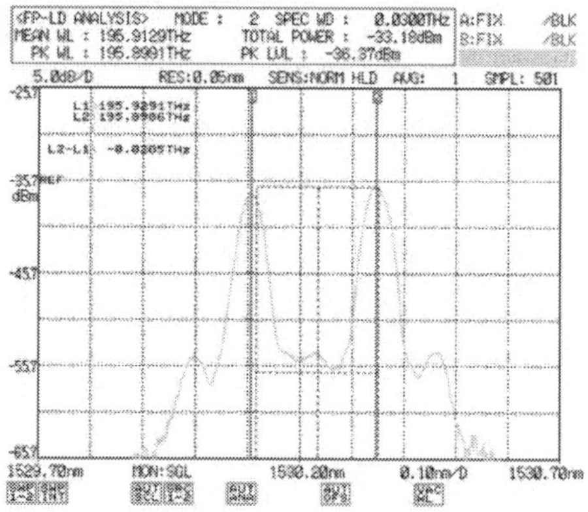

Fig. 7. The optical spectrum of subcarrier after pass through FBG.

The optical spectrum of the subcarrier and the central carrier for downstream transmission are shown in Figs. 8 and Fig. 9, respectively. To compare with intensity modulation and phase modulation, we reuse part of the downstream optical signal with phase modulation for the upstream signal.

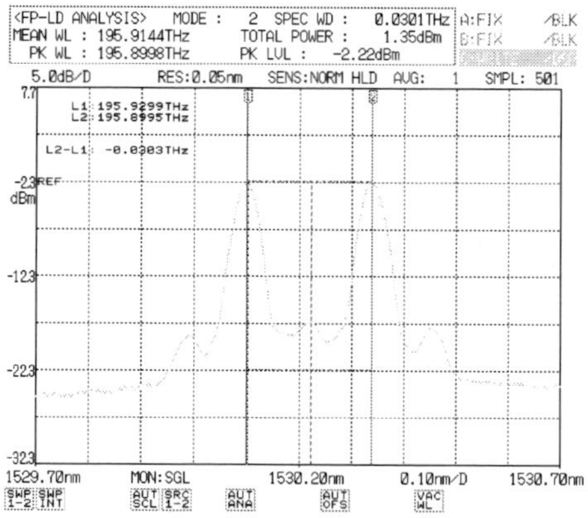

Fig. 8. Optical spectrum of subcarrier amplified by EDFA and 25km SMF transmission.

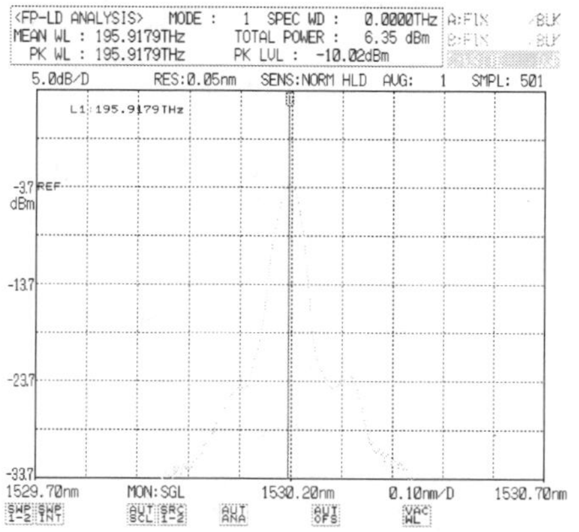

Fig. 9. Optical spectrum of central carrier after 25km SMF transmission.

The optical spectrum of the central carrier is remodulated by the phase modulator then amplified by EDFA, which is shown in Fig. 10. The central carrier via 25 km SMF is presented in Fig. 11.

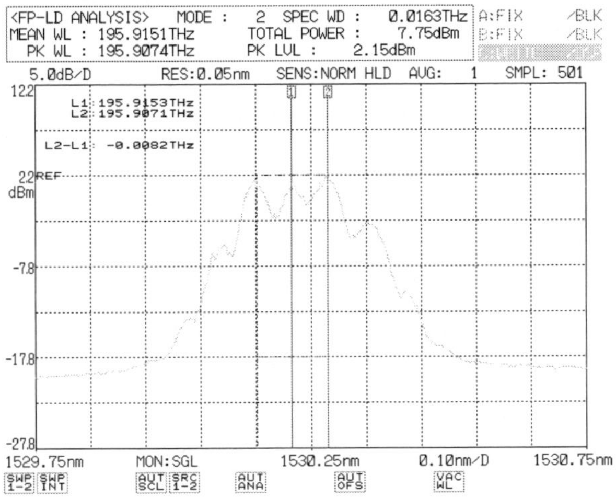

Fig. 10. The optical spectrum of central carrier remodulation by phase modulator and amplify by EDFA.

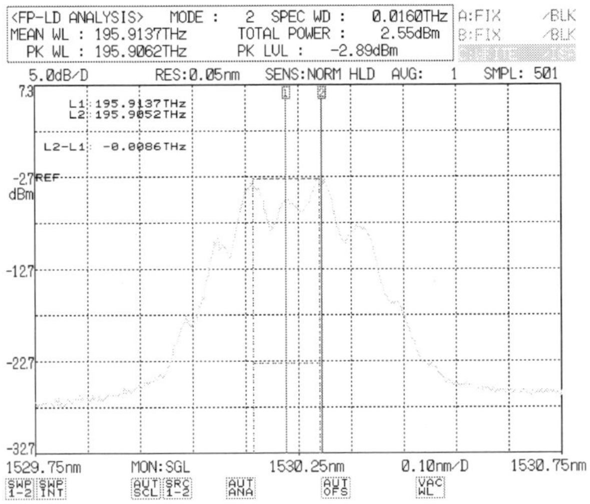

Fig. 11. The optical spectrum of remodulated central carrier used for upstream data after 25km transmission.

Figs. 12-14 illustrate the eye diagrams of downlink and uplink transmissions. Fig. 12 shows the eye diagram for the central carrier downstream data while Fig. 13 shows it for the subcarrier downstream data. Fig. 14 depicts the eye diagram for the central carrier upstream data. From these eye diagrams observation, we see that phase modulation is better than intensity modulation. The system power penalty of the central carrier for downlink and uplink is seen to be < 0.5 dB. The downlink and uplink transmission of BER values are lower than 10^{-9}.

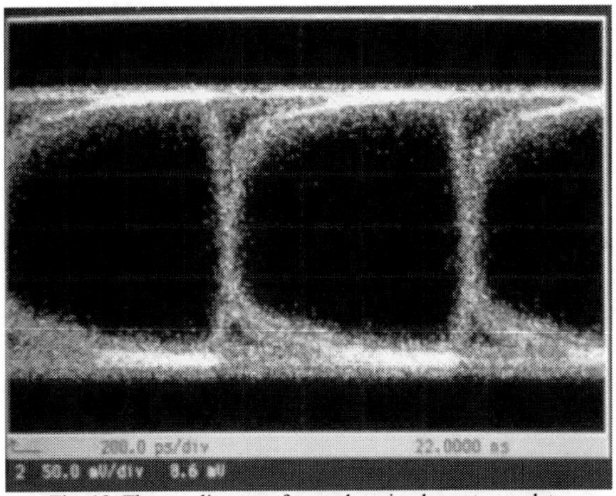

Fig. 12. The eye diagram of central carrier downstream data.

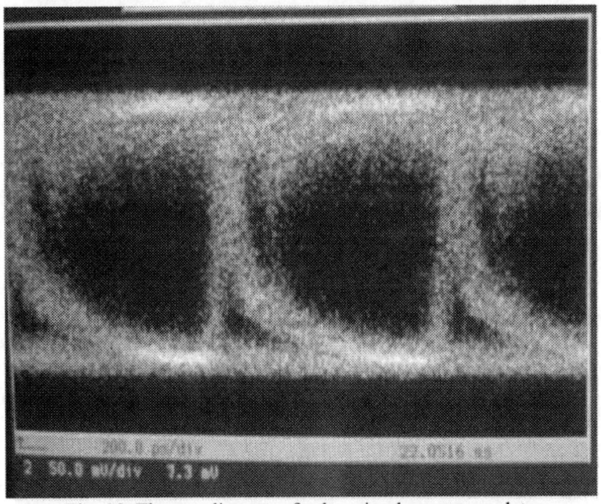

Fig. 13. The eye diagram of subcarrier downstream data.

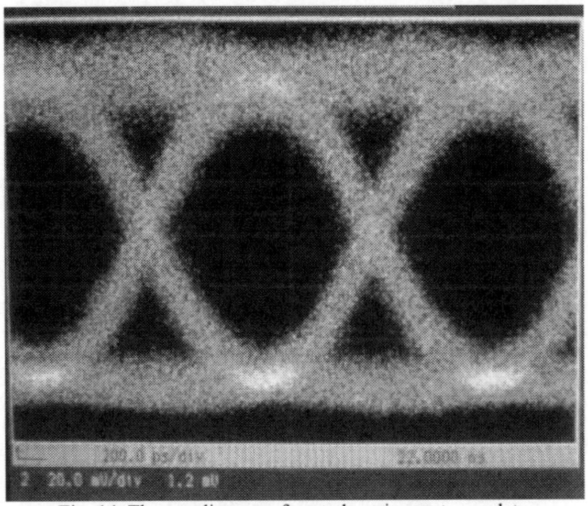

Fig. 14. The eye diagram of central carrier upstream data.

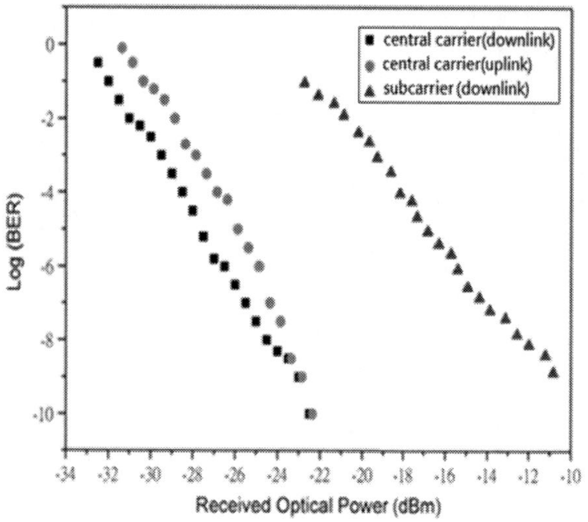

Fig. 15. The measure BER curves.

The measured BER curves of received optical power are presented in Fig. 15.The received optical power levels at the BER of 10^{-9} are −22.5dBm (central carrier downlink), −22.4dBm (central carrier uplink), and −10.6dBm (subcarrier downlink). A power penalty of approximately <0.1 dB (central carrier for downlink and uplink) for the fiber link is observed during the BER test for 25 km SMF transmission.

IV. CONCLUSION AND FUTURE WORK

We have proposed and demonstrated a bidirectional ROF-PON system. The system has simple and low cost features. Due to the RB effect, using FBG and OC achieve different transmission path to improve power fading in the OLT. We reuse part of the downstream signal as upstream optical carrier in BS to achieve low cost. Compared to phase modulation and intensity modulation for transmission, we could observe the eye diagram from high speed oscilloscope. Phase modulation is better than intensity modulation because PM has better anti-noise interference. The power penalty of the system is < 0.1 dB, downlink and uplink transmission of BER values are lower than 10^{-9}. The system can be combined with optical network and radio frequency in the future, such as fiber to the home (FTTH), Wi-Fi and antenna to implement long-haul transmission.

REFERENCES

[1] J. Yu, Z. Jia, T. Wang, G. K. Chang, and G. Ellinas "Demonstration of a Novel WDM-PON Access Network Compatible with ROF System to Provide 2.5Gb/s per Channel Symmetric Data Services," 2007 Optical Fiber Communication and National Fiber Optic Engineers Conference (OFC/NFOEC 2007), pp. 1-3, March 25-29, 2007.

[2] J. Prat, J. Lazaro, P. Chanclou and S. Cascelli, "Passive OADM Network Element for Hybrid Ring-Tree WDM/TDM-PON," the 35th European Conference on Optical Communication(ECOC 2009), pp.1-2, Sept. 20-24, 2009, Vienna, Austria.

[3] Y. Liao and W. Pan, "All-optical OFDM Based on Arrayed Grating Waveguides in WDM Systems," International Conference on Electronics, Communications and Control (ICECC), pp.707 – 710, Sept. 9-11, 2011.

[4] K. Hogari, I. Baraki, S. Tetsutani, J. Zhou and F. Yamamoto, "Optical-transmission characteristics of optical-fiber cables and installed optical-fiber cable networks for WDM systems, "IEEE Journal of Lightwave Technology, vol. 21, no. 2, pp.540-545, February 2003.

[5] T. Yoshida, S. Kimura, H. Kimura, K. Kumozaki and T. Imai, "A New Single-Fiber 10-Gb/s Optical Loopback Method Using Phase Modulation for WDM Optical Access Networks," IEEE Journal of Lightwave Technology, vol. 24, pp. 786-796, no. 2, February 2006.

[6] H. H. Lin, C. Y. Lee, S. C. Lin, S. L. Lee and G. Keiser "WDM-PON Systems Using Cross-Remodulation to Double Network Capacity with Reduced Rayleigh Scattering Effects," 2008Optical Fiber *communication (OFC) /National Fiber Optic Engineers Conference (NFOEC)*, pp.1-3, March 24-28, 2008.

Lightwave Robot Positioning based on Composite Codes Acquisition and Evolutionary Computations

Chun-Chieh Liu, Cheng Jhe-Ren, Jen-Fa Huang
Advanced Optoelectronic Technology Center,
Institute of Computer and Communications Engineering,
Department of Electrical Engineering,
National Cheng Kung University, Tainan, Taiwan.
email: {Q38021115@mail.tut.edu.tw; huajf@ee.ncku.edu.tw; Q36041402@mail.ncku.edu.tw}

***Abstract*—Lightwave robot positioning with composite codes acquisition is investigated in this paper. The indoor robot positioning system was previously examined with single Pseudo-Noise (PN) signal sequence. In views of correlation acquisition, the longer the code acquisition time, the longer the path estimation distance, and the worse the robot positioning accuracy. Under comparable period lengths, acquisition time for composite PN codes can be shorter than that of pure PN codes, thus can largely enhance the robot positioning accuracy. In the devised system configuration, three transmitters continuously send out their light coding signals to the robot receiver. The robot evaluates its current position by measuring time difference of arrival (TDOA) among the three paths. Memetic algorithms (MA) can then be used with the measured TDOAs to obtain a more accurate robot location. Finally, we provide a general analysis of the relationship between correlation value and robots position.**

***Keywords- M-sequences; Parallel codes acquisition; Time difference of arrival (TDOA); Memetic algorithms (MA)*.**

I. INTRODUCTION

With the mature technology, the functionality of robots is more and more complex. For example, different service types of robots, such as the navigation robot, the cleaning robot, etc. need to move around when they execute their tasks. Therefore, the accuracy of positioning is very important, and the error of measurements between robot and sensor must be solved. For example, the multipath propagation is caused by interference, because the light is transmitted in all directions. As a result, multipath propagation will occur when the light collides with obstacles. Transmitting signals may be cut by obstacles so that a longer distance and a large time delay are produced. Time of Arrival (TOA) [1][2] and Time Difference of Arrival (TDOA) [3][4] in positioning are easily influenced by errors so that the positioning accuracy is reduced.

We need to improve indoor lightwave positioning accuracy, so the robot object can be more precisely positioned, and capture light signals in the process. How to confirm the capture of light signals to the correct sources and reduce errors is the most important issue to study.

Several previous works have used the coding techniques of the light signal to determine the robot position, using Pseudo-Noise sequences (PN sequences) [5][6], Gold sequences [7], Loosely Synchronous sequences (LS sequences) [8], Golay codes [9] and Barker codes [10].

This paper proposes a new coding scheme of Composite Pseudo-Noise code sequences [11], which uses composite codes to encode the transmission signals. We constructed indoor light positioning based on Direct Sequence Spread Spectrum (DSSS) system, and a different orthogonal code is assigned to every transceiver. Using composite codes, we can determine the approximate position of a robot by hyperbolic triangulation of the distance obtained from the measurement of the difference in TDOA between a transceiver and the others. By using composite codes acquisition [12], we analyze the accuracy of the positioning and expect to improve the accuracy of the indoor positioning systems. We utilize Memetic algorithm (MA) to look for the absolute position of the object.

MA, which is similar to Genetic algorithm (GA), is also called Genetic algorithm combined with local search. The speed and changes of cultural evolution are more dramatic and alarming than the biological evolution, such as the basic structure of the genetic algorithm, generated populations carry out crossover and mutation to produce offspring. Differently from GA, the information of the previous generation is passed to the next generation, and this operation is called local search [13]. Local search finds local optimum values among the offspring, and the value of the global optimum is searched from all local optima. The proposed method is a wireless communication positioning system to reach the goal of improving positioning accuracy.

In this paper, we combine the positioning method with MA to estimate the location of MS. The code acquisition is described in Section II and how MA works is discussed in Section III. The compared correlation value and the robot are described in Section IV. Section V presents our conclusion.

II. ROBOT POSITIONING SYSTEM ARCHITECTURE

Figure 1 depicts a conceptual schematic of the proposed indoor robot positioning system. The reason we use light instead of other signals is for making use of LED to realize the positioning of the robots. Because the place is too small, we choose suitable chips rate for indoor positioning of robots. Take as comparative numerical figures for the high or low modulation rates. With 21-chip lengths per code frame and suppose 5-frames time is needed to confirm code acquisition. On using RF chips rate of 2000-kHz ($2x10^6$ chips/sec), the estimated object distance will be $21x5/2x10^6$ = $5x10^{-5}$m. This figure is hardly distinguishable on the robot distance to the transceiver. We make the chips rate the same as ultrasonic, 20-Hz (20 chips/sec), the same code length and acquisition frame will yield an estimated object distance of 21x5/20 = 5m. This figure is something acceptable. In practice, acquisition chips period length in mobile positioning can reach up to 2^{13}-1 = 8191 chips per frame to yield a distinguishable object distance.

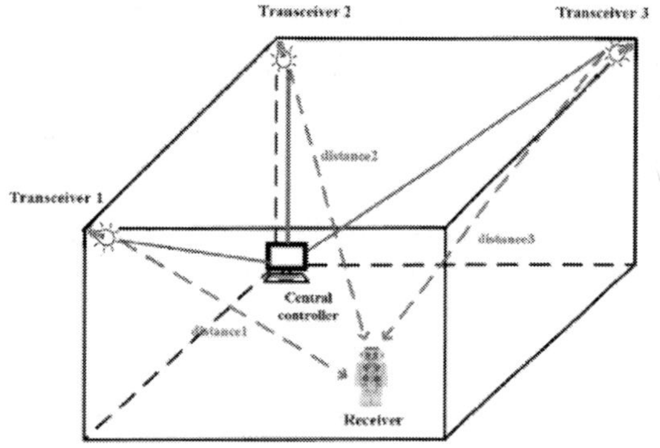

Figure 1. Overview of the indoor positioning system.

In the robot receiver, so as to calculate the distance from each transceiver, the robot needs to separate the incoming signals from different transceivers. The robot bears the same signal carrier wave and composite code sequences as those of the transceiver signals, which are called the replica signals. When correlating the received code signals with local replica signals, the robot can separate correlation peaks for the matched transceiver code from correlation nulls for the unmatched ones. This procedure for correlation detection of code signals is called code acquisition.

A. *Code acquisition with correlation detection*

In the code acquisition, we note that the correlation characterizations of the assigned composite codes are related to their code weights. If code vectors $T^iC_1(X)$ and $T^jC_2(X)$ have the respective code weights w_1 and w_2, then composite code $C^{(i,j)}(X) = T^iC_1(X) \oplus T^jC_2(X)$ possesses the following code weights

$$W(C^{(i,j)}) = w_1(n_2 - w_2) + w_2(n_1 - w_1) \quad (1)$$

$$= \begin{cases} \frac{n_1(n_2+1)}{2}, & if\ w_1 = 0,\ w_2 = (n_2+1)/2. \\ \frac{n_2(n_1+1)}{2}, & if\ w_1 = (n_1+1)/2,\ w_2 = 0. \\ \frac{(n_1n_2-1)}{2}, & if\ w_1 = (n_1+1)/2,\ w_2 = (n_2+1)/2. \end{cases} \quad (2)$$

Here, we have taken advantage that a binary ($n_l=2^{ml}$-1, $k_l = m_l$) M-sequence code has all of its n_l nonzero code vectors the same code weight of $(n_l+1)/2 = 2^{ml-1}$. Corresponding to the weight distribution of (2), the periodic correlation between composite codes $C_u^{(i_u,j_u)}$ and $C_v^{(i_v,j_v)}$ can be derived to be

$$\theta_{u,v} = \begin{cases} \left(\frac{n_1n_2-1}{2}\right), if\ u = v \\ \left(\frac{n_1n_2-n_2-2}{4}\right), \left(\frac{n_1n_2-n_1-2}{4}\right), \left(\frac{n_1n_2-1}{4}\right), if\ u \neq v \end{cases} \quad (3)$$

From the correlation distribution of (3), we see that correlations between reference transceiver and interfering transceivers can be separated by the correlation operation to track the desired transceiver sequences.

The robot positioning block chart for acquiring signal codes and estimating their flight time is shown in Figure 2. Figure 2 depicts every transceiver performed light signal modulation with assigned signature code, and emits this light signal continuously. Once the signal is received by the robot, the receiver turns the signal from analog to digital, and demodulates it into a corresponding code sequence. Since the receiver needs to identify the intended sequence code among all received signals, the demodulated code sequence is connected to three parallel correlators to calculate each assigned code. The output correlation passes through a peak detector to estimate the time of flight from transceiver to the robot. The robot then evaluates its current position by measuring TDOA from the three transceiver paths.

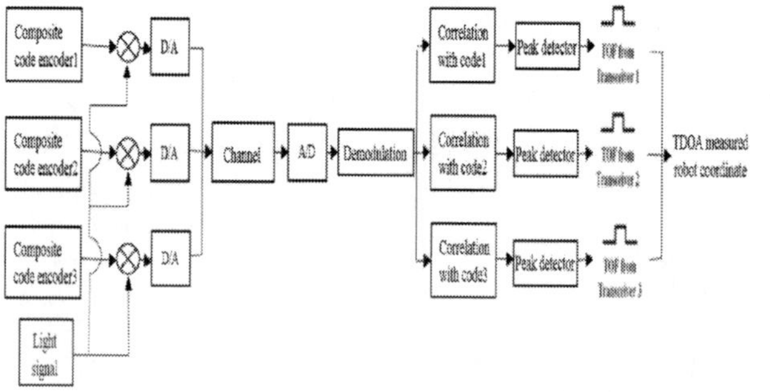

Figure 2. Block chart for robot positioning system.

With regard to the block diagram of Figure 2 for robot positioning system, we will give detailed descriptions on codes correlation acquisition/detection, acquisition time difference and time error, and relative distance/locations determination of robot object in the following subsections.

B. *Code acquisition time difference and time error*

A flow chart for the above composite codes correlation acquisition processes is shown in Figure 3. For the purpose of finding relative code sequences, the parallel correlator uses a local replica code sequence to perform correlation computations. Next, the system determines whether the correlation results are the peak of interval n_i=3 or n_j=7. If the correlation results meet the peak of interval n_i=3 or n_j=7, the system will immediately determine whether the correlation results meet the common peaks of interval n_{ij}=21, and confirm the code sequence. These results, which do not meet the correlation peaks. will advance chips and then perform correlation computations again. And these results, which meet the correlation peak will execute the two steps. One step is estimating the time error of code acquisition, and the other is estimating the time of flight.

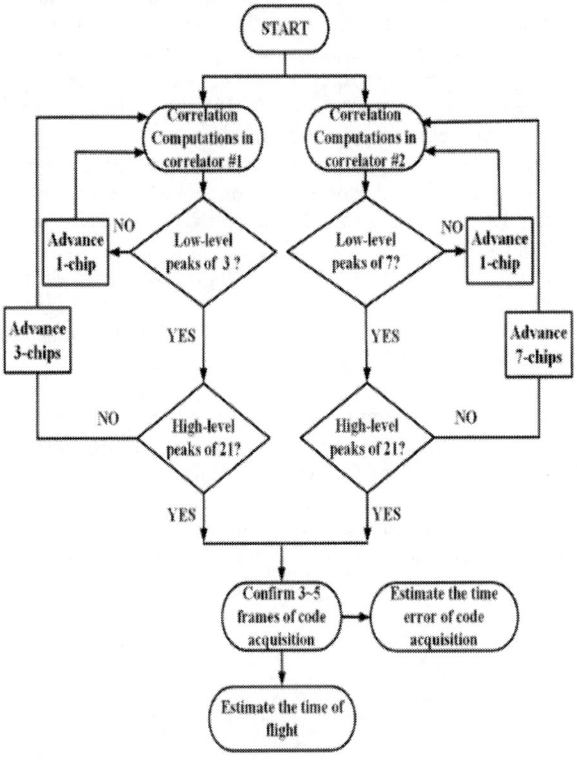

Figure 3. Flow chart for PN codes' correlation acquisition processes.

On estimating the flight time of coding signals, we note that the distance estimation between transmitters and the mobile robot is based on the cross-correlation method. Through the cross-correlation method, the robot calculates the number of frame peaks between the local replica sequence and the transmission sequence, and then offer robot to estimate the distance of transmitters. The information of the distance of transmitters will further perform optimization algorithms to obtain the absolute location of the robot.

C. *Determine the position of the robot receiver*

In order to obtain the position of the robot, the range measurement is acquired by TDOA of the light signals of the transceivers. In the TDOA scheme, the system locates a receiver by processing signal arrival-time measurements at three or more transmitters. Instead of the absolute arrival time, TDOA determines the relative difference on distance by measuring the difference in arrival time at any two transmitters. Each TDOA measurement can be regarded as a hyperboloid curve, and the receiver location must lie on this hyperbola.

Since there are more than two TDOA measurements, at least two hyperbolas can be drawn. Hence, the receiver location is at the intersection of the hyperbolas. Generally speaking, any two transmitters produce a hyperbola. Therefore, to get the intersection as the receiver location, it is required that more than three transmitters be detected. The TDOA will be biased by the time error of code acquisition that can degrade the positioning estimate. Therefore, the time error of code acquisition needs to be included in the calculation.

In this paper, we determine the receiver location by utilizing the intersection of the two hyperbolas in 2D environments, where r_1, r_2 and r_3 are the estimated values of the time of flight that we obtain from the number of frame peak between local code and received sequence. And then, once we get these estimated values, we take these values to subtract with each other to obtain the values ΔT_{12}, ΔT_{13} and ΔT_{23}. These values will substitute into (4) to solve the TDOA equation.

$$r_1 - r_2 = \Delta T_{12},\ r_1 - r_3 = \Delta T_{13},\ r_2 - r_3 = \Delta T_{23},$$
$$d_{ij} = c * (\Delta T_{ij} + e_{ij}),\ i \neq j$$
$$= \sqrt{(x_i - x)^2 + (y_i - y)^2} - \sqrt{(x_j - x)^2 + (y_j - y)^2} \quad (4)$$

where (x, y) is the real position of mobile robot while (x_i, y_i) and (x_j, y_j) are respectively the estimated position of robot receiver to the i-th and the j-th indoor transmitter, i, j = 1, 2, 3. The term d_{ij} are the value of TDOA; c is the ultrasonic wave speed; ΔT_{ij} is time difference measured by code acquisitions; and e_{ij} is the value of the time error of code acquisition to subtract with each other. The equations above represent hyperbolas, and their intersection gives the estimated positioning of the receiver. The area is enclosed with hyperbola represented the possible position of the receiver.

III. EVOLUTIONARY COMPUTATION MEMETIC ALGORITHM

MA is motivated by Dawkin's notion of a meme. Meme as a unit of information is processed on behalf of the evolution of culture. Instead of genes, the elements of MA are called memes. It is used to include an extensive class of metaheuristics, such as combing evolutionary algorithms with local search. In the unique viewpoint of MA, all individuals of offspring desired the information from the previous generation by local search [14]. MA reduces the probability of divergence and computation complexity. It combines the power and superiority of genetic algorithm and local search at the same time. Similar to the GAs, MA also needs the evolution mechanisms such as reproduction, crossover and mutation, as shown in Figure 4. The following steps describe the processes of MA approach.

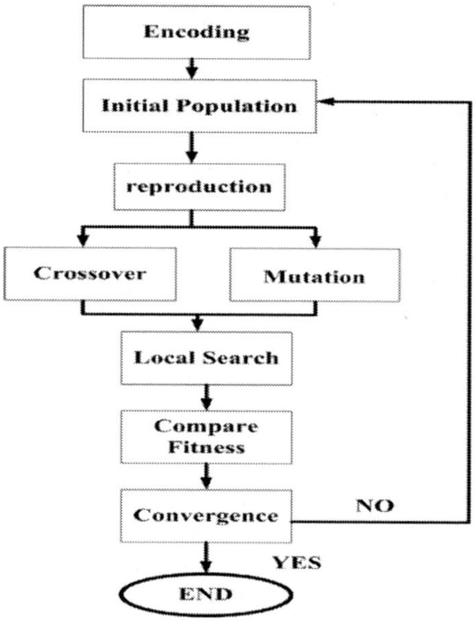

Figure 4. The flow diagram of Memetic Algorithm.

Step 1: Encoding:

To make evolution more convenient, the optimization parameters are always transformed to the binary sequences. The straight binary algorithm transforms the real numbers to the binary bits in this step. The range of real number and the bit length should be defined. For example, a variable is ranging from 0 to 10, and the bit length is 3. The range of real numbers is assigned to each code uniformly. By utilizing the coding schemes, the real numbers of horizontal coordinate is transformed to the binary sequence. Each binary sequence represents as a different individual.

Step 2: Initial Population:

After encoding, the individual is represented as a bit sequence. The first generation is generated through the random bit string generator from the overlap of three circles.

Step 3: Reproduction:

Based on comparing the object function value, a new population of individuals is generated by the selecting schemes. Individuals with better performance based on object function have a higher chance of being selected for the next generation.

Step 4: Crossover and Mutation:

Crossover and mutation operators are applied, similar to GA. These schemes are designed to promote the performance of individual's multiplicity. Especially, individuals avoid trapping in the local optimum of the object function by mutation in MA.

Step 5: Local Search:

In MA, local search is an important step. The mission of local search in MA is to search the optimum solution efficiently. By searching the neighbor individuals, the initial coordinate is changed to the neighbor coordinate with better performance. In local search, each individual is tuned by changing bits near the tail of the sequence to constrain the local search range. It ensures that the local search individuals are close to the original one, as shown in Fig. 5. Most of existing MA uses some local search procedures to generate solutions discovered from the neighbors of offspring individuals [15]. It helps to generate a better individual with lower object function value. Local search is applied on all the offspring individuals in every generation. A local search procedure is implemented on top K neighbor individuals, where K is the number of individuals that we will search.

The number of neighbor individuals is also affected by the local search range d, whose units depend on the number of bits. Local search range means the number of tuned bits. The end of bits is changed preferentially. Different searched bits are also discussed, and the searched bits are less than two in this paper. With increasing the local search bits d, the number of searching neighborhoods K is also increasing.

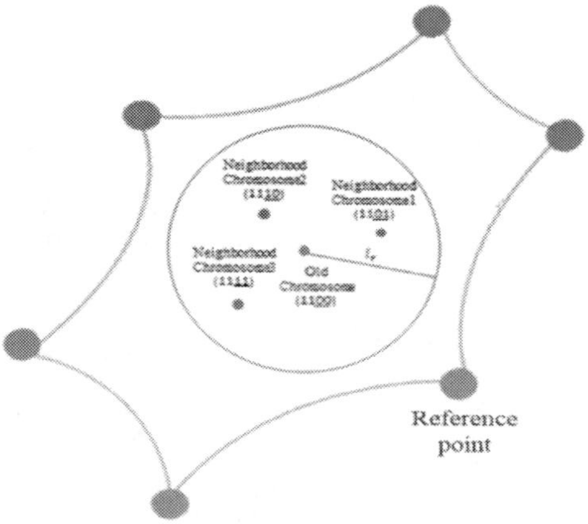

Figure 5. The local search procedure by comparing with neighborhoods.

Local search is applied for searching a better individual near each offspring individual. S is defined as the old individual, which is the offspring individual after the crossover and mutation step in Figure 5. We apply and discuss three different methods of local search sequentially.

IV. SIMULATION

We consider the problem of indoor positioning using TDOA measurements and utilize MA algorithm to improve the positioning accuracy in 2D environment. In the following, we analyze how the correlation value will be affected by the position of the robot.

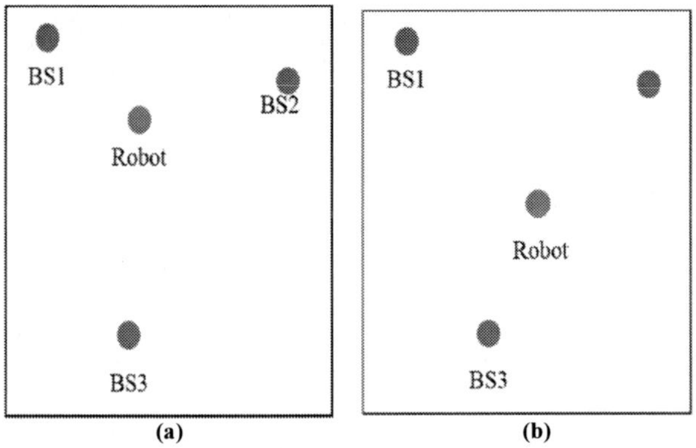

Figure 6. The possible position of robot. (a). Possible position #1. (b). Possible position #2.

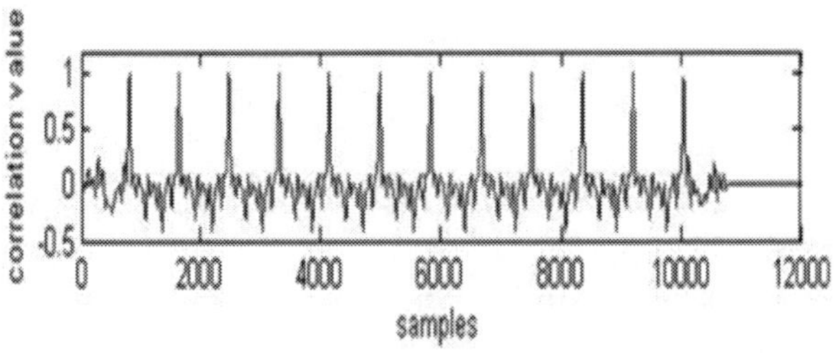

(a).

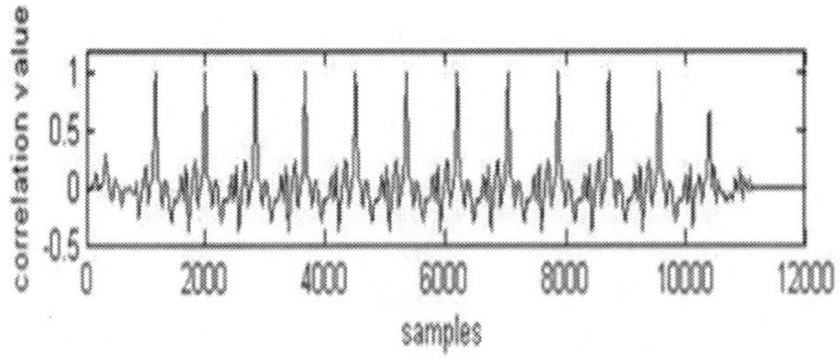

(b).

Figure 7. The correlation value. (a). for the possible position #1; (b). for the possible position #2.

Figure 6 (a) is a possible robot position and the matched correlation value is base station 1 in Figure 7 (a). The same discussion applies for the possible position #2 in Figure 8 (b). Figures 6 and 7 represent robot position makes the correlation value difference. Also, we describe the situation of correlation value and illustrate the different between two possible positions of robot.

IV. CONCLUSIONS AND FUTURE WORK

We have proposed a composite code acquisition to implement indoor lightwave robot positioning based on DSSS system. Each transceiver is modulated the light signal with a 3×7 bits composite code, which has a particular auto-correlation and cross-correlation in a cycle. By using code acquisition, the robot receiver detects the arrival time of codes and the error time of code acquisition, and the robot will use information to determine its absolute location.

Through comparing with traditional M-sequence code, we find that composite codes have more advantages. First, the code length is more flexible, it is not limited by 2^m-1. Second, other robot users are difficult to acquire the location of the designated robot because the code combination is more complex. Third, with the same location distance, the positioning accuracy and the error time of code acquisition of composite coding is more precise than the conventional M-sequence coding. In this paper, we used a location algorithm based on MA to determine the location of MS. We also improve the positioning accuracy by memetic algorithm.

V. REFERENCE

[1] P. C. Chen, "A non-line-of-sight error mitigation algorithm in location estimation," Proc. IEEE Wireless Communications and Networking Conference, vol. 1, pp. 316-320, Sept. 1999.

[2] S. Al-Jazzar, J. Caffery, and H.-R. You, "A scattering model based approach to NLOS mitigation in TOA location systems," Proc. IEEE Vehicular Technology Conference, vol. 2, pp. 861-865, May 2002.

[3] M. Aatique, "Evaluation of TDOA Techniques for Position Location in CDMA Systems," Thesis, Available:http://scholar.lib.vt.edu/theses/available/etd-82597-03345/ unrestricted/aatique.pdf.

[4] S. Kim; J. Lee; M. Yoo; Y. Shin, "An improved TDoA-based tracking algorithm in mobile-WiMAX systems," 20th IEEE International Symposium on Personal, Indoor and Mobile Radio Communications, pp. 561-565, Sept. 13-16, 2009.

[5] J. Klaus-Werner, B. Markus, "Using Pseudo-random Codes for Mobile Robot Sonar Sensing," IAV'98, Madrid, Spain; pp. 231-236, March 25-27, 1998.

[6] H. Andrew, K. Lindsay, "A Sonar Sensing with Random Double Pulse Coding," Australian Conference on Robotics and Automation," pp. 81-86, Melbourne, Australia, Aug. 30 – Sept. 1, 2000.

[7] J.M. Villadangos, J. Urena, M. Mazo, A. Hernandez, F. Alvarez, J.J. Garcia, C. de Marziani, D. Alonso, "Improvement of ultrasonic beacon-based local position system using multi-access techniques," IEEE International Symposium on Intelligent Signal Processing (WISP 2005), pp. 352-357, Algarve, Portugal, 2005.

[8] M.C. Pérez, J. Urena, A. Hernández, C. De Marziani, A. Jimenez, J.M. Villadangos, F. Alvarez, "Ultrasonic

beacon-based Local Positioning System using Loosely Synchronous codes," IEEE International Symposium on Intelligent Signal Processing, (WISP 2007), vol. 1, no. 6, pp. 3-5, Oct. 2007.

[9] A. Hernández, J. Ureña, J. J. García, V. Díaz, M. Mazo, D. Hernanz, J. P. Dérutin, J. Serot, "Ultrasonic signal processing using configurable computing," 15th Triennial World Congress of the International Federation of Automatic Control (IFAC'02), Barcelona, 2002.

[10] J. Ureña, "Contribución al Diseño e Implementación de un Sistema Sonar para la Automatización de un a Carretilla Industrial, ". PhD. Thesis, Electronics Department, University of Alcalá, 1998.

[11] H. Jen-Fa, C. Kai-Sheng, L. Ying-Chen, L. Chung-Yu, "Reconfiguring Waveguide-Gratings-based M-Signature Codecs to Enhance OCDMA Network Confidentiality," Optics Communications, vol. 313C, pp. 223-230, February 2014.

[12] G. De Angelis, G. Baruffa, S. Cacopardi, "Parallel PN code acquisition for wireless positioning in CDMA handsets," the 5th Advanced satellite multimedia systems conference (asma) and the 11th signal processing for space communications workshop , pp.343-348, Sept. 13-15, 2010.

[13] P. Moscato, M. G. Norman, "A memetic approach for the travelling, salesman problem – implementation of a computational ecology for combinatorial optimization on message-passing systems," Proc. of International conference on parallel computing and transputer application, pp. 177–186, 1992.

[14] P. Merz and B. Freisleben, "A Genetic Local Search Ap-proach to the Quadratic Assignment Problem," Proc. of the 7th International Conference on Genetic Algorithms, pp. 465-472, 1997.

[15] K. Ghoseiri, H. Sarhadi, "A memetic algorithm for symmetric travelling salesman problem," International Journal of Management Science and Engineering Management, Vol. 3, pp. 275-283 , Feb. 2008

Micro-CI: A Critical Systems Testbed for Cyber-Security Research

William Hurst, Nathan Shone, Qi Shi
Department of Computer Science
Liverpool John Moores University
Byrom Street
Liverpool, L3 3AF, UK
{W.Hurst, N.Shone, Q.Shi}@ljmu.ac.uk

Behnam Bazli
School of Computing
Staffordshire University
Beaconside
Stafford, ST18 0AD
Behnam.Bazli@staffs.ac.uk

Abstract— **A significant challenge for governments around the globe is the need to improve the level of awareness for citizens and businesses about the threats that exist in cyberspace. The arrival of new information technologies has resulted in different types of criminal activities, which previously did not exist, with the potential to cause extensive damage. Given the fact that the Internet is boundary-less, it makes it difficult to identify where attacks originate from and how to counter them. The only solution is to improve the level of support for security systems and evolve the defences against cyber-attacks. This project supports the development of critical infrastructure security research, in the fight against a growing threat from the digital domain. However, the real-world evaluation of emerging security systems for Supervisory Control and Data Acquisition (SCADA) systems is impractical. The research project furthers the knowledge and understanding of Information Systems; specifically acting as a facilitator for cyber-security research. In this paper, the construction of a testbed and datasets for cyber-security and critical infrastructure research are presented.**

Keywords—Critical Infrastructure, SCADA, Testbed, Security

I. Introduction

Interconnected control systems such as SCADA (Supervisory Control and Data Acquisition) monitor and govern public infrastructures, such as power plants and water distribution networks [1]. A constant assessment of the security of working control systems is necessary to ensure critical infrastructures are secured against external cyber-threats. However, this assessment process can impact the availability and performance of the control system. These types of environment require constant service provision and any disruption can be costly, and impact upon the end-users. For that reason, alternative approaches to assessing the security of automated control systems are needed.

Non-virtualised physical testbeds are costly and inaccessible, and are often location constrained [1]. As such, modern education and research for control system security is becoming increasingly reliant on virtualised labs and tools [2]. Any learning or research undertaken using these tools, however, is based around the limitations and characteristics of such tools, as well as any assumptions made by their developers. Additionally, the accuracy of data resulting from emulations and models may be further decreased if used outside of their intended usage scenario. It is for that reason that projects such as SCADAVT propose testbed frameworks for cyber-security experimentation, based on a simulation approach [1].

A virtualised approach offers significant cost savings and a self-paced and active approach to learning. However, it also has several key limitations including: no hands-on experience, no real-world training with specific equipment and no experience in identifying and interpreting incorrect or uncharacteristic data. Simulation is effective at representing "*correct*" behaviour. However, critical infrastructure systems need to be protected against situations where they are exposed to extreme abnormal events. Unfortunately, in such circumstances, systems do not always behave in the way expected or respond in the same consistent manner. Similarly, it is therefore difficult to accurately model how a system's erratic behaviour might cascade and impact other parts of the infrastructure.

The research presented in this paper provides an ideal solution. The practical element involved in the Micro-CI project introduces a level of realism that is difficult to match through simulation alone. It allows for the advantages of both physical and virtual tools to be combined, and some of these are discussed below.

- Pedagogical benefits: The Micro-CI approach offers students and researchers hands-on experience and first-hand knowledge of the unpredictability of a system under attack or stress. It will also help them to refine their problem solving and practical skills.
- Cost effectiveness: The Micro-CI project has been designed to be as cost effective as possible. For example, at the time of writing, we estimate that at the time of writing, the design presented in this paper can be replicated at low cost.
- Portability: As the project components are on a miniaturised bench top scale, it enables them to be packed away, stored and transported with ease. Projects can still be moved and/or stored whilst partially assembled.

- Platform independency: The Micro-CI project does not require any specific requirements, dependencies or operating systems to interact with the testbeds developed. Additionally, it is not tied or restricted by any licencing model, so it can be used on an infinite number of different machines, without incurring additional costs.

In this paper, the architecture for the Micro-CI testbed, which replicates a water distribution plant, is outlined. Both the physical design and construction of the testbed are detailed. A case study and evaluation, in which cyber-attacks are launched against the water distribution plant, are also presented.

The remainder of this paper is organised as follows. Section 2 presents a background discussion on testbed and critical infrastructure modelling. Cyber-security and cyber-threats are also highlighted. Section 3 presents the approach used to construct the Micro-CI testbed and a case study of the impact of an attack on the system. The resulting data is evaluated in Section 4. Finally, the paper is concluded and the future work is highlighted in Section 5.

II. BACKGROUND

As automation grows in all areas of critical infrastructures [4], increased pressure is put on control systems to oversee and monitor operations at all times. A central control unit has the job of governing the behaviour of a vast system, ensuring the infrastructure is run smoothly and automated efficiently [7].

A. *Control Systems*

Centralised control systems enable operators to control components from remote locations without physically needing to be there [5]. The requirement of operators having to travel to distant locations has been replaced by carefully designed user interfaces that allow the operator to interact with the system. The interfaces are often comprised of off-the-shelf components constructed to a specification suitable for the type of infrastructure being used [6]. The use of off-the-shelf components is a cause for concern, as the technology used in infrastructures is readily available for anyone to use, which can make them more vulnerable to attack [6].

A typical modern control system consists of a network of sensors acquiring data, which are used to control devices using programmable logic controllers (PLC). They are typically composed of three parts, the master terminal unit (MTU), remote terminal units (RTU) and the communication links. The MTU acquires data and sends instructions between various components such as a Human Machine Interface (HMI), databases for storing past information, workstations for engineers and business information systems for industrial applications. RTUs are essentially PLC devices that automate the actions ordered by the master terminal unit. The communication links are responsible for proficient communication and usually consist of fibre optics, microwave, telephone lines, pilot cables, radio or satellite.

Figure 1 provides a simplified illustrative overview of a control system, whereby the RTU provides the communication link between various components of the infrastructure and the MTU, which is linked to the graphical user interface.

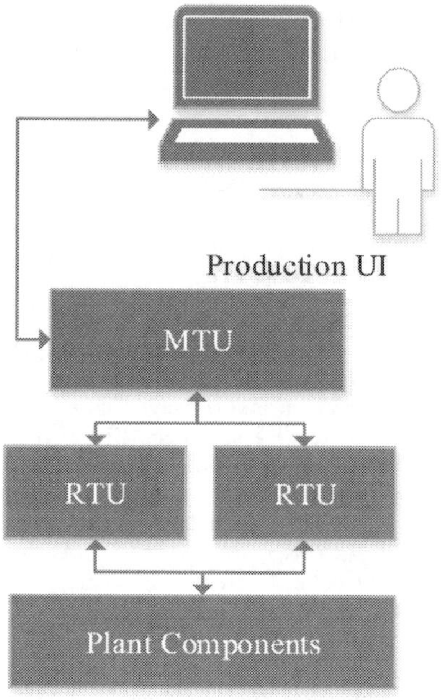

Figure 1 Control System Overview

At this stage, the SCADA system is typically software that enables the operator to interact with the MTU and observe the on-going activities in the infrastructure [10]. Other approaches to control system construction can include a DCS (Distributed Control System) layout, which tends to have no central controller but is operated by various control components working together to decide the required action [8], [9]. However, the Micro-CI testbed detailed in this paper follows the traditional centralised control system structure for the purposes of simplicity and replicability.

B. *The Cyber Threat*

Control system data is coded in protocol format to exchange information with components and RTUs. The protocol formats provide automation and send information back to the control user interface to deliver a status of system operations. Communication protocols are designed for real-time operation [11]. Two examples of industrial control network protocols include Modbus (Modicon Communication Bus) and DNP3 (Distributed Network Protocol). They are commonly used in modern day critical infrastructures and able to match the specific requirements of the system. However, they are susceptible to disruption and security breaches [11]. One of the most common methods of attack is the Distributed Denial of Service (DDoS) attack, where systems are sent large volumes of traffic that is intended to make the system fail by overloading it. This attack is effective. It is a challenge to distinguish between good and bad requests, making attacks problematic to block [13].

Often cyber-attacks are specifically targeted at individual parts of infrastructures. For example, various attacks are designed with the precise intention of disrupting or infiltrating SCADA systems [12]. One such attack is known as a Process Network Malware Infection (PNMI), which involves injecting a worm into the process network. The process network is often used for hosting the whole of the SCADA where communication is conducted through protocols like ModBus or DNP3 [12]. Another common technique is the Man in the Middle attack (MITM) [14] where false commands or system instructions and fake responses are inserted into the system. Not only can a MITM attack be used to cause disruption; it can also be used to provide a way of eavesdropping; making it important to use authentication protocols to ensure the confidentiality and integrity of the communications [15].

C. *Related Projects*

The growing cyber-threat has led to a switch in research focus from physical protection to digital infrastructure security measures. However, this cyber-security research is hampered by a lack of realistic experimental data and opportunities to test new theories in a real-world environment [16]. For that reason, projects such as SCADAVT, have developed simulation-based testbed, which builds upon the CORE emulator, for building realistic SCADA models [1].

In their approach, Almalawi *et al.*, develop a framework to construct a water distribution system [1]. The testbed consists of SCADA components, including the Modbus/TPC slave and master, and the Modbus/TPC HNI server. Functioning together, the testbed employs the use of the dynamic link library (DLL) of EPANET to simulate the water flow within the system. The testbed combines the use of existing techniques to produce a novel testbed application. The system tested through a case study involving a DDoS attack to demonstrate that convincing data-construction is possible. Software-based simulation data, such as this approach, is often used to test theoretical cyber-security systems; however, data constructed through emulators is inherently lacking in realism and a hands-on learning experience is missed.

In addition to the aforementioned water distribution testbed approach, there are several existing proposals for critical infrastructure testbed architectures, which focus on specific systems, such as electricity substations [17]. However, our long-term goal is not to constrain our testbed to a single role, but to adopt a modular approach; whereby new critical infrastructure roles can be integrated at a later stage. This would make it suitable and useful to a wider audience. Specifically, the proposed system focuses on a water distribution plant; however, the design is extendable and testbeds can be extended to incorporate other infrastructure types, such as an ecologically-aware power plant.

This project provides research opportunities for the testing and development of security enhancements in a real-life scenario. As such, the aim of the research is to have a practical output; a fully working critical infrastructure testbed. The goal is to demonstrate the suitability of the datasets generated by the Micro-CI testbed, which can also provide a benchmark for future comparison against those created by industry-standard software.

III. APPROACH

The Micro-CI project addresses the lack of both access to experimental data and the hands-on experience needed to properly understand the challenges involved in an era of growing digital threats. As such, the intended output of this project is to support the construction of a bespoke bench-top testbed for data generation; consisting of a model critical infrastructure and control system. The testbed will be used for cyber-security research purposes and testing new experimental methods for enhancing the level of security in cyber-critical systems, specifically those under current exploration by the investigators. In this section, an outline of the architecture of the Micro-CI project is presented.

A. *System Design*

The design displayed below in Figure 2, presents a rudimentary water distribution plant. The specification is modest, meaning there is scope for future expansion; yet is sufficient in size to produce realistic infrastructure behaviour datasets for research purposes. As illustrated in the diagram, there are two reservoir tanks, which are fed by two pumps moving water from external sources. The remote terminal unit (RTU) is used to monitor the outgoing flow rate and water level, to dynamically adjust the pump speed ensuring adequate replenishment of the reservoir tanks. However, vulnerabilities exist in the system, meaning that it is possible for an external source to cut off the water supply or flood the reservoir tanks. This can be achieved by switching off or speeding up either of the pumps used to control the water flow.

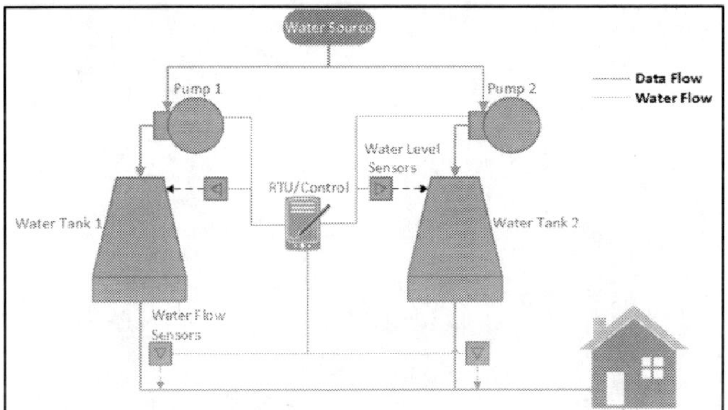

Figure 2. Water distribution plant testbed architecture

B. *Practical Micro-CI implementation*

The practical implementation of the testbed includes the following physical components: an Arduino Uno Rev. 3 as the RTU, two 12v peristaltic pumps as the water pumps, two liquid flow meters, two water level sensors, two amplification transistors, diodes, resistors and an LCD.

In the schematics shown in Figure 3, potentiometer symbols have been used in place of sensors; this is due to the limited symbols available in the blueprint software. As the maximum output of the Arduino is only 5v, transistors amplify this to the 12v required by the pumps. Lastly, the diodes are used to ensure the current can only travel in one direction, thus preventing damage to the Arduino. The hardware specification used is modest, meaning there is scope for future expansion; yet is sufficient in size to produce realistic infrastructure behaviour datasets for research purposes.

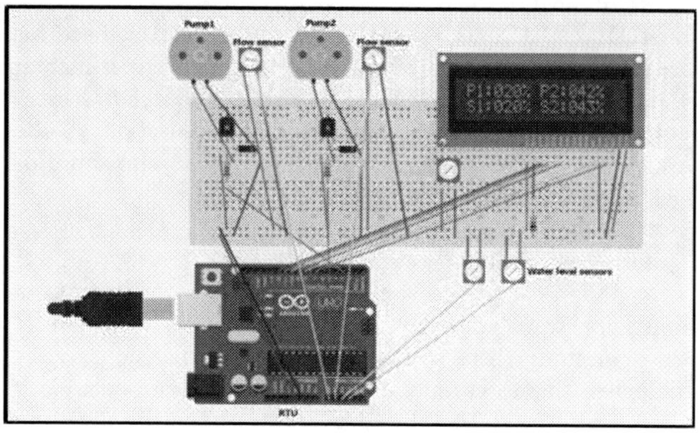

Figure 3. Physical wiring schematics

The construction is displayed in Figure 4. For the purpose of this experiment, the Arduino board remains connected to a PC via a USB cable (although this could be replaced with a network connection for similar experiments). The system is also inactive.

Figure 4. Testbed Construction

Through this USB connection, a serial connection is established to supply a real-time data feed, which is recorded and preserved by the PC (as illustrated in Figure 3). The metrics collected in this instance include: Water level sensor1/2 readings, Flow meter1/2 readings and Pump1/2 speeds. These readings are taken from each sensor every 0.25 seconds (4Hz) and written to the serial data stream.

To examine the quality of the data produced by the Micro-CI implementation, a dataset was recorded over the period of 1 hour. During this time, the testbed was operating under normal parameters (i.e. no cyber-attacks were present).

Essentially, this means that the pump speeds are configured to slowly continue filling the tanks at a controlled speed until full (even if no water is being used) and to cover the current rate of water consumption (if possible). The outflow (water being consumed) is a randomly applied value within a specific range (to make usage patterns more realistic). In this instance, the water source pipe is 60% smaller than the outflow pipes, which allows for a more accurate representation and to enable water tank starvation in case of overload. A sample of the data collection process is displayed in Figure 5, which shows the Arduino Serial Monitor.

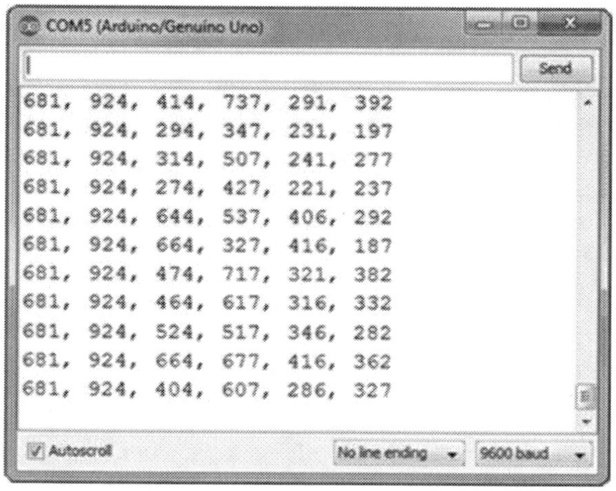

Figure 5. Example Serial Data Stream

The datasets produced by the testbed are evaluated in the following section, as a demonstration of their applicability in a critical infrastructure research setting.

IV. EVALUATION

Similar to the SCADAVT project, this testbed is evaluated through the demonstration of a Distributed Denial of Service attack [1]. The effect of a DDoS attack in comparison with normal behaviour of the testbed is evaluated.

A. Data Construction

As such, for the first part of this case study, data for the water distribution plant is recorded whilst operating under normal conditions. This enables the building of a behavioural norm profile for the system. Within the testbed, during the DDoS attack, only intermittent readings from the sensors are received, forcing it to make drastic (and therefore uncharacteristic) changes to the pump speeds, rather than gradual as when operating normally.

A small sample of the data obtained at 00:10.5 in run time is shown in Table 1. There is no significant variation present in the data. All the metrics maintain consistent trends in operation.

Within Table 1, C1 to C6 denote the system components used for data collection. As such, C1 and C2 denote the water level in tank 1 and 2 correspondingly; C3 and C4 signify the water levels in tank 2 and 3; C4 represents the water flow from tank 2; C5 denotes the speed of pump 1 and C6 indicates the speed of pump 2.

TABLE 1. NORMAL PHYSICAL TESTBED DATA SAMPLE

Sample(*t*)	C1	C2	C3	C4	C5	C6
00:10.5	65.0	69.9	47.3	55.4	81.9	85.1
00:10.7	65.0	69.9	39.4	48.5	74.1	78.8
00:11.0	65.0	69.9	39.4	53.4	74.1	83.1

Table 2 represents the distribution of values for each of the components over the 1 hour simulation. The unique value, max, min, median, mean and standard deviation of the values are demonstrated.

TABLE 2. DISTRIBUTION VALUES FOR NORMAL DATA

Assessment	C1	C2	C3	C4	C5	C6
unique (est.)	23.00	4.00	55.00	52.00	51.00	53.00
min:	65.00	69.99	34.82	44.86	68.91	74.83
max:	66.14	70.19	38.19	47.96	72.91	77.92
median:	65.59	70.09	36.86	46.69	71.30	76.64
mean:	65.58	70.07	36.72	46.54	71.14	76.50
std:	0.328	0.063	0.691	0.694	0.772	0.695

B. Attack Data Construction

The DDoS attack on the system, which is launched against the RTU's communications channel, results in intermittent sensor readings. Whilst no new values are readily available, the RTU continues to maintain the previous pump speed. As before, Table 3 represents the distribution of values for each of the components over the 1 hour simulation during the cyber-attack scenario. The unique value, max, min, median, mean and standard deviation of the values are again demonstrated.

TABLE 3. DISTRIBUTION VALUES FOR ATTACK DATA

Assessment	C1	C2	C3	C4	C5	C6
unique (est.)	25.00	7.00	52.00	51.00	58.00	59.00
min:	65.00	69.89	34.91	44.69	56.42	56.84
max:	66.18	70.02	38.16	47.98	85.05	91.45
median:	65.69	69.99	36.86	46.69	71.64	75.51
mean:	65.62	69.99	36.71	46.54	72.07	74.88
std:	0.36	0.015	0.689	0.705	6.832	7.327

Whilst under attack, the testbed continues to function, service is disrupted and the output is visible in the dataset constructed. For example, the min and max values from C5 are considerably different. This change is data is identifiable in a visual comparison of the pump speeds.

Figure 6 presents a two feature scatter plot of the normal and abnormal operation of the two testbed pumps. Pump speed 2 is displayed along the y-axis with pump speed 1 detailed on the x-axis.

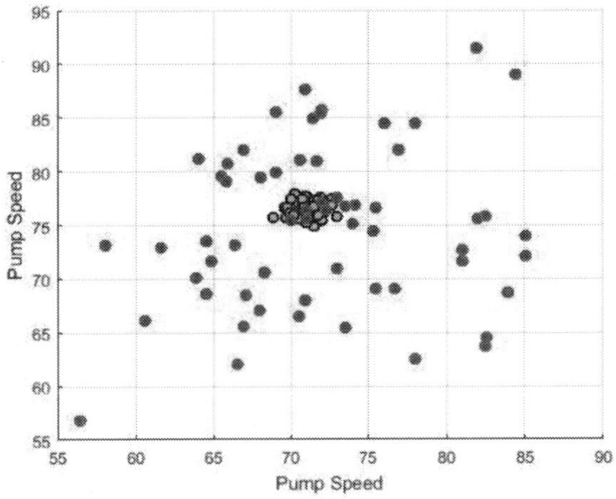

Figure 6. Scatter Plot for Normal and Abnormal Operation of Pumps

Variance can be seen in the clustering of the data. The colour indicates the grouping. The normal behaviour of pump shows a deviation in the operational speed to adjust for water flow changes and maintaining the water level in the tanks. This is displayed in the red circles, distributed throughout Figure 6. Within the attack data, the RTU's communications channel is unable to maintain active communication the water levels meaning that pump 2 is unable to adjust efficiently to match the tank water levels. This is reflected in the small data cluster in the centre of Figure 6.

C. Discussion

Current anomaly detection systems function by identifying a deviation from established patterns within given datasets. For example, in the case of network security, algorithms compare network flow with historical flows and outliers in the datasets are subsequently identified. Threats are marked as an anomaly. Supervised learning algorithms are generally employed to learn about the threats and establish patterns of attack behaviour, which are labelled as signatures. This allows for the detection of novel attacks. Based on the above evaluation, we envision that this testbed would be ideal for training and research which focuses on anomaly and signature-based detection. Specifically, this testbed offers the following benefits:

- Normal/Abnormal dataset construction: Normal datasets can be constructed to act at the established pattern of system behaviour. Abnormal dataset can be constructed to act as deviation from normal patterns of behaviour. This can allow for experimentation with novel detection algorithms. Both types of data are needed for the core functionality for how anomaly detection practice is done.
- Diverse application: The testbed is applicable to a range of CI scenarios and cyber-attack types. The above evaluation focuses on DDoS on a water plant; however, Denial of Service, Signature Injection, are further examples of attack scenarios which can be implemented for dataset construction. The main components of the system, for

example the pumps, can also be altered to change the CI infrastructure type.

V. CONCLUSION

As previously discussed, one of the aims of this project is to devise a testbed, which is suitable for cyber-security training and research. It is our belief that the use of real-life data is more suitable for cyber-security research, than that of simulation only. One of the most effective aspects of the Micro-CI testbed is its expandability; meaning that in future work the scale of the testbed can be expanded to incorporate additional components and sensors.

However, as with all solutions, there are some drawbacks to our approach. The first is that the use of low cost hardware reduces the level of accuracy that can be achieved. For example, the Arduino Uno uses an ATMega microcontroller, which is only capable of recording 4-byte precision in double values. This can present problems if precision is a crucial part of the research being undertaken. However, this can be mitigated by purchasing more expensive hardware. Another limitation is that in comparison to simulation software, the practical approach may require a greater level of improvement to students' skillsets (which is not a detrimental attribute), and a longer initial construction time, to accomplish a working implementation.

One of the main challenges for governments around the globe is the need to improve the level of awareness for citizens and businesses about the threats that exist in cyberspace. The arrival of new information technologies has resulted in different types of criminal activities, which previously did not exist, with the potential to cause extensive damage to internal markets.

Society is becoming increasingly reliant upon critical infrastructure systems, which is forcing them to become more accessible and interconnected, in a short space of time. When this is combined with the growing sophistication of cyber-attacks, this poses a considerable physical and digital security threat. Hence, critical infrastructure security is a key area of much-needed research that is under-supported. We hope that Micro-CI will provide a cost-effective, yet realistically accurate tool for future cyber-security research and learning. In our future work, we will compare the results from Micro-CI against existing industry-specific simulation software. We will also make the datasets available for cyber-security and critical infrastructure research. In addition, the construction design and instructions will be made available to other researchers.

VI. ACKNOWLEDGEMENTS

The authors would like to thank the UK Academy for Information Systems (UKAIS) as the funding body for this research project (http://www.ukais.org.uk/).

REFERENCES

[1] A. Abdulmohsen., Z. Tari., I. Khalil., and A. Fahad., SCADAVT-A framework for SCADA security testbed based on virtualization technology, Proceedings of the 38th IEEE Conference on Local Computer Networks (LCN), pp639-646, 2013

[2] L. Topham, K. Kifayat, Y. A. Younis, Q. Shi and B. Askwith, Cyber Security Teaching and Learning Laboratories: A Survey, Information & Security: An International Journal, vol. 35, 2016.

[3] D. Lewis, The pedagogical benefits and pitfalls of virtual tools for teaching and learning laboratory practices in the Biological Sciences, HE Academy, 2014

[4] L. H. de Melo Leite, L. de Errico, and W. do Couto Boaventura, Criteria for the selection of communication infrastructure applied to power distribution automation, Proceedings of the IEEE PES Conference on Innovative Smart Grid Technologies (ISGT Latin America), pp. 1–8, 2013.

[5] O. Gerstel, AControl Architectures for Multi-Layer Networking: Distributed, centralized, or something in between? Optical Fiber Communications Conference and Exhibition (OFC), pp 1-16, 2015.

[6] C. Esposito, D. Cotroneo, R. Barbosa, and N. Silva, Qualification and Selection of Off-the-Shelf Components for Safety Critical Systems: A Systematic Approach, Proceedings of the Fifth Latin-American Symposium on Dependable Computing Workshops, pp. 52–57, 2011.

[7] V. Urias, B. Van Leeuwen, and B. Richardson, Supervisory Command and Data Acquisition (SCADA) system cyber security analysis using a live, virtual, and constructive (LVC) testbed, Proceedings of the IEEE Military Communications Conference, (MILCOM), pp. 1–8, 2012.

[8] Z. Liu., D. Li., L. Yun., and S. Xu., An assessment method for reliability of distributed control system, Proceedings of the IEEE International Conference on Information and Automation, pp. 1300-1304, 2015.

[9] H. Fayyaz Abbasi., N. Iqbal., M. Rehan, Distributed Robust Adaptive Observer-Based Controller for Distributed Control Systems with Lipschitz Nonlinearities and Time Delays, Proceedings of the 13th International Conference on Frontiers of Information Technology (FIT), pp. 185–192, 2015.

[10] J. Adrian Ruiz Carmona., J. César Muñoz Benítez and J. L. García-Gervacio., SCADA system design: A proposal for optimizing a production line, Proceedings of the International Conference on Electronics, Communications and Computers (CONIELECOMP), pp. 192-197, 2016.

[11] R. Gao and C. Hwa Chang, A scalable and flexible communication protocol in a heterogeneous network, Proceedings of the 13th International Conference on Computer and Information Science (ICIS), pp 49-52, 2014.

[12] Y. Zhang., L. Wang., Y. Xiang and C. Ten, Inclusion of SCADA Cyber Vulnerability in Power System Reliability Assessment Considering Optimal Resources Allocation. IEEE Transactions on Power Systems, Vol:PP, No 99, pp 1-16, 2016.

[13] Q. Yan., F. R. Yu., Q. Gong., and J. Li., Software-Defined Networking (SDN) and Distributed Denial of Service (DDoS) Attacks in Cloud Computing Environments: A Survey, Some Research Issues, and Challenges, IEEE Communications Surveys & Tutorials, Vol. 18 No. 1, pp. 602–622, 2015.

[14] A. Sahi Khader., and D. Lai., Preventing man-in-the-middle attack in Diffie-Hellman key exchange protocol, Proceedings of the 22nd International Conference on Telecommunications (ICT), pp. 204–208, 2015.

[15] R. Divya., and S. Muthukumarasamy., An impervious QR-based visual authentication protocols to prevent black-bag cryptanalysis, Proceedings of 9th IEEE International Conference on Intelligent Systems and Control (ISCO), pp. 1–6, 2015.

[16] T. Benzel, R. Braden, D. Kim and C. Neuman, Experience with DETER: a testbed for security research, in Proceedings of the 2nd International Conference on Testbeds and Research Infrastructures for the Development of Networks and Communities, 2014.

[17] Z. L. H. Wei, G. Yajuan, and C. Hao, Research on information security testing technology for smart Substations, in Proceedings of the International Conference on Power System Technology (POWERCON), pp. 2492–2497, 2014.

[18] M. Ficco, G. Avolio, L. Battaglia, and V. Manetti, Hybrid Simulation of Distributed Large-Scale Critical Infrastructures, Intell. Netw. Collab. Syst., pp. 616–621, 2014.

A Cyber-Support System for Distributed Infrastructures

Sahar Badri
School of Computing and Mathematical Sciences
Liverpool John Moores University
Liverpool, UK
S.K.Badri@2010.ljmu.ac.uk

Paul Fergus
School of Computing and Mathematical Sciences
Liverpool John Moores University
Liverpool, UK
p.fergus@ljmu.ac.uk

William Hurst
School of Computing and Mathematical Sciences
Liverpool John Moores University
Liverpool, UK
w.hurst@ljmu.ac.uk

Abstract— **The Internet is now heavily relied upon by the Critical Infrastructures (CI). This has led to different security threats facing interconnected security systems. By understanding the complexity of critical infrastructure interdependency, and how to take advantage of it in order to minimize the cascading problem, enables the prediction of potential problems before they happen. Our proposed system, detailed in this paper, is able to detect cyber-attacks and share the knowledge with interconnected partners to create an immune system network. In order to demonstrate our approach, a realistic simulation is used to construct data and evaluate the system put forward. This paper provides a summary of the work to-date, on the development of a system titled Critical Infrastructure Auto-Immune Response System (CIAIRS). It provides a view of the main CIAIRS segments, which comprise the framework and illustrates the functioning of the system.**

Keywords— ***Critical Infrastructure; Distributed System; System of Systems; Data Analysis; Cyber-attack.***

I. INTRODUCTION

The role of one infrastructure influences the functioning of others. This can be referred to as interdependency. Interdependency is considered the main challenges for Critical Infrastructures (CI). Operating as a mutually interdependent network, treated as a system of systems, failures and successful cyber-attacks have the potential to cause a cascading effect. Understanding the interconnectivity behaviour between the critical infrastructures, and how it changes depending on the complexity, can reduce the effect before cascading occurs. Moreover, this would control the damage and limit the impact [1].

The risk of cascading failure among distributed systems is the main influential factor behind this research. To date, our previous work has involved creating a support system against cyber-attacks, using the human immune system mechanism as inspiration for the design [2]. The system is titled Critical Infrastructure Auto-Immune Response System (CIAIRS); in this paper, the framework for CIAIRS is presented. The operation process and design for CIAIRS is discussed, along with the evaluation of CIAIRS using a simulation testbed. The simulation is established using a professional plant simulator, where realistic data is constructed through its operation. The data is subsequently used to further our investigation into a support framework for distributed and interconnected systems [2] [3].

Simulation is considered to be a key role in the advancement of critical infrastructure protection. Currently, there are some simulation programs, which contain smart built-in models for many common real systems. These programs can be used to test new security techniques within a safe environment. Specifically, simulation test beds can be used to analyse the inputs and outputs and do all the required challenging work and give realistic and comprehensive results. In addition, simulations are not held back by the use of real-time data construction and can carry out complex models of operation in a relatively short period of time. As such, it is becoming a common technique for the testing of cyber-attack prevention measures and for improving the level of the security techniques [4]. A large critical infrastructure can be represented by creating a simple system and allow for realistic testing to take place [5].

Within this paper, realistic data constructed from a simulation of 8 critical infrastructures is presented in order to test the CIAIRS system. Furthermore, the big data analysis techniques used to identify patterns of abnormal behaviour and share threats between infrastructures are detailed. As such, the remainder of the paper is divided as follows: Section 2, presents a background on Critical Infrastructures (CI), CI modelling and highlights the important of the simulation. Section 3 introduces the CIAIRS framework components and an overview of the system route. Subsequently, Section 4 contains the evaluation of the system. Finally, Section 5 will conclude the paper.

II. BACKGROUND

In this section, a discussion on critical infrastructure growth and its interdependency characteristics is put forward. The focus is on the interdependency between the critical infrastructures and a number of modeling examples are discussed.

A. Critical Infrastructures Interdependency

The National Institute of Standards and Technology (NIST) defines critical infrastructures as any physical or virtual systems that would affect the national security, public economy and health service by their failure or if damage occurred to them [6]. Critical infrastructure assets, as explained by Command et al., and can be divided into three categories [7]. Firstly, the physical assets, which could be tangible or intangible. Secondly, human assets, that can represent vulnerabilities by having privileged access to important information or systems. Thirdly, cyber assets, which include hardware, software, data, and which all, serve the network functionality.

Infrastructure is the main source of development and economic construction process of any country [8]. Different types of urban developments depend on the size and the provision of infrastructure elements, which help guide the development of new areas. Critical infrastructures are considered to be the head of the development process and the driving force behind economic construction. Urban development depends on the size and the provision of infrastructure elements of style, which contributes to guiding the development of new areas. However, many infrastructures, such as power plants, are considerably outdated and are therefore difficult to repair [6]. This means that disruptions in service provision and weaknesses in security are apparent.

Yusufovna et al., discuss energy resources, finance, food, health, government services, manufacturing, law and legislation, transportation [9]. As Yusufovna et al. discussed, there is a risk of these security weaknesses causing failures, which can cascade across borders. For example, they present a survey on different groups of critical infrastructure and detail how many are international and national as well as local and individual. This means that any successful attack may have a political and economic impact, which spams across borders.

As previously discussed, in the result of the global expansion, and with the Internet revolution, infrastructures have become highly complex and have increased the interdependency at the physical and network layers. Therefore, the interdependency is considered to be one characteristic that can raise several concerns; in particular the analysis and modelling of interdependencies due to the complicated interactions [10][11]. For that reason, accurate critical infrastructure modelling techniques are imperative for the testing of new security metrics.

B. CI Modelling

Depending on the infrastructure type, the task of an accurate modelling is a challenge. This has led to develop simulation programs that can help diagnose infrastructure weaknesses and simulate their behaviours and interactions. This includes software, such as Tecnomatix [12], and the adaptation of existing software-based simulators, such as OMNET++, Simulink and Matlab [13], just to name a few. These simulators allow for affordable representations of critical infrastructure systems, by modelling their behaviour, interactions and the integration of their specific protocol types such as Modbus and DNP3.

The interest in simulation has increased as an appropriate and effective education process in recent years. Simulation has become a process to test concepts, activities, and experiments done through the computer. It has an increasingly important and prominent role in the cyber-security and critical infrastructure educational process [14]. Al-essa et al., defines simulation as a method for teaching students that bring elements from the real world, overriding difficulties such as material cost or human resources [15]. For that reason, the system proposed in this paper is evaluated through a simulation testbed rather than through a real-world application.

C. A Cyber Framework for CI

Simulations helped in enhancing the security level by using new framework concepts. For example, the NIST developed a framework to reduce the risk of cyber-attacks to critical infrastructure [16]. The NIST framework includes sets of procedures and methodologies that help to understand the cyber risks. Moreover, the approach involves flexible, classified, performance-based, and cost-effective method with more security measures. Finally, the framework helps the possessor and specialist of the critical infrastructure to recognize, classify, assess and control the cyber risk [16]. Specifically, the NIST cybersecurity framework has been set up to strengthen security through the following:

- Diagnose the security status of a system.
- Mend and form a cyber-security program.
- Detect new chances for new or known standard.
- Support the critical infrastructure organisation, to use the cyber-security framework with tools and technologies.

Critical infrastructures have benefited from the NIST cybersecurity framework. This has been recognised by some notable improvements, such as reducing the time of starting the security program, reduce the risk by recognize the improving areas in the program and improving the efficient relationship between law and critical infrastructure [16].

Depending on the previous different frameworks and more which were used in order to improve the critical infrastructure level of security the next section will present our framework.

III. APPROACH FOR CIAIRS

In our research to date, a system framework titled Critical Infrastructure Auto-Immune Response System (CIAIRS), which is able to identify threats to a network and communicate the potential impact, has been put forward [2]. The quality of the framework depends on four main features: Simplicity, Clarity, Boundaries, Expandability [17]. Therefore, these features were taken in mind while forming the research approach.

CIAIRS functionality relies on identifying attacks, then the system assists and guides critical infrastructures on how to behave when abnormal behavior is detected. Furthermore, inspired by the human immune system characteristic the information is then shared to other infrastructures to create an immune system network [2]. In the following sub-sections, the CIAIRS structure is presented along with a detailed account of the various components, which work together to predict the abnormal behaviours and share them with other infrastructures. Then, high level of the CIARIS process is presented. Finally, a simulation of 8 critical infrastructures is presented to construct data for the evaluation of CIARIS.

A. *CIAIRS Design Overview*

Fig. 1 indicates the CIAIRS framework design and the interaction between the various modules, which function together to perform the security and communication services. The module linked together comprises the system as a whole and works together in order to detect abnormal behaviours in one infrastructure and share them with others. In doing so the aim is to prevent cyber-attacks from having a cascading impact and spreading to other infrastructures. Threat information can be communicated to allow operators in other infrastructures to take appropriate measures to prevent an attack having an impact.

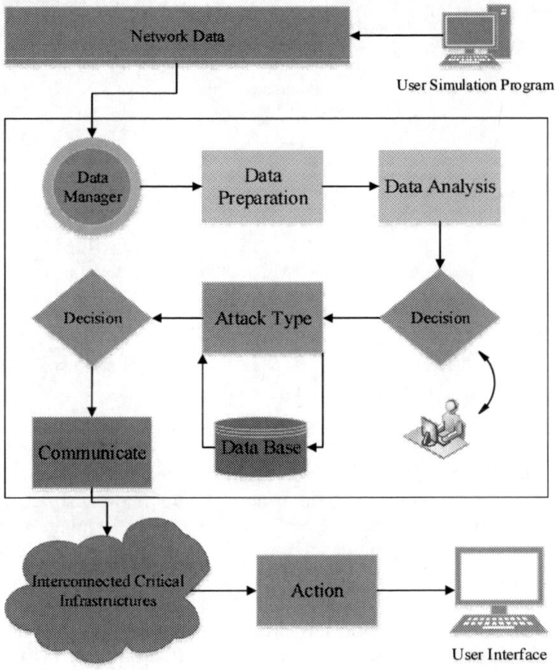

Figure 1. CIAIRS Design

CIAIRS is composed of several mechanisms, interconnected processes and a data collection modules. The different components that form the system, and the flow between the components, are displayed in Fig. 1. By extracting the data from the network, which, for the purposes of this research, is provided by the simulation, the data manager is responsible for controlling the intake of information. Extracting the data in blocks prevents overload of the system.

Subsequently, the data passes through a cleaning process to make sure there is no missing information; this stage called the Data Preparation stage. At this point, the data needs to have features extracted and be analysed. The features correspond to the system behaviour and present the behaviour in a simplified view of the overall network.

By using the features, a data classification process is involved in order to indicate the normal and the abnormal behaviour. In order to compare the attack type, the data is sent to a temporary database until needed. Each block of data is stored as a block of column data, which would help in comparing the CI data collection to the CI database.

Depending on the decision, the network uses the connectivity between infrastructures to share the new abnormal behaviour with interconnected partners. This would assist other infrastructure in planning for an emerging attack or cascading impact. At all times an administrator overviews the system functionality. This whole process is clarified further in the next subsection, which presents two key module components from the CIAIRS design. The Data Manager and the Communication Manager are explained in detail.

1) *CIAIRS Data Manager*

Fig. 2 presents a Data Flow Diagram for the CIAIRS processing of the infrastructure data. The data manager is responsible for data collection, validation and checking, purifying and storage. Each of these methods requires time (T) and data status (S).

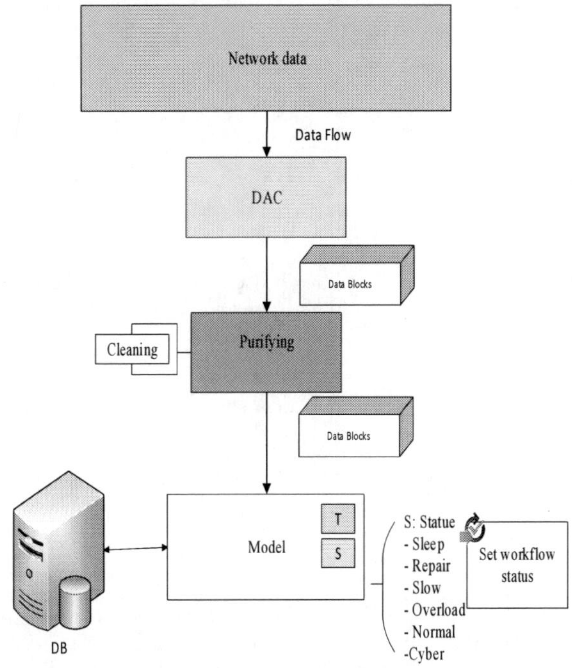

Figure 2. CIAIRS DFD Process

2) *CIAIRS Communication*

Fig. 3 presents the communication process for sharing attacks information between the different partners. This is one of the novelties of the design. After identifying abnormal behavior in one of the critical infrastructures, the attack information and characteristics are shared with interconnected partners in order to prevent cascading failures. After indicating an abnormal behaviour the CIAIRS communication process starts by checking the connectivity list in order to send an inherited script to the connected infrastructure.

The script, which includes the abnormal behaviour information from features, ID and source are compared to the data source of each interconnectivity CI. By comparing the database source, an indicator selects the corresponding information cell and adds to the database. Base on the result an action of recommendation is distributed order to suggest the right reaction for any future attacks.

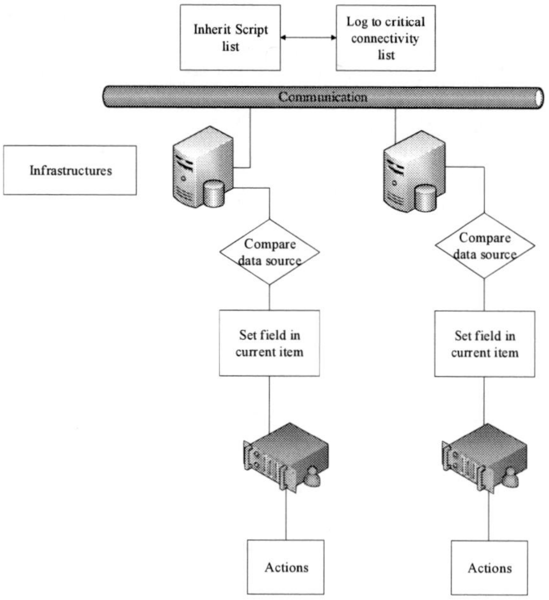

Figure 3. CIAIRS Communication

B. CIAIRS Simulation

In order to evaluate the discussed system design, as simulation testbed is constructed. Fig. 4 presents an emulation of 8 critical infrastructures, which include key service providers, such as an Electricity Grid and Water Distribution service. The full simulation is outlined in our past work [2][3]. Each of the critical infrastructure systems is given a graphical icon to represent its function more clearly. They can be expanded within the simulation, to show the different objects, which comprise the system as a whole.

Fig. 5 displays one of the presented critical infrastructures: The Water Distribution System. The Water Distributed System consists of a main water resource, the sea, a main electricity cable from the power plant and a transport system to send the water through pipes and feed both the houses in the compound and a factory. The Water Distribution System is controlled by a FlowControl to pump the water for both the Houses and the Factory, divided equally.

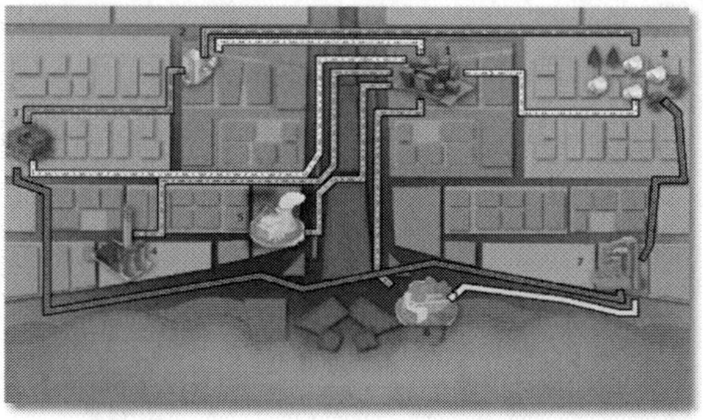

Figure 4. Simulation Overview

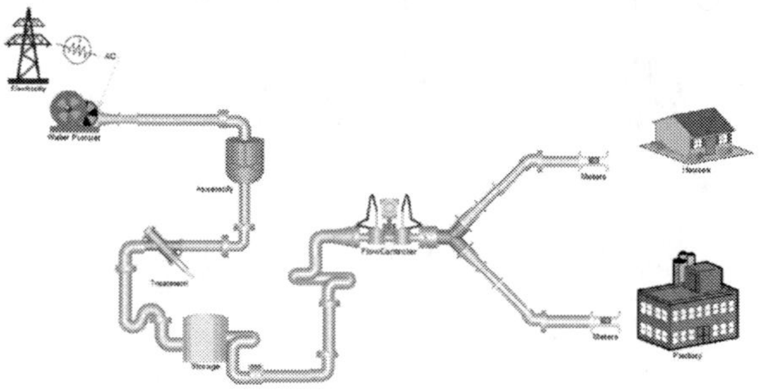

Figure 5. Water Distribution System

The experiments detailed in Section 3 are used to evaluate the proposed system, form the process layout and construct the product lifecycle management. As such, the evaluation is presented in the following section.

IV. EVALUATION

This section presents the evaluation process for CIAIRS. The evaluation can be either formative or summative [18]. A formative evaluation takes place during the project itself. On the other hand, a summative evaluation takes place after the project is done in order to assess if the outcomes met the aim of the project [18]. Therefore, a summative evaluation is used to improve the service within the CI's. The system is evaluated using data constructed through a simulation of a network of critical infrastructures. Data analysis is conducted using data visualisation to identify system anomalies and demonstrate that models of behaviour can be constructed and shared with other infrastructures.

In order to reach the aim of the research, two critical infrastructures are chosen as a case study, the Water Distribution System and the Electricity Grid. The impact on service provision to a housing compound is illustrated. The trends in data patterns for both normal and abnormal behaviour can be identified and communicated to prevent future impacts.

The first phase is data collection that conducts with a sampling rate of 4 Hertz (which is every 0.25 of a second). Blocks of data are extracted to prevent data overload and to support building the features from both normal and abnormal datasets [3]. In the next subsection, a data sample is presented, data trends and a statistical production report for one of the CIAIRS infrastructures is also provided as an example.

A. *Data Sample*

In order to understand the behaviour of the system, two data sets are constructed from The Water Distribution Infrastructure System. A normal system set constructed from a two days simulation. Then faults were introduced to the system as abnormal behaviours in order to construct a dataset of the system under attack. For this paper, a fault is introduced into the water pipe 1 and the water pipe connected to the houses compound inside the water distributed critical infrastructure. Tables I and II display data samples from normal behaviour mode and the abnormal mode in the Water Distribution Infrastructure, consecutively.

TABLE I NORMAL SIMULATION DATA SAMPLE

Time	F1	F2	F3	F4	F5	F6	F7	F8	F9	F10
Normal Data Set										
1:10:59:14.50	0	3	1	0	0	2	1	3	0	2
1:10:59:14.75	0	3	1	0	0	2	1	3	0	2
1:10:59:15.00	0	3	1	0	0	2	1	3	0	2
1:10:59:15.25	0	3	1	0	0	2	1	3	0	2
1:10:59:15.50	0	3	1	0	0	2	1	3	0	2

TABLE II ABNORMAL SIMULATION DATA SAMPLE

Time	F1	F2	F3	F4	F5	F6	F7	F8	F9	F10
Abnormal Data Set										
1:10:59:14.50	3	3	1	3	50	3	1	3	0	2
1:10:59:14.75	3	3	1	3	50	3	1	3	0	2
1:10:59:15.00	3	3	1	3	50	3	1	3	0	2
1:10:59:15.25	3	3	1	3	50	3	1	3	0	2
1:10:59:15.50	3	3	1	3	50	3	1	3	0	2

The simulation consists of 147 components in total. The numbers in the tables represent the units, which flow in the water pipe. It is clear that the between the time 1:10:59:14:50 to 1:10:59:15:50 the level of the water was fluctuated.

B. *Data Trends*

Based on the data collected, a number of features were extracted from both normal and abnormal behaviours. However, for the purpose of this paper, The Water Distribution Infrastructure system relative standard deviation (RSD) was chosen to indicate the change in behavioural patterns between normal and abnormal, which is displayed in Fig. 6. RSD is a statistical trend that helps in indicating how far the data from the mean and measure the distance for every value from the mean in order to employ the quality assurance. Fig. 6 displays the relative standard deviation for data trend for the Water Distribution Infrastructure with normal and one signal and two failures: water pipe 1 and the water pipe connected to the houses compound inside the water distributed critical infrastructure.

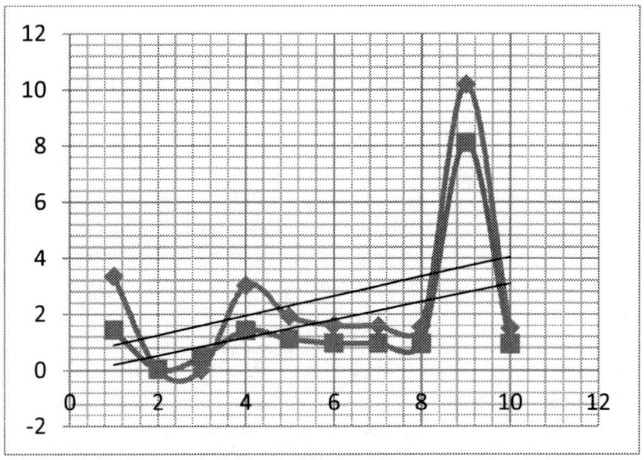

Figure 6. The normal and abnormal RSD Water Distribution

Fig. 6 clarifies the difference between the water rate in a normal system and a failure system with two failures in water pipe 1 and the water pipe connected to the houses compound inside the water distributed infrastructure. The red line, with squares, presents the abnormal behaviour trend while the blue, with diamonds, presents the normal behaviour trend. It is clear that the data does not follow a normal distribution. Moreover, that the failures had a significant impact on the water pipe from the Water Distribution Infrastructure system to Houses component in the Water Distribution Infrastructure system more than any other component.

V. STATISTICAL PRODUCTION REPORT

As the previous subsection presents, the data trends between the normal and abnormal behaviour can be seen. It is this information which can be commutated using CIARIS to interconnected infrastructures. In this case, the faults in the system have affected the percentage of the production for some components in different CI.

TABLE III THE NORMAL PRODUCTION STATISTICAL REPORT FOR THE WATER DISTRIBUTION INFRASTRUCTURE

Object	Name	Mean Life Time	Production	Transport	Storage	Value added	Portion
nuedearpower.vipor	steamvapor	25:48.4231	7.81%	92.19%	0.00%	3.94%	
nuedearpower.vipor	water	1:41:52.1647	3.85%	19.52%	76.63%	0.98%	
houses.house1.Drainelechouse1	electricity	1:51.8491	71.75%	27.35%	0.89%	37.20%	
houses.house2.Drainelechouse2	electricity	1:51.8118	71.75%	27.36%	0.89%	37.22%	
houses.house3.Drainelechouse3	electricity	4.2426	0.00%	100.00%	0.00%	0.00%	
houses.house4.Drainelechouse4	electricity	2.8284	0.00%	100.00%	0.00%	0.00%	
houses.house5.Drainelechouse5	electricity	2.8284	0.00%	100.00%	0.00%	0.00%	
houses.house6.Drainelechouse6	electricity	2.8284	0.00%	100.00%	0.00%	0.00%	
houses.Drain	car	1:42.2102	0.00%	100.00%	0.00%	0.00%	
houses.Drain1	car	1:40.6394	0.00%	100.00%	0.00%	0.00%	
factory.Drain	electricity	1:43.7490	78.44%	20.60%	0.96%	41.16%	

By comparing Tables III and IV, which show the statistical service production report, it is clear that the production of the electricity in the houses hains dropped from 71.75% to 61.19% and the production of the electricity in the factory also decreased by 10%. The result indicates that the attacks, which accrued in the Water Distribution Infrastructure faults, have affected the production of the electricity in two other infrastructures including a factory and the housing complex.

TABLE IV THE ABNORMAL PRODUCTION STATISTICAL REPORT FOR THE WATER DISTRIBUTION INFRASTRUCTURE

Object	Name	Mean Life Time	Production	Transport	Storage	Value added	Portion
nueclearpower.vipor	steamvapor	25:48.4231	7.81%	92.19%	0.00%	3.94%	
nueclearpower.vipor	water	1:41:52.1647	3.85%	19.52%	76.63%	0.98%	
houses.house1.Drainelechouse1	electricty	2:12.2814	61.19%	38.05%	0.76%	31.73%	
houses.house2.Drainelechouse2	electricty	2:08.6905	61.79%	37.43%	0.78%	32.06%	
houses.house3.Drainelechouse3	electricty	4.2426	0.00%	100.00%	0.00%	0.00%	
houses.house4.Drainelechouse4	electricty	2.8284	0.00%	100.00%	0.00%	0.00%	
houses.house5.Drainelechouse5	electricty	2.8284	0.00%	100.00%	0.00%	0.00%	
houses.house6.Drainelechouse6	electricty	2.8284	0.00%	100.00%	0.00%	0.00%	
houses.Drain	car	1:42.2102	0.00%	100.00%	0.00%	0.00%	
houses.Drain1	car	1:40.6394	0.00%	100.00%	0.00%	0.00%	
factory.Drain	electricty	1:59.9414	68.27%	30.89%	0.83%	35.82%	

VI. CONCLUSION

The development and evaluation of CIAIRS are presented in this paper. The simulation put forward can be used to create substantial datasets. Critical infrastructure interconnectivity is one of the main challenges. Systems such as CIAIRS can assist to countering the growing cyber-threats and the risk of cascading failures. This paper presented the CIAIRS's framework. The various components and mechanisms were highlighted in order to present the role of the CIAIRS, which shares information with other infrastructures, using the human immune system as a reference model, to create a distributed support network for enhanced cyber-security.

REFERENCES

[1] A. Laugé, J. Hernantes, and J. Mari Sarriegi, "The Role of Critical Infrastructures' Interdependencies on the Impacts Caused by Natural Disasters," Crit. Inf. Infrastructures Secur., vol. 8328, pp. PP50–61, 2013.

[2] S. Badri, P. Fergus, W. Hurst, and B. Street, "Critical Infrastructure Automated Immuno-Response System (CIAIRS)," in 3rd International conference, Malta, p. 6, 2016.

[3] S. Badri, P. Fergus, and W. Hurst, "A Support Network for Distributed Systems," n 10th Int. Conf. E-Learning Games., p. 16, 2016.

[4] E. Commission, "Digital Agenda: cyber-security experts test defences in first pan-European simulation," Eur. Comm. Press Release, no. November, 2010.

[5] C. M. Davis,et al., "SCADA cyber security testbed development," in 2006 38th Annual North American Power Symposium, NAPS-2006 Proceedings, pp. 483–488, 2006.

[6] National Institute of Standards and Technology, "Framework for Improving Critical Infrastructure Cybersecurity," Natl. Inst. Stand. Technol., vol. 1, pp. 1–41, 2014.

[7] D. Command and F. Leavenworth, "Critical Infrastructure Threats and Terrorism," in DCSINT handbook No. 1.02, 1st ed., no. 1, Distribution Unlimited, 2006.

[8] S. Marrone, R. et al., "Vulnerability modeling and analysis for critical infrastructure protection applications," Int. J. Crit. Infrastruct. Prot., vol. 6, no. 3–4, pp. 217–227, 2013.

[9] F. S. Yusufovna, et al., "Research on Critical Infrastructures and Critical Information Infrastructures," in 2009 Symposium on Bio-inspired Learning and Intelligent Systems for Security pp. 97–101, 2009.

[10] S. M. Rinaldi, "Modeling and Simulating Critical Infrastructures and Their Interdependencies," in System Sciences, 2004. Proceedings of the 37th Annual Hawaii International Conference on,vol. 00, no. C, pp. 1–8, 2004.

[11] B. S. M. Rinaldi, J. P. Peerenboom, and T. K. Kelly, "Identifying, Understanding, and Analyzing: Critical Infrastructure Interdependecies," Control Syst. IEEE, vol. 21, no. 6, pp. 11–25, 2001.

[12] Siemens, "www.siemens.com/tecnomatix," 2011. Access on: March 2016

[13] S. Bangsow," Manufacturing Simulation with Plant Simulation and SimTalk", vol. 1. 2015.

[14] D. Asteteh and O. Sarhan, Education and e-Learning Technology. Jorden: darwael, 2007.

[15] A. AL-esaa, "The effect of using simulation Implementing strategy through computer teaching assistant in the immediate and delayed achievement," Jorden, 1993.

[16] National Institute of Standards and Technology, "Framework for improving critical infrastructure cybersecurity," no. April, 2015.

[17] A. R. McGee, S. Rao Vasireddy, C. Xie, D. D. Picklesimer, U. Chandrashekhar, and S. H. Richman, "A framework for ensuring network security," Bell Labs Tech. J., vol. 8, no. 4, pp. 7–27, 2004.

[18] R. Hartson and P. Pyla, The UX Book: Process and Guidelines for Ensuring a Quality User Experience. USA: Elsevier, 2012.

Impact of Topology on Service Availability in a Smart Grid Advanced Metering Infrastructure

Bashar Alohali, Kashif Kifayat, Qi Shi, William Hurst
School of Computing and Mathematical Sciences,
Liverpool John Moores University, Liverpool, UK,
B.A.Alohali@2012.ljmu.ac.uk{K.Kifayat, Q.Shi, W.Hurst}@ljmu.ac.uk

***Abstract*— over the last decade, Wireless Sensor Networks (WSNs) have brought radical changes to the means and forms of communication for monitoring and control of a large number of applications including Smart Grid (SG). Traditional energy networks have been modernized to Smart Grids to boost the energy industry in the context of efficient and effective power management, performance, real-time control and information flow using two-way communication between utility provides and end-users. However, integrating two-way communication in smart grid comes at the cost of cyber security vulnerabilities and challenges. In the context of SG, node capture is a severe security threat due to the fact that a compromised node can significantly impact the operations and security of the SG network. In this paper, node compromise attack is explored on Advance Metering Infrastructure (AMI) with smart meters for Neighbor Area Networks (NANs) in star and mesh network topologies. Simulation of node compromise/failure for a SG network, using ZigBee nodes in simulation indicates that a partial mesh topology is more resilient to node capture attacks as compared to star topology. A larger number of nodes are reachable from the control center of the SG in a partial mesh topology compared to that in a star topology.**

Keywords- Smart meter; Smart Grid;, Node Capture, Mesh Smart Meter, Start Smart Meter

I. INTRODUCTION

The swift development of information and communication technology (ICT) has not only changed the way we live our lives but also changed the industrial automation system including Smart Grid (SG) to an effective, efficient and reliable system. The integration of ICT has been of great importance to transform the traditional energy networks into SGs to ensure a reliable system and to overcome the limitations and challenges experienced by traditional energy networks. The U.S department of energy has defined the smart grid as an "electricity delivery system (from point of generation to point of consumption) integrated with communication and information technologies for enhanced grid operations, customers' services and environmental benefits [1]."

Recently, wireless sensor networks (WSNs) have shown great potential for various applications including in SGs. The SG applications can include a range of devices/systems such as smart meters (SMs), advance metering infrastructure (AMI), wide area measurement system (WAMS), substation automation system, common information models (CIF), and fault diagnosis to achieve seamless, efficient energy transmission and distribution, effective and reliable remote monitoring due to its easy deployment in remote locations, low cost, low date rates and low energy consumption [2-5]. Regardless of the economical and functional benefits exploited by SGs, its adoption, deployment and resiliency has been of great challenge due to potential lack of adequate security and vulnerable attacks like node capture to damage confidentiality, integrity and availability [6-7]. SMs, deployed in domestic and commercial location, required to be interconnected for communication and data flow to management entities. The deployment (i.e. star, tree, partial/full mesh) will vary as per the distribution of SMs in NANs environment and can severely impact the network resiliency due to network threats. The aim of this paper is to explore the node compromise attack on AMI and so smart meters for NANs star and mesh network topology. SG network segments in different topologies are simulated using OPNET. The simulation results show that a partial mesh topology is more resilient to node capture (NC) attacks.

The paper is organized as follows. Section 2 presents the related work followed by architecture and the functionality of SGs and its components in section 3. Section 4 describes the NC attack and its impact on NAN star and mesh topology is analyzed in section 5 and 6. Finally, Section 7 concludes the paper and future work is outlined.

II. SMART GRID OVERVIEW

A SG network permits services to have bi-directional interaction with devices on their electric grid as well with end-users and distributed power generation and storage facilities. To achieve the detailed view of the Smart Grid, it can be considered as a heterogeneous network (Fig. 1) based on the interconnection of multiple networks segments such as, the Home Area Networks (HANs) for effective energy at consumer end; the Neighborhood Area Network (NAN) for providing advance metering infrastructure; and the Wide Area Network (WAN) to distribute automation and the SG backbone [14]. The HAN interconnects to the WAN via a SM, which is part of NAN. Majority of the devices in the HAN and NAN are wireless communicating nodes. The interconnectivity of SMs into NAN is collectively referred to as advanced metering infrastructure (AMI) and is the main focus of this paper. NAN can be a network of smart meters creating a star, tree, or mesh network, which consists of smart meters and gateways that relay data.

AMI facilitates the critical communication and control functions required to implement important energy management services such as pricing schemes, demand response, automatic meter reading, and management of power quality. AMI, integrated with million number of low-cost nodes being placed in insecure, uninterested and unsophisticated locations, make smart metering vulnerable to cyber-attacks such as spoofing, eavesdropping, Denial-of-Service (DoS), man-in-the-middle attacks and node compromise [13,15]. To ensure secure communication and resiliency in SM infrastructure and so AMI is one of the critical requirements.

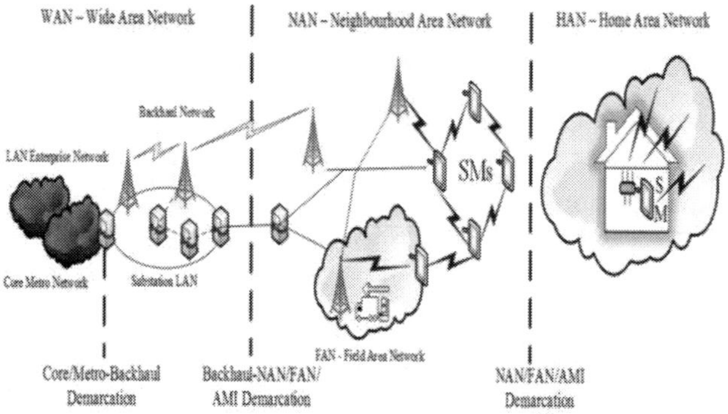

Figure 1 Smart Grid Network

III. RELATED WORK

According to The U.S. Department of Energy, an emerging SG system must possess seven critical properties including resiliency to vulnerable attacks [8]. Over the last decade, malicious security threats on SG system have raised serious concerns. In 2003, due to Slammer worm attack from dial-up connection, Davis-Besse nuclear plant in Ohio was turned off to limit the impact of the threat [9]. In Iran, due the Bushehr power plant was infected due to one of the very first malicious coding attack known as Stuxnet worm [10]. The recent cyber-attack on Ukraine's power network also highlighted the security and system resiliency as major requirement for smart grid [11].

In [12], a binary tree based topology has been considered to introduce an efficient and scalable key management scheme for secure unicast, multicast and broadcast communication in SGs. The scheme demands considerable manual tasks to create the binary tree and transmit it together with secret key to each node. Due to binary tree nature, this scheme is vulnerable to NC attack where a compromised node can put network resiliency at risk due to unavailability of an alternative route. In [13] tree attack has been explored on tree topology and highlighted the tree topology as vulnerable for energy theft in AMI. There have been various studies to highlight and enhance the security of Smart Grids based on encryption techniques and key management approaches against different attacks. However, the analysis of NANs resiliency considering tree and mesh topology against attacks like NC has been overlooked.

IV. NODE COMPROMISE / CAPTURE ATTACK

Among various attacks in SGs, node compromise attack is a severe threat due to unattended nature of the sensor nodes. In a NC threat, an intruder can capture/compromise a node (SM) to get the access to secure cryptographic keys, node identification, communication between node and the network and monitor by re-deploying the compromised node into the network [16-17]. Once a node is compromised, it allows an intruder to execute various operations/attacks on the network and easily compromise the entire network. According to [18], there are three critical factors as mentioned below, which can lead intruder to compromise the entire network while triggering the node capture threat.

1. Cryptography technology has been of great interest to secure data transmitted across the AMI and authenticates the different entities involved in the communication flow. Node capture threat can result into a massive threat if the key(s) used to encrypt/decrypt data among neighboring nodes are deployed with weak key security and management.
2. The node deployment/topology play a critical role as it affects the scope of the node capture attacks. Generally, the scope can be defined based on the number of communication links such as, fewer the communication links between neighboring nodes (i.e. tree topology), the greater the possibility that an intruder can threat entire network. At the other end, higher the communication links between neighboring nodes (i.e. full/partial mesh topology), the smaller the possibility that an intruder can threat entire network. Therefore, node capture attacks seem to be less effective to mesh topology as compared to star topology, where there is only route from a child node to parent node.
3. The node density also plays a critical role as it affects the scope of the node capture attacks. A node compromised in the larger density network can threat the larger section of network.

Therefore, security of SM nodes and so the AMI is a critical issue to maintain the security and resiliency. Cryptography mechanisms based on symmetric (single share key) and asymmetric (public and private key) represents a crucial technology to secure the data transmitted across the nodes. A key (responsible to encrypt and decrypt data) plays a critical role and therefore an unauthorized access to key through a compromised node can threat entire network. In this paper, it is assumed the NANs use encrypted communication based on random redistribution key approach.

SMs, deployed in domestic and commercial location, required to be interconnected for communication and data flow to management entities. The deployment (i.e. star, tree, partial/full mesh) will vary as per the distribution of SMs in NANs environment. Fig. 2, 3 shows the example of star and mesh NAN topology.

Star-based network deployment is characterized by central root node, connected at the highest level in the hierarchy as show in Fig.3. Top-level node is connected to 2nd level, whereas 2nd level nodes are connected to 3rd level and so forth. The levels of the star topology can be denoted by $n \in N := \{1, 2, \ldots N\}$, where the 0^{th}level is for top root.

In a mesh network deployment, a node in each of the smart meter in NANs will communicate (transmit / receive) data by hoping from one node to another node until either the receiving node is reached or transmitted data reached to mesh gateway from node to node as shown in Fig. 3. The data from the gateway is typically transmitted to central data station via a backhaul network. The GWs are connected as start topology to backhaul network and SMs are connected as partial mesh as each SM is not directly connected to each of the other SM in the network.

V. METHODOLOGY

A. Network Security Model

It is considered that a group of Smart Meters (SMs) with one SM taking on the role of a gateway (GW) is interconnected in a manner that some SMs have a multi hop path to the gateway (GW). The GW interconnects to the central authentication point over the backhaul network. SMs that are children of other SMs use the multi-hop path to reach the GW node as shown in Fig. 2. It is assumed the NANs use encrypted communication based on random redistribution key approach. Each node is configured with a set of (K) different keys from a key pool of (P) keys. A pair of nodes with the range (R) can initiate a secure connectivity only if appropriate assigned keys are shared between them. It is also assumed that every node is deployed in a promiscuous approach and is able to recognize sources of all messages initiating from its neighboring nodes. Based on this assumption, each node will inspect only the source node ID therefore this assumption will not incur significant communication overhead.

B. Network Threat Model and Performance Metrics

It is assumed that an intruder can physically capture a limited number of SM nodes in a target region Ŗ and turn them into threat node by extracting secure keys and measured data for NAN. Considering Ç represents a set of nodes captured by intruder and for each node in set Ç, a set of secure keys are considered to be compromised. When a node is compromised, its connectivity to other nodes is affected. If the node is not an end node, a larger number of nodes lose connectivity. It allows intruder to clone a captured node and collaboratively deploy them in the NAN. The resiliency of NAN star and mesh topology in Smart Grid against NC attack will be evaluated based on following metrics; hop count, availability of SM, End to End Delay, and Energy Consumption.

C. Network Topology and Simulation Setup

To carry out evaluation of NC attacks, two NAN topologies, star and mesh as shown in Fig. 2 are considered. The NAN made of (N) nodes is deployed over a region of $(A \subseteq \mathbb{R})$. Considering that SMs in the AMI are fixed nodes, there is no mobility aspect included. Each node is assumed to be equipped with an omni-directional radio with fixed communication range (R) based on the Zigbee standard. To evaluate the resiliency of star and partial mesh topology in NAN in smart grid based on Zigbee network against node capture attack, OPNET simulation tool has been used. In both star and mesh topology simulation of NAN, network consist of a Zigbee coordinator (Gateway) and Zigbee end devices (SMs).

Case 1 – Star Topology: In this case, Zigbee nodes are deployed in a star topology for NAN.

Case 2 – Tree Topology: In a NAN tree topology, there is a relationship of root (GW) and child (SM) node. The child node can communicate only with their parent node whereas the parents can communicate with their child and their own parent node. Therefore, child node (SM) always depends on the parent node for data availability as there are no alternative routes for SM node to get target.

Case 3 – Mesh Topology: In this case, Zigbee nodes are deployed as partial mesh topology for NAN. NAN Mesh topology is more flexible as it can allow each node to choose between multiple routes to transmit/receive data to the target location. It also allows the network to self-heal and search for other paths and so that data can be relay through.

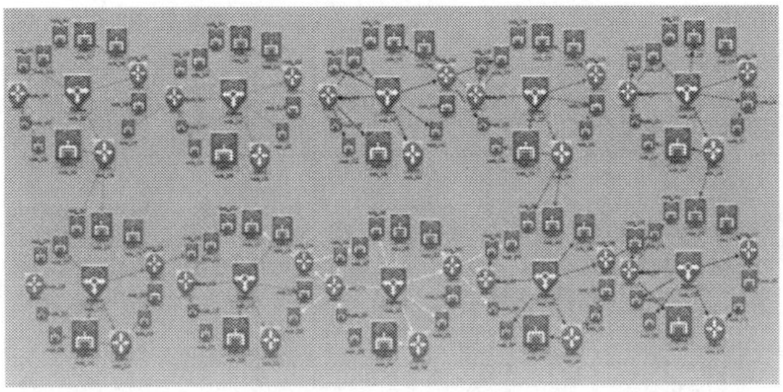

Figure 2 Mesh Topology scenarios

VI. PERFORMANCE ANALYSIS AND DISCUSSION

In this section, the OPNET simulation [19] of both star and mesh NAN topologies against node capture attacks are discussed to highlight which NAN topology is more resilient against node capture attacks.

A. Node Capture Attack and Impact on Reachability

Node capture attack involves capturing a node and incapacitating it. Often the data in the node is retrieved for malicious use, but in case of tamper-resistant hardware, the access to data on the ROM of the device is avoided. Therefore, the primary impact of a node capture is the loss of the node. In addition to the loss of the sensed data from the node, the reachability from/to the central reporting node, the NOC, is impacted. This happens when the captured node provides a path for the downstream nodes to reach the NOC.

In order to assess the impact of the reachability in the event of a node capture, star and mesh topologies are used to create a large network. For each node captured or a group of nodes captured, the number of nodes that are unreachable are noted.

A network comprising ten ZigBee coordinator nodes, thirty ZigBee router nodes and a hundred ZigBee devices are used to create the network to test the impact of the node capture attack. The topology at the coordinator node is set to mesh and star respectively for each simulation run, in its network parameters.

The coordinator node sends packets to the routers and end devices in each case.

Nodes are randomly chosen to fail and the reachability from the NOC to all nodes is checked. The simulations are run for the two topologies separately and in each case, up to 9 nodes are failed. The corresponding numbers of nodes that are unreachable are noted. The figure plots the number of unreachable nodes against the number of captured nodes.

The plotted results indicate that the mesh topology of the ZigBee network fares better than the star topology. The results are dependent upon which nodes are captured in the mesh topology. If an attacker succeeds in capturing and incapacitating all the ZigBee router nodes, then the impact could be more intense. It could turn out that the mesh topology could fare worse than the star topology.

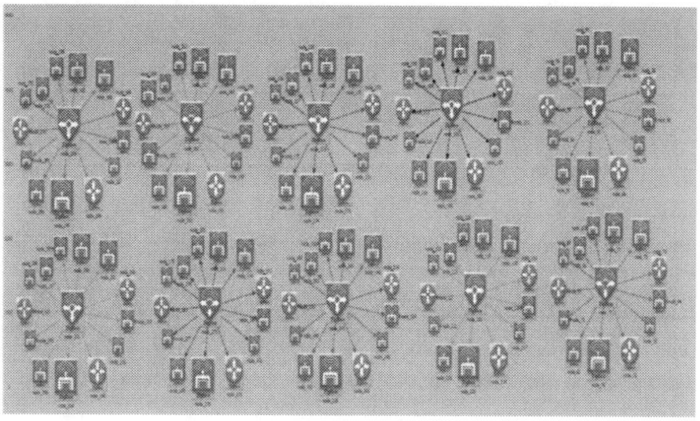

Figure 3 Star Topology scenarios

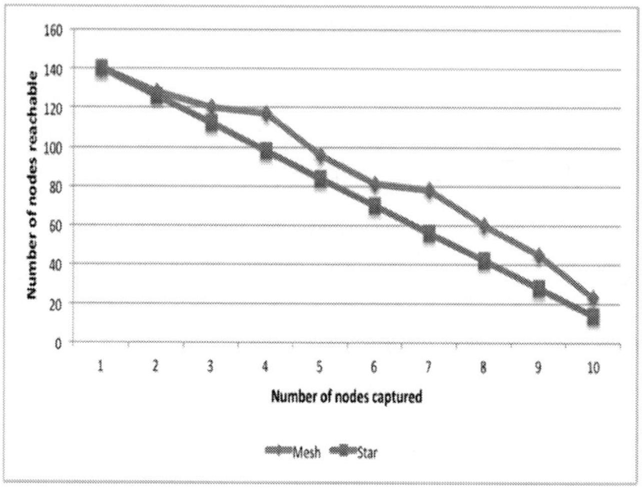

Figure 4 Reachability of nodes after node captures

VII. Conclusion

Node capture attacks in Smart Grid can significantly degrade network performance and threaten network security. Based on the simulation results, it is identified that partial mesh topology is more resilient topology as compared to star topology in NAN in Smart Grid against node capture attacks. As compared to NAN star, NAN mesh topology is more flexible as it can allow smart nodes to choose between multiple routes to transmit/receive data to the target location, if one of the node(s) compromised. Due to the flexibility offered by mesh topology, it is not only resilient but also an ideal solution with easy to deploy in NAN environment.

This study has been focused on simple star and partial mesh topology for NAN along with NC attack. For future work, the study will be extended to complex topology star, star and mesh topology along with advance threat model and security scheme to detect and avoid node capture attacks to enhance the network resiliency as well as security.

References

1. Sioshansi, F. O, *Smart Grid: Integrating Renewable, Distributed & Efficient Energy*, Academic Press, 2012, p. 89.
2. V. C. Gungor, B. Lu and G. P. Hancke, "Opportunities and Challenges of Wireless Sensor Networks in Smart Grid," *IEEE Transactions on Industrial Electronics*, vol. 57, no. 10, pp. 3557-3564, 2010.
3. E. Fadel, V.C. Gungor, L. Nassef, N. Akkari, M.G. Abbas Malik, S. Almasri, I. F. Akyildiz, "A survey on wireless sensor networks for smart grid", *Computer Communications*, Vol. 1, pp. 22-33, 2015.
4. Z. Popovic and V. Cackovic, "Advanced Metering Infrastructure in the context of Smart Grids," *IEEE International Energy Conference (ENERGYCON)*, pp. 1509-1514, 2014.

5. L. Nian, C. Jinshan, Z. Lin, Z. Jianhua, and H. Yanling, "A Key Management Scheme for Secure Communications of Advanced Metering Infrastructure in Smart Grid," *IEEE Transactions on Industrial Electronics*, vol. 60, pp. 4746-4756, 2013.
6. M. Amin, "Guaranteeing the security of an increasingly stressed grid," *IEEE Smart Grid Newsletter*, Feb. 2011.
7. NIST, "Guidelines for Smart Grid Cybersecurity, Volume 1 - Smart Grid Cybersecurity Strategy, Architecture, and High-Level Requirements, The Smart Grid Interoperability Panel – Smart Grid Cybersecurity Committee, 2014, National Institute of Standards and Technology, U.S. Department of Commerce.
8. U.S. Department of Energy, National Energy Technology Laboratory, *A Systems View of the Modern Grid*, 2007.
9. Y, Yang, T, Littler, S. Sezer, K. McLaughlin, H. F. Wang, "Impact of cyber-security issues on Smart Grid", *2nd IEEE PES International Conference and Exhibition on Innovative Smart Grid Technologies*, vol., no, pp.1,7, 2011.
10. D. Kushner. (2016, 8/3/2016). *The Real Story of Stuxnet*, 2013, Available: http://spectrum.ieee.org/telecom/security/the-real-story-of-stuxnet
11. L. Tomkiw. (2016, 8/3/2016). *Russia-Ukraine Cyberattack Update: Security Company Links Moscow Hacker Group To Electricity Shut Down*. Available: http://www.ibtimes.com/russia-ukraine-cyberattack-update-security-company-links-moscow-hacker-group-2256634
12. J. Y. Kim, and H. K. Choi, "An efficient and versatile key management protocol for secure smart grid communications," *IEEE Wireless Communications and Networking Conference (WCNC)*, pp. 1823-1828, 2012.
13. S. McLaughlin, D. Podkuiko, P. McDaniel, "Energy Theft in the Advanced Metering Infrastructure", *Critical Information Infrastructures Security*, Vol. 6027 of the series Lec Notes in Computer Science, pp 176-187, 2009.
14. W. Meng, R. Ma, and H.-H. Chen, "Smart grid neighbourhood area networks: a survey," *IEEE Network*, vol. 28, pp. 24-32, 2014
15. S.H. Seo, X. Ding and E. Bertino, "Encryption key management for secure communication in smart advanced metering infrastructures," *IEEE International Conference on Smart Grid Communications (SmartGridComm)*, Vancouver, BC, pp. 498-503, 2013
16. M. V. Bharathi, R. C. Tanguturi, C. Jayakumar and K. Selvamani, "Node capture attack in Wireless Sensor Network: A survey," *IEEE International Conference on Computational Intelligence & Computing Research (ICCIC)*, Coimbatore, pp. 1-3, 2012.
17. K.Venkatraman, J.Vijay Daniel, G.Murugaboopathi, "Various Attacks in Wireless Sensor Network: Survey", *International Journal of Soft Computing and Engineering (IJSCE)*, Vol. 3, No. 1, pp. 208-212, 2013.
18. K. Kifayat, M. Merabti, Q, Shi, and D. Llewellyn-Jones, *Security in Wireless Sensor Networks, Chapter 26, Handbook of Information and Communication Security*, Springer Science & Business Media, 2010.
19. RIVERBED. 2014. Riverbed Modeler Version 17.5, PL6,, Riverbed Software [Online]. Available: http://www.riverbed.com/.

Smart Monitoring: An Intelligent System to Facilitate Health Care across an Ageing Population

Carl Chalmers, William Hurst, Michael Mackay, Paul Fergus
School of Computing and Mathematical Sciences
Liverpool John Moores University
Byrom Street
Liverpool, L3 3AF, UK
{C.Chalmers, W.Hurst, M.I.Mackay, P.Fergus}@ljmu.ac.uk

Abstract— **In the UK, the number of people living with self-limiting conditions, such as Dementia, Parkinson's disease and depression, is increasing. The resulting strain on national healthcare resources means that providing 24-hour monitoring for patients is a challenge. As this problem escalates, caring for an ageing population will become more demanding over the next decade. Our research directly proposes an alternative and cost effective method for supporting independent living that offers enhancements for Early Intervention Practices (EIP). In the UK, a national roll out of smart meters is underway, which enable detailed around-the-clock monitoring of energy usage. This granular data captures detailed habits and routines through the users' interactions with electrical devices. Our approach utilises this valuable data to provide an innovative remote patient monitoring system. The system interfaces directly with a patient's smart meter, enabling it to distinguish reliably between subtle changes in energy usage in real-time. The data collected can be used to identify any behavioural anomalies in a patient's habit or routine, using a machine learning approach. Our system utilises trained models, which are deployed as web services using cloud infrastructures, to provide a comprehensive monitoring service. The research outlined in this paper demonstrates that it is possible to classify successfully both normal and abnormal behaviours using the Bayes Point Machine binary classifier.**

Keywords*— *Smart Meters, Profiling, Early Intervention Practice (EIP), Data Analysis, Patient Monitoring, Anomaly Detection, Assistive Technologies.

I. INTRODUCTION

Smart meters are the foundation of any smart electricity grid, used for balancing grid load and demand. They also provide consumers with highly reliable and accurate metering services. Energy usage readings are taken at 10 second intervals [1] and monitor the electrical usage of appliances in the home; specifically, their operation time and duration of use. All data is produced to a granular level. Their introduction has brought about new technological opportunities, which can be applied to a health care environment.

In the UK, around one in five adults are registered disabled. More than one million of those is currently living alone [2]. Providing a safe and secure living environment places a considerable strain on social and healthcare resources. Effective around the clock monitoring of these conditions is a significant challenge and affects the level of care provided. Consequently, a safe independent living environment is hard to achieve. Current public policy enables sufferers to live independently in their homes for as long as possible. However, it faces significant challenges. For example, current monitoring services are expensive and are met, often, with patient resistance, as the equipment is intrusive and complex. Substantial research gaps in non-invasive and cost effective monitoring technology exist [3]. Specifically, for safe and effective monitoring solutions, that are beneficial to the patient and healthcare providers alike. Any remote monitoring system must facilitate EIP, enabling front line services in the community to intervene much earlier.

As such, the method put forward in this paper presents the concept of smart meter analytics for the detection of anomalies in a patient's electricity usage. Using the Bayes Point Machine binary classifier, we demonstrate how the identification of abnormal behaviour provides an accurate solution for patient monitoring. The remainder of this paper is as follows. Section 2 provides a comprehensive assessment of current assistive living technologies while highlighting the significant caps in each of the methods. In addition, the different components that are used to facilitate the profiling of patients using smart meters is discussed. Section 3 discusses the proposed system methodology. Section 4 presents a detailed patient monitoring case study utilising the system. The paper in concluded in Section 5.

II. BACKGROUND

The use of smart technologies in primary care delivery is significantly increasing. In recent years, there has been rapid developments in monitoring technologies for independent living, early intervention services and condition management. In this section, an overview of these technologies, along with their feasibility, is provided.

A. Assistive Technologies and limitations

The term assistive technology covers a wide range of applications and tasks [4]. Assistive technology refers to devices or systems that support a person to maintain or improve their independence, safety and wellbeing. Typically, existing monitoring technologies can be divided into two categories. Firstly, physical aids, which assist the sufferer in performing specific tasks. Secondly, monitoring and surveillance, whereby electronic devices keep track of a person's medical condition and automatically alert health care staff when required. Although no official standardisations exist for assistive technologies, it is widely agreed that technology should be personalised, adaptive and non-intrusive. Current assistive living technologies involve the deployment of various sensors around the home [5]. These include motion sensors, cameras, fall detectors and communication hubs. However, installing, maintaining and monitoring these devices can be costly and a technical challenge [6].

In addition, diverse wearable technology exists. These include personal emergency response systems, wearable body networks, ECG, pulse oximeter, blood pressure and accelerometers. The main objective of these sensors is to obtain essential medical data to assist in the overall assessment of a patient's wellbeing. These readings enable clinical staff to assess remotely, while determining if there is a requirement for intervention.

There are many limitations and challenges with existing solutions, as many of them are impractical. Affordability and associated costs with existing technologies mean they cannot be implemented on a large scale. This leaves many solutions inaccessible to health care trusts, councils and social services. In addition, the use of sensors and cameras around the living environment raise many privacy and protection concerns [7]. This leads to a general reluctance to use the technology. Often technical solutions are tailored to a specific application and do not meet the ongoing changing requirements of a patient. Many solutions fail to adequately identify tends in behaviour, which may indicate health problems. This inhibits early intervention.

B. *Deploying Cloud Computing for Patient Monitoring*

One of the most significant limitations in existing solutions is the absence of personalisation. The inability to learn the unique characteristics of each individual and condition degrades the effectiveness of any solution. A person's habits and routines are clear indicators of their wellbeing. The ability to model routines and understand them is imperative for any patient monitoring system.

With the emergence of cloud infrastructures, the ability to analyse large data and model behaviour in real-time has become feasible. Smart meters like many other sensors generate large amounts of data [8]. Being able to extract and analyse useful information is an imperative requirement for any system. In order to achieve this requirement, the use of smart and scalable analytics services are needed. Big data is often unstructured and is often difficult to process using conventional tools. Cloud based analytics utilise complex and demanding algorithms which require vast computational power [9].

Using a cloud infrastructure removes the historical constraints associated with data analysis, as vast storage and flexible computational resources is offered. Using cloud services enables the real-time interpretation of data intelligence through the integration of front-end applications. This can be achieved by deploying analytical services, such as ready-to-use web services. These web services enable the integration of apps, which can be utilised to provide critical information to the patients support network. Our solution takes advantage of the cloud infrastructure and big data analytics, to provide a personalised patient monitoring system. The following section introduces our dataset and discusses the system methodology.

III. METHODOLOGY

In this section, the components of the system and their specific roles are highlighted. A case study is presented, along with the data analytics being used.

A. *End to End Processing*

The system directly interfaces with a patient's smart meter to learn and detect changes in routine. It operates in two separate modes. Firstly, mode one, which is used for training and, secondly, mode two which is used for the prediction of health deterioration. The method has a modular design in order to cater for different circumstances of healthcare monitoring. Smart meter data is collected in an unstructured way. Therefore, the data is processed by collecting energy usage readings that represent a specific behaviour. Figure 1 shows this overall process.

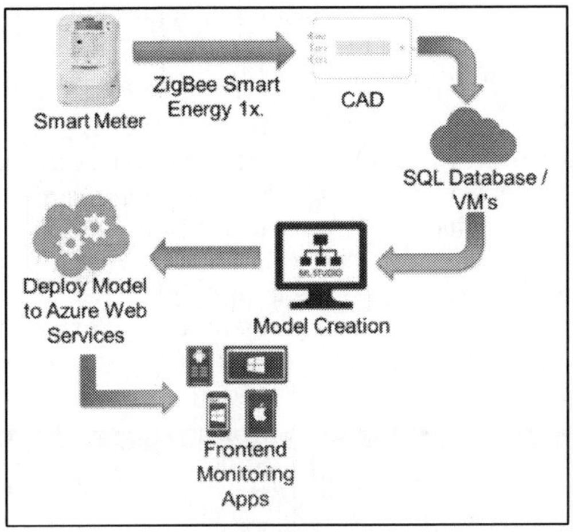

Figure 1. End-to-End Process.

The process starts with the smart meter, which resides within the patient's home. The main function of this device is to record accurately and store electricity consumption information for defined times (to a minimum of 10 seconds). Table 1 shows example readings obtained from a smart meter at 10 second intervals. The date time column illustrates the date and time of the reading, while the reading column displays the amount of electrical load in watts.

TABLE 1. DATA SAMPLE

Date Time	Reading
01/03/2016 21:25	1217
01/03/2016 21:25	1224

In order to collect the energy usage readings from the smart meter a Consumer Access Device (CAD) is required. Smart meters utilise ZigBee smart energy. The UK Department of Energy & Climate Change (DECC) has announced Smart Metering Equipment Technical Specifications (SMETS) 2, which cites the use of ZigBee Smart Energy 1.x.

Smart meters establish a wireless Home Area Network in a consumer's home. This is a local ZigBee wireless network (the SM HAN), which gas and electricity smart meters and in-home displays use to exchange data. Consumers are also able to pair other devices that operate the ZigBee Smart Energy Profile (SEP) to the network. Once a consumer has paired the device to their HAN, a CAD is able to access updated consumption and tariff information directly from their smart meter; a CAD can request updates of electricity information every 10 seconds and gas information every 30 minutes.

All of the obtained data from the CAD is logged remotely to a cloud SQL database. Here the data is used to create, test and deploy the classification models. Once the model is generated the classification models need to be accessible to the end user applications to provide real-time monitoring. This is achieved by deploying trained models, as ready-to-use web services. Once the web service is deployed, data from the SQL database can be directly sent to the service for active monitoring. The generated monitoring applications interface with the service API key to receive real-time monitoring alerts about the patient's wellbeing.

To further support individual health monitoring, a mobile application is provided to the patient. The patient is asked to log any unplanned interactions with medical services, such as visits to GPs, A and E and Walk-in Centres. The app records the visit type and date; this is undertaken so the patient's energy reading can be assessed prior to the visit and to highlight any noteworthy changes in behaviour directly to the medical practitioner. Figure 2 displays a screen shot of the mobile application.

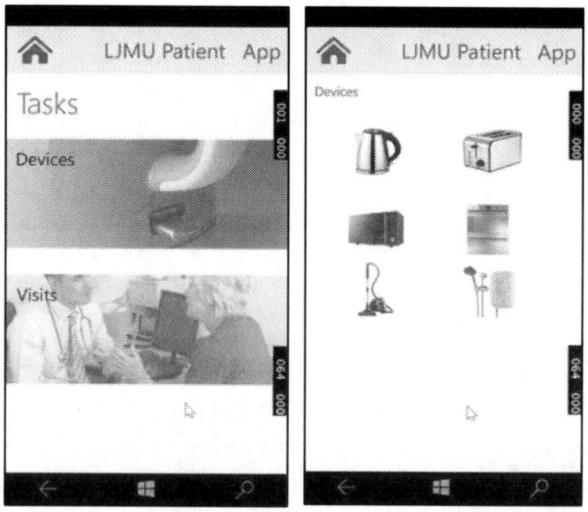

Figure 2. Application Screenshot.

B. Data Case Study

In this sub section, a case study presents the real-time data gathering capabilities of a smart meter. An energy monitor is installed in a person's home to perform the collection of real-time energy usage data. The installation is used to model a person's daily routine and to identify any noteworthy trends in device utilisation. Figure 3 shows the patient's energy usage taken at ten second intervals. The y-axis shows the amount of energy being consumed in Watts, while the x-axis shows a snap shot of the time. Each individual colour represents one week's electricity usage, which has been overlaid to show correlation over a three-week period.

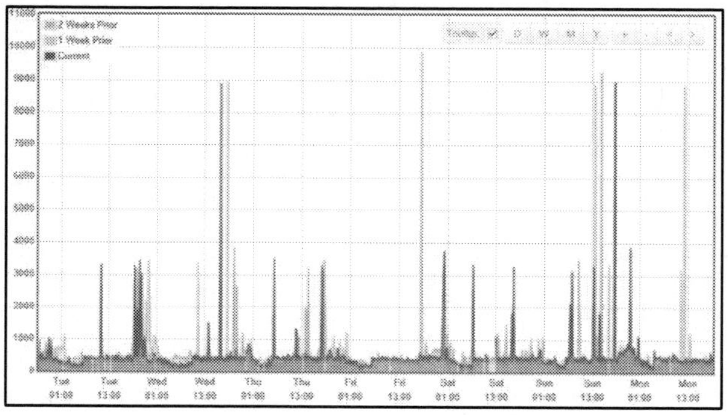

Figure 3. Energy Usage over a 3 Week Period.

Obtaining energy readings at 1 to 10 second intervals provides energy signatures for each device. Figure 4 displays the amount of electricity being consumed for a kettle and its duration of use. Identifying the use of specific electrical devices enables the assessment of a patient's wellbeing.

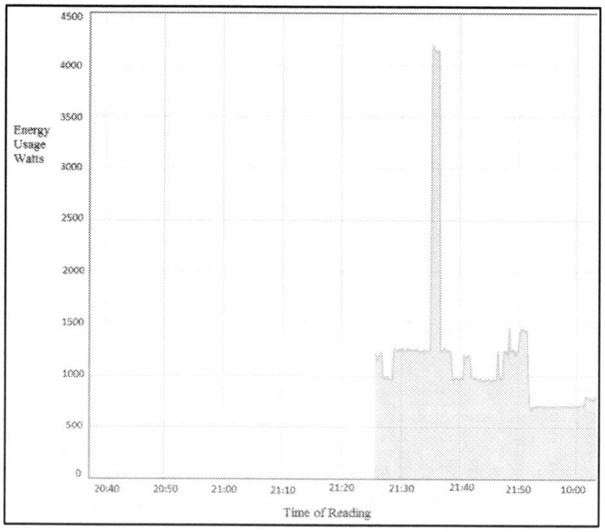

Figure 4. Kettle Usage.

C. Behavioural Analysis

Knowledge about a person's ability to undertake normal Activities of Daily Living (ADL) is an essential part for the overall assessment [10]. This is imperative in determining the diagnosis. The following list highlights the main ADL's that can be detected through a patient's interaction with their electrical devices:

- Eating patterns – for the purposes of detecting abnormal or altering changes in eating habits. These types of behavioural changes provide key indicators regarding the general health of the patient.
- Sleep patterns – changes in sleep patterns can provide insights into a patient's mental and physical wellbeing. Sleep disturbances are often key indicators for various mental health problems.
- Behavioural changes – provide impotent indicators for the detection of new conditions while providing information about the progression of existing medical problems.
- Changes in activity – can highlight possible periods of inactivity. These types of changes would require intervention to prevent additional complications and worsening of a patient's condition.
- Routine alteration – is vital for detecting changes in a patient behaviour and forms a key part in our system for the purposes of facilitating independent living. The identification of a route change especially in more serious conditions such as dementia can indicate the need for immediate intervention.
- The effects of social interaction on consumers and if the benefits are short or long lasting. This is important for assessing the mental wellbeing of a patient.

Being able to detect subtle changes early and predict future cognitive and non-cognitive changes facilitate much earlier intervention. Often, dementia sufferers in hospital are admitted due to other poor health caused by other illnesses [11]. These illnesses are often a result of immobility in the patient. Most commonly infections cause additional complications and can also speed up the progression of dementia [12]. Additionally, immobility leads to pressure sores, which can easily become infected, other serious infections and blood clots, which can be fatal. With any of these complications early intervention for both preventative care and early treatment is vital to ensure a good prognosis and safe independent living.

D. *Mode One*

When the system is in training mode, learning a user's personalised behaviour, features are extracted from the collected data. Features represent the dataset's characteristics as a whole and are needed for training the classifiers. While in the training mode, the information clearing component runs a set of SQL queries against the data store for the specific condition or application. Each query returns a balanced data set for both normal and abnormal behaviours. A balanced dataset is required for the classification process as it removes the possibility of a bias prediction and misleading accuracies.

The period and type of energy usage data collected varies. Each training iteration is application specific. A high-level view of the data collection process is shown in figure 5.

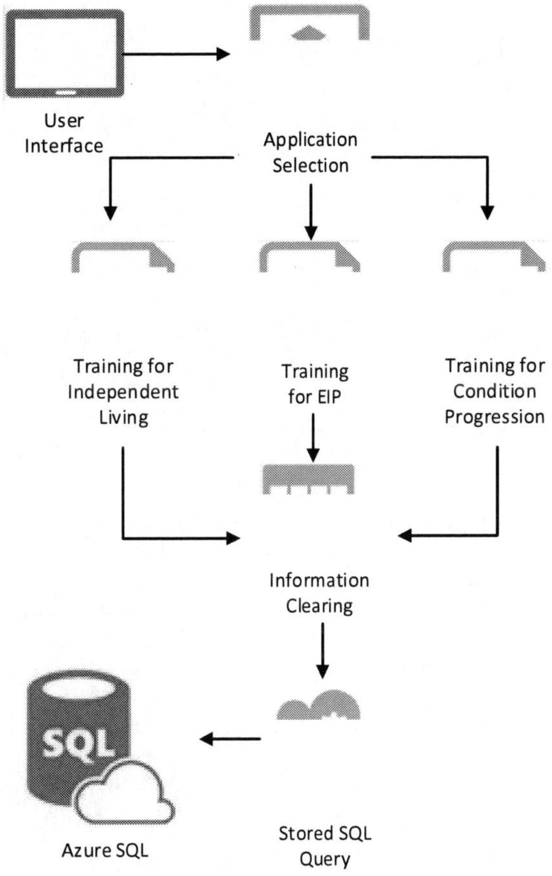

Figure 5. Information Clearing Data Collection Process.

E. *Mode Two*

Using the trained classifiers and generated models, the system automatically detects both normal and abnormal patient behaviour in real-time using web services. Where appropriate the system alerts the patient's support network if potential problem if detected. In the first instance, the system alerts the patient to check in, by performing specific device interaction. This reduces any possible false alarms and verifies that the patient requires no further assistance.

The system identifies if interaction has taken place; if this is not the case an alert is communicated to a third-party health care practitioner. Enabling patients to check in helps to reduce the number of false positives while allowing the system to retrain. Figure 6 shows the workflow for the prediction mode. Regular medical review is required to assess the condition or revaluate the patient's condition were appropriate. This could alter the type of health data included in the classification process, as different observations from the data might be required.

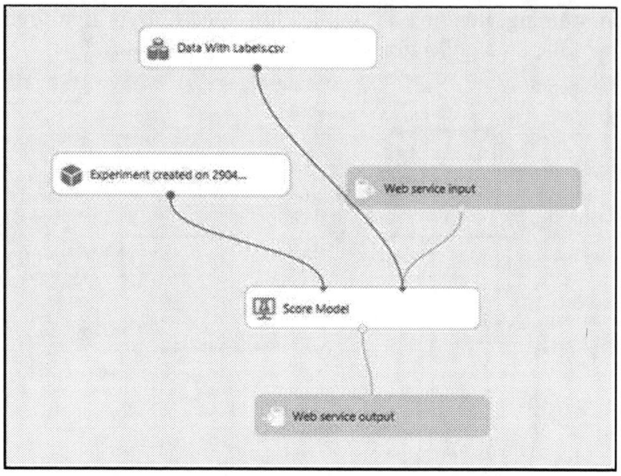

Figure 6. Azure Data Flow for Prediction Mode.

IV. CASE STUDY

In this section, a case study is presented utilising the data set generated from the energy monitor outlined above. Each 24-hour period has 86400 individual readings, as the data is recorded at 10 second intervals. Figure 7 shows an example morning highlighting usage of 2 individual devices. Firstly, a kettle, which is represented by the black dot, secondly the toaster, which is represented by the orange dots. Understanding the energy consumption and duration of usage enables the identification of an individual device. This is important to ascertain the amount of ADL's the patient is performing.

In addition to appliance monitoring, profiling the lighting within a home enables the detection of a patient's location. Lights, light fittings and bulbs create specific profiles based on the type of light and the amount of bulbs fitted. This type of monitoring is extremely beneficial in assessing a patient's wellbeing. Being able to determine how many times a patient visits the bathroom during the night can provide useful insights into their current health. For example, frequent visits may indicate a urinary tract infarction.

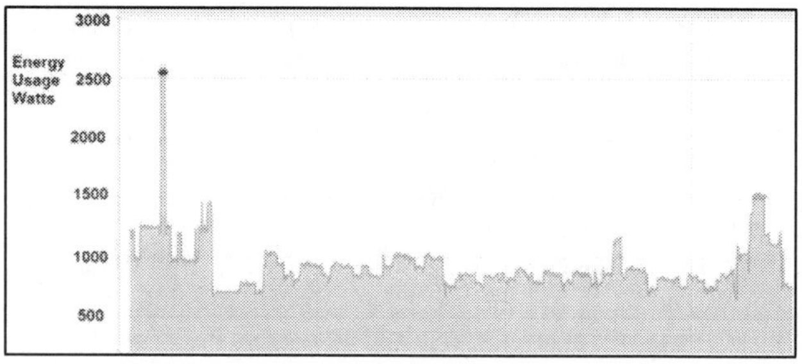

Figure 7. Morning Energy Usage.

In order to detect reduced ADL's, which is a key indicator in assessing the wellbeing of a patient, a balanced data set is created. The data set contains a total of 20 days' energy usage readings taken at 1 minute intervals equating to 1440 readings per 24-hour period. This reading frequency is selected, as it is granular enough for the detection of significant energy usage reductions. 10 days have combined daily energy usage exceeding 720000 watts while the remaining 10 days have usage readings below 620000 watts representing significant reduction in device interaction.

A. *Classification*

The system employs classification methods to identify both normal and abnormal energy usage patterns. The specific classifier used for this experiment is a Bayes Point Machine binary classifier. The classifier was selected for its ability to reduce the chance of over fitting during the training process, as it deploys a Bayesian classification model [13]. In addition, Bayes point machines often outperform Support Vector Machines (SVM) on both surrogate data and real-world benchmark data sets. Figure 8 shows a diagram of the training process. The classifier is conducted 50 times against randomly sampled training and testing sets for each iteration [14]. The hold out cross validation technique was deployed using 80% of the data for training while the remaining 20% is used for testing.

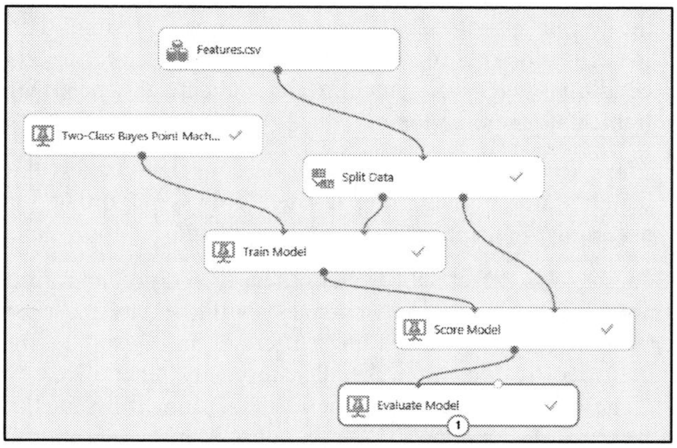

Figure 8. Training Process.

B. *Results*

In this section, the results from the training process are presented. The classifiers performance is calculated using a confusion matrix. This allows the Accuracy (AUC or Area Under Curve), Sensitivity, Specificity and error to be considered. The results from the classifier are shown in Table 2.

TABLE 2. CLASSIFICATION RESULTS 50 REPETITIONS.

Classifier	AUC (%)	Sensitivity	Specificity	Error
Bayes Point	75.00	1	0	0.25

The Bates Point classifier was able to classify 75.00% of the data accurately, with an overall error rate of 0.25. The results of the classification can largely be attributed to the use of a linear classifier. This is due to the fact that most observations are separable due to their large split in values. It is clear from the results that the classifier was able to identify the different behaviours with a reasonable degree of accuracy.

V. CONCLUSION

This paper discussed the challenges in providing a safe and secure independent living environment. Especially for an ever increasing proportion of the population living with self-limiting conditions. It highlighted significant gaps that exist in remote patient monitoring that is not intrusive, cost effective and facilitates EIP. There is an ever-growing focus on these disorders; both from public awareness, health, charitable and social organisation. It is widely accepted that patients should be able to live for as long as possible in their own homes. In order to address this problem, the paper introduces the concept of using smart meters for actively monitoring a patients wellbeing.

Every household in the UK will have a smart meter installed by 2020. The cost of the roll out and ongoing maintenance is being funded by energy suppliers and the UK government. The paper highlighted, that by utilising this infrastructure, energy usage reading can be obtained in real-time to identify any deviation in a patient's habit or routine. Therefore, a system framework that utilises the Azure Cloud platform to train our classification models was presented. This process demonstrates the ability to detect reduced patient activity, which would arguably be cause for concern. The paper demonstrated that the use of the Bayes Point Machine binary classifier to detect a reduction in a patient activity is possible. Using a classification approach enables alterations in routine and reduced ADLs to be detected.

Any reduction in activity would often go undetected with traditional monitoring systems. Using the techniques described in this paper monitoring both the physical and mental wellbeing of a patient becomes possible. This is important for providing a true representation of their welfare. In order to improve the classification performance, future work includes incorporating significantly larger feature sets to create a system, which is scalable. In addition, experimenting with, dimensionally reduction techniques will be undertaken. Deploying these techniques enables a reduction in the noise and the identification of the most valuable features in the dataset. This will involve the use of Principle Component Analysis (PCA) to improve the overall classification.

REFERENCES

[1] Eoghan McKenna, Ian Richardson and Murray Thomson, Smart meter data: Balancing consumer privacy concerns with legitimate applications, Energy Policy, pp. 807-814, 2012.

[2] Mental Health Foundation, The Fundamental Facts The latest facts and figures on mental health, [Available at: http://www.mentalhealth.org.uk/content/assets/PDF/publications/fundamental_facts_2007.pdf?view=Standard], Accessed June 2015.

[3] Mert Bal, Weiming Shen, Qi Hao1 and Henry Xue1, Collaborative Smart Home Technologies for Senior Independent Living: A Review, Computer Supported Cooperative Work in Design, pp.481-488, 2011.

[4] Alzheimer's Society, Assistive technology - devices to help with everyday living, [Available at: https://www.alzheimers.org.uk/site/scripts/documents_info.php?documentID=109], Accessed June 2016.

[5] Julie Doyle, Cathy Bailey and Ben Dromey, Experiences of In-Home Evaluation of Independent Living Technologies for Older Adults, The 3rd Annual Irish Human Computer Interaction Conference (I-HCI), 17-18 September 2009.

[6] Grguric, Andrej. ICT towards elderly independent living. Research and Development Centre, Ericsson Nikola Tesla, 2012.

[7] Jaromir Przybylo, Landmark detection for wearable home care ambient assisted living system, 8th International Conference on Human System Interaction (HSI), pp.25-27, 2015.

[8] Soma Sherkara Sreenadh Reddy Depuru, Lengfeng Wang and Vijay Devabhaktuni, Smart meters for power grid: Challengers, issues, advantages and status, Renewable and Sustainable Energy Reviews, ELSEVIER, pp. 2736-2742, 2011.

[9] Kenneth E. Covinsky, Robert M. Palmer and Richard H. Fortinsky, et al., Loss of Independence in Activities of Daily Living in Older Adults Hospitalized with Medical Illnesses: Increased Vulnerability with Age, Journal of the American Geriatrics Society,Vol 51, 4, pp 451-458, April 2003.

[10] Domenico Talia, Clouds for Scalable Big Data Analytics, Computer, pp98-101, 2013.

[11] Sandra Selikson, Karla Damus and David Hameramn, Risk Factors Associated with Immobility, Journal of the American Geriatrics Society, April 2015.

[12] Alzheimer's Association. 2013 Alzheimer's disease facts and figures. Alzheimer's & dementia 9.2 pp 208-245, 2013.

[13] Herbrich, Ralf, Thore Graepel, and Colin Campbell. Bayes point machines. Journal of Machine Learning Research 1.Aug 245-279, 2001.

[14] P. Fergus, A. Hussain, D. Hignett, D. Al-Jumeily and K. Abdel-Aziz, A Machine Learning System for Automated Whole-Brain Seizure Detection, Applied Computing and Informatics, Volume 12, Issue 1, pp. 70-89. 2016.

Recommendation Method to Make Combined Video from Video Segments

YunKyung Park, KyungDuk Moon
Electronics and Telecommunications Research Institute
Daejeon, South Korea
{parkyk, kdmoon}@etri.re.kr

Jungtaek Kim, Seungjin Choi
Pohang University of Science Technology
Pohang, South Korea
{jtkim,seungjin}@postech.ac.kr

***Abstract*—In this paper, we propose a recommendation scheme for media framework, which enables users to make their own videos by writing a story and reusing parts of accumulated videos. To reuse part of videos, we split a video into semantic segments based on an analysis of relations among objects in a video and store the segments with semantics in repository. To create a new video, the user sends queries based on his/her own story, then the framework recommends appropriate video segments for each query. To determine the rank of searched segments, the recommendation engine uses the degree of coincidence between the segment and the query. Also, it uses the degree of similarity between the searched segment and previously selected segment. By doing this, we can recommend a segment, which is consistent with user's intent and harmonized with the other parts of the new video.**

Keywords-component; Recommendation; Combined Video; Video Segment; Similarity; Conformity.

I. INTRODUCTION

Nowadays, it is common to take photos and shoot videos to record events in everyday life, and consequently visual data has been rapidly accumulating. Roughly 500 million photos are uploaded per day on social sites and 100 hours of videos per minute on YouTube. As visual data is accumulated, it has been reevaluated as new digital asset to trade and the most appropriate medium to represent one's thinking. This is because visual data can be intuitively understood, easily combined and transformed without any degradation of quality. To represent one's thinking, the parts of video should be selected and reconstructed freely by user. Also, new recommendation method is needed to minimize user effort.

Until now, recommendation algorithms are best known for their use on e-commerce Web sites [1], where they use input about a customer's interests to generate a list of recommended items. To recommend items, many applications use the items that customers purchase and explicitly rate to represent their interests, or use other attributes, including items viewed, demographic data, subject interests, and favorite artists [2]. Recommendation systems can be classified into two broad groups, content-based system and collaborative filtering system. Content-based systems examine properties of the items recommended. For instance, if a Netflix user has mainly watched cowboy movies, the system recommends a movie in cowboy genre. Collaborative filtering systems recommend items based on similarity measures between users and/or items. The items recommended to a user are those preferred by similar users [3]. In this paper, we propose a recommendation scheme for new media framework, which enables any user to make a new video through reusing parts of videos. The outline of this paper is as follows: in section II, we describe the proposed architecture in detail. In section III, we present the recommendation system and conclude in section IV.

II. MEDIA FRAMEWORK FOR COMBINED VIDEO

The proposed media framework enables the reuse of videos without user intervention. The framework consists of 4 subsystems: video analysis subsystem, search engine based on semantics, video segment recommendation subsystem and visualization subsystem which interfaces with the user. The video analysis subsystem analyzes the correlation of multi-modalities from an input video in order to precisely analyze the semantics of objects and splits a video into segments. The features of each modality are analyzed, after separating modalities from an input video. Noises and ambiguities of an object can cause an incorrect analysis. If each modality is only considered independently, it is difficult to overcome those factors, despite extensive efforts by researchers to address this. Video analysis subsystem then analyzes the correlations of modalities by fusion of modalities at the feature- and decision-level in order to overcome the effects of those factors [4][5]. Semantic search subsystem infers semantics of segment based on the objects and their trajectory in the segment, and stores the video segment with annotations. Moreover, semantic search subsystem searches all segments that matched user query.

The recommendation subsystem recommends a segment, which is the most appropriate segment to make a new video, among searched results. Many studies on recommendation, mainly confined to movies, consider not only information of persons, such as demographic data and behavior pattern, but also information on related content and persons, such as content with a similar subject or categories, and information on social relations [6][7]. Since the framework makes a new video using segments from different videos, the similarity among segments and the development of the story should be considered for a better recommendation. To choose the most appropriate segment, it considers semantic accuracy and similarity of back and forth segments. The visualization subsystem provides the user interface for describing a story, and dynamically reconstructs a series of segments according to the story. The subsystem extracts keywords and segment-sequence from the user story. Next it sends keywords to the search engine, and receives metadata for the recommended segment. Using Uniform Resource Identifier (URI) of original video, start and end point of the segment in the metadata, it makes video plot. The player plays the video according to the plot.

III. Recommendation System

We determine the proper segment through a 3-step process. First, when the subsystem receives searched segments from the search engine, the subsystem filters the segments based on some contexts in profile, such as guidance rate, using device, user defined attributes, etc. Second, it analyzes semantic correspondance between query and searched segments, and similarity between previously selected segment and searched segment. To reflect user preference, user ranks are predicted and used as weights. Third it ranks the segments depend on previous learning, how much the factors effect user selection.

Each query consists of <Subject, Predicate, Object> triples which describe the segment, Action State (AS) which describes movement direction of the objects and some user Designated Features (DF). To compute the semantic correspondance between the query and the searched segments, we created vector space for SPO, DF and AS. To compute degree of correspondance, we used euclidean distance in SPO, DF vector space and cosine similarity in AS vector space. Fig. 1 shows an example of semantic correspondance.

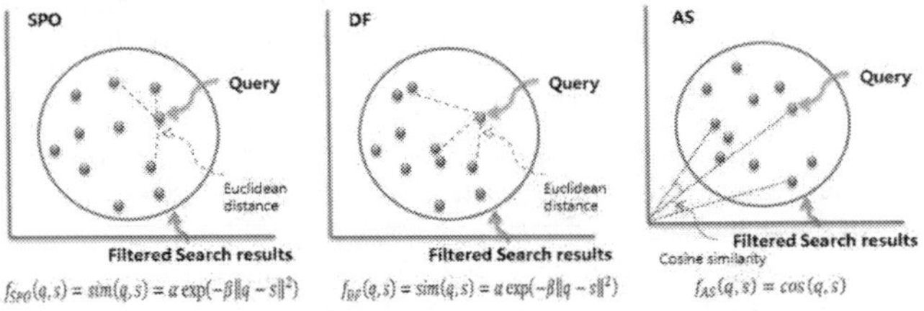

Figure 1. Example of a Semantic Correspondance.

The similarity between previously selected segment and searched segment is computed using euclidean distance in SPO space, Low-level Features (LF) space and cosine similarity in AS space. Fig. 2 shows an example of similarity between previously selected segment and searched segment.

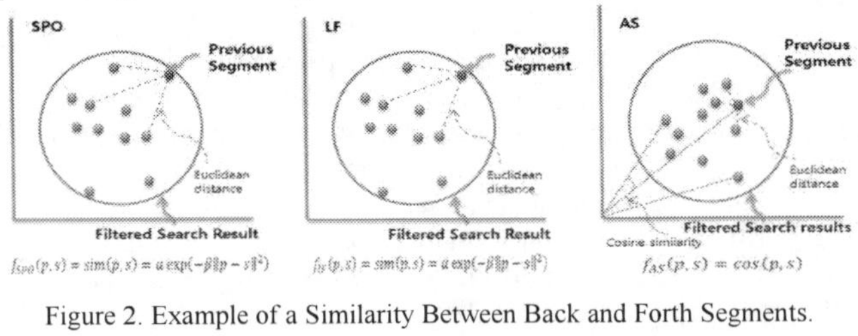

Figure 2. Example of a Similarity Between Back and Forth Segments.

In filtered search results, some segments have user rank and other segments have no rank. To predict the user rank for unranked segments, we propagate the known rank to unknown rank using a matrix, which is composed of rank propagation probability based on similarity. Fig. 3 shows an example of preference prediction using distance. In the figure, l_{spo}, l_{as}, l_{df}, l_{lf} are predicted preference values for unlabeld segment in each space. They show how much the user is going to like the segment. The values are computed using label propagation algorithm. As a result, every segment has forur preference values.

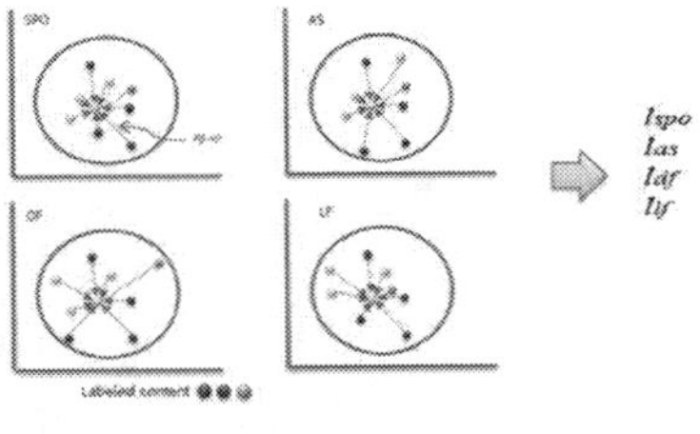

Figure 3. Example of Preference Prediction Using Distance

The final score of a segment is determined by weighted semantic correspondance and similarity. In equation (1), w_{qi} and w_{pi} are weights which are learned from user history. And $f_{space}(q,s)$, $f_{space}(p,s)$ are consistency and similarity measure in each space, respectively.

$$S = w_{q1} l_{spo} f_{SPO}(q,s) + w_{q2} l_{df} f_{df}(q,s) + w_{q3} l_{as} f_{as}(q,s) + w_{p1} l_{spo} f_{spo}(p,s) + w_{p2} l_{lf} f_{lf}(p,s) + w_{p3} l_{as} f_{as}(p,s) \quad (1)$$

IV. Conclusion and Future Works

Here, we propose a recommendation scheme for media framework, which enables users to create their own video by analyzing semantics of video and combining segments from different videos. In this recommendation system, the key differences are that it uses similarity between previously selected segment and recommending segment, and consistency between query and recommending segment. It can diminish awkwardness that occurs when the framework combines segments. To customize the recommendation, more research is needed on implicit user behavior. To assess the developed subsystem, more research on the evaluation method is also needed.

Acknowledgment

This work was supported by the ICT R&D program of MSIP/IITP. [R0126-15-1112, Development of Media Application Framework based on Multi-modality which enables Personal Media Reconstruction].

References

[1] J. B. Schafer, J. A. Konstan, and J. Reidl, “E-Commerce Recommendation Applications” Data Mining and Knowledge Discovery, Kluwer Academic, pp 115-153, 2001.

[2] G. Linden, B. Smith, and J. York, “Amazon.com recommendations item-to-item collaborative filtering”, IEEE Internet Computing, pp 76-80, January • February 2003.

[3] A. Rajaraman and J. D. Ullman, “Mining of Massive Datasets”, Cambridge University Press, 2011.

[4] R. Frcke, J. Thomsen, "LinkedTV Platform and Architecture", LinkedTV, 2012.

[5] P. K. Atrey, M.. A. Hossain, A. E. Saddik, and M. S. Kankanhalli, "Multimodal fusion for multimedia analysis: a survey", Multimedia Systems, Volume 16, Issue 6, pp345-379, 2010.

[6] W. W. Cohen, "Collaborative Filtering: A Tutorial,"Carnegie Mellon University, https://www.cs.cmu.edu/~wcohen/collab-filtering-tutorial.ppt, [retrieved: Aug, 2016].

[7] D. Tsatsou et al., "Specification of user profiling and contextualization", LinkedTV, 2012.

Study on Effective Management of Cyber Incidents in Graph Database

Seulgi Lee, Hyeisun Cho, Byungik Kim, and Taejin Lee
Security R&D Team 1
Korea Internet & Security Agency
Seoul, Republic of Korea
{sglee, hscho, kbi1983, tjlee}@kisa.or.kr

***Abstract*—Nowadays, cyber incidents are becoming increasingly intelligent, and they have escalated dramatically. For this reason, our research focuses on finding a solution to counter cyber incidents. We decided to build a multiple- and unified data warehouse, one of the many ways of controlling massive information and gathering meaningful intelligence to respond to cyber incidents. The major idea of this paper consists in correlating information based on the massive data set in a graph database. We concentrated on managing massive information in the cyber area and solving the problem when managing malicious information in a relational database. This project is also developing the system based on the architecture in a graph database. We expect the system to contribute to creating various intelligence types. This paper describes how to manage correlated information for building a data warehouse, which is meant to be a kind of infrastructure for responding to cyber-attacks effectively.**

Keywords- information management; cyber incidents; graph database; cyber threat intelligence

I. INTRODUCTION

Nowadays, cyber incidents are becoming increasingly intelligent, and they have escalated dramatically. Recently, many studies have been done on intelligence for cyber incidents. This is still very much a work in progress. Intelligence is generally accepted to be useful for tracking bad guys who conduct espionage in the cyber area [1]. In achieving this goal, there are many changes in the course of the process derived from past research. The purpose of this study is to describe some problems in the established analysis systems and solutions. The methodology proposed in this study is expected to be used for the management of massive correlated information in a graph database. The expectation is that the established systems will be able to provide intelligence for forecasting cyber incidents. We have developed a unified hub system to counter cyber incidents in a relational database. The system has structural characteristics and consists of two parts: a gathering subsystem and an analysis subsystem. The subsystems are suitable to deploy and operate independently, since the data structure with several gathering channels was designed to offer flexible extension; the same is true for the gathering subsystem. The rest of this paper is organized as follows: Section II introduces the previous studies on intelligence analysis system in a relational database; Section III presents ideas for management in a graph database as proposed in this paper; we conclude in Section IV.

II. RELATED WORK

A. Data warehouse for cyber incidents

This section describes the overall organization of the developed intelligence system. In a recent study, there was an attempt to react to potential cyber incidents in the future [2]. This study proposed a cyber defense operation framework which can classify attack groups and predict cyber incidents. It also suggested 5 type keys of attack group identification such as Email, attached file, malware, and OSINT (Open Source Intelligence). However, there are many more indicators showing the characteristics of cyber incidents; we have studied effective management using more diverse information. We have constructed a data warehouse for cyber security. The system can be divided into two main subsystems: gathering and analysis. Fig. 1 shows the system overview. The gathering system consists of gathering, scheduling, and management modules. The essential function in the gathering system is collecting information for cyber incidents, which is opened to the public. Following the collected information, the system groups derived pieces of information for managing their relationships, such as landing site, phishing email, and malware.

The analysis subsystem periodically pulls in information from the gathering subsystem into its database. As the system is pulling, resources and attributes are given unique IDs and stored. For instance, if information with the same value is already stored in a database, the system will not store that. It also extracts essential information from pulling data. The essential information originates from the intelligence report presented by leading antivirus vendors. Using this extracted information, we expect to be able to identify and cluster identical hackers or hacking groups. Through this past research, we could analyze the infrastructure used by most hackers to procure some zombie PCs for attacking victims.

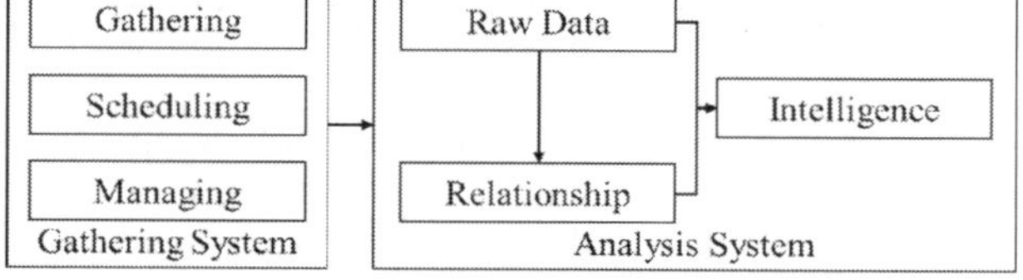

Figure 1. Data warehouse in a relational database

Since there are various and numerous information feeds for cyber security in public, the system needs to manage the massive correlated information. In a DNS (Domain Name System) based blacklist, for example, a gathering subsystem usually collects around two million pieces of data per day. Because we have focused on tracing the relationship with cyber incidents, we have concentrated on a graph database that need not do a JOIN operation like a relational database. In the data warehouse, which uses a relational database, the clustering method of identical hacker was running with difficulty. Hackers experience difficulty with complex infrastructures which are used for cyber incidents. Therefore, hackers usually attack victims from a previously generated infrastructure. A relational database is barely suitable for analysis of these relationships. For this reason, there is still room for improvement in analysis performance. The approach we have used in this study seeks to improve analysis performance and enables effective management through a graph database.

B. *Requirement for Improving the Existing System*

1) Performance: In one of the proposed ways, the major analysis method creates a venn diagram-based stored relationship. Moreover, the sets in a diagram were extracted by recursive JOIN operations. Therefore, the system tends to produce a result slowly when much information is calculated. Although the system architecture considered huge amounts of information, the system did not work well.

2) Hard Grouping: The relationships between resources and attributes are grouped in a hard manner. The system computes groups by relationship. Moreover, these groups are originated by connected information derived by the initial resource. When the system analyzes and creates groups, the component parts of groups may be overlapped. Therefore, the system has difficulty supporting long-distance information from initial data.

3) Uncomfortable Visualization: The intelligence is caused by connected information. Or, put differently, the information is extracted from raw data collected by the gathering system. GUI, which has its own roles for control with users, has to present stored and created intelligence effectively. Unfortunately, it is hard to imprint users with intelligence.

III. Management in Graph Database

A. *Proposed Scheme*

We propose a scheme in graph database for building the management system that responds to cyber incidents. In earlier times, we thought that the information simply migrates to a graph database from a relational database. To apply information to a graph database, however, a hybrid architecture should be considered for the management of classified data like ordinary NoSQL. In this manner, we decided to divide data into two-tier information. Being a traditional database, the relational database has its own advantages with the effect of storing structured and patterned data. Such could commit massive data. This allows us to make a data warehouse from the raw data stored. Note, however, that a relational database makes managing the relationship between essential information and extracted gathering data difficult. That being the case, we structuralize architecture in a graph database whose structure needs to store the worked data. Effective management leads us to determine atypical information that should be stored in a graph database [3].

Fig. 2 shows the hybrid architecture that we structuralized. The node as entity in a relational database is a defined resources and attributes. Moreover, the relationship in a graph database is the relationship between resources and attributes just as it is.

Since the information is composed of fragmented information, there is a need to do preprocessing for managing the information collected by each channel in a graph database. For instance, the one with various channels in the gathering system, which could collect massive URLs for landing malware, stores raw data in a relational database as shown in Fig. 3. The developed system processes the information secured throughout the collected information in refined form and conducts relationship analysis in order to check for cyber-attacks, which seemed to be irrelevant superficially. The system then disassembles the information and analyzes cyber-attacks.

B. *Stage for Building the Management System*

1) Migrating Existing Information: If we want to manage data in a graph database, we should first mitigate the data pulled in from the gathering system from a relational database. If we do that, we would have to begin with the resource. We tried migrating information using a binay protocol called Bolt, which is served from Neo4j [4].

2) Reconstruction of Relationship: In the existing structure, we have to establish a relationship directly. For this reason, we could not use migration tools, which were used by most graph database communities. Therefore, the new system has to recreate the relationship. Furthermore, because infringement information (attack resources and attributes) is disassembled, the method of control relationship needs to be improved. TABLE I shows the components in a graph database as defined on grounds of APT (Advanced Persistent Threat) reports. As stated above, resources and attributes are stored as nodes on the system; relationship is configured in the same manner. This work makes a fundamental prototype in a graph database.

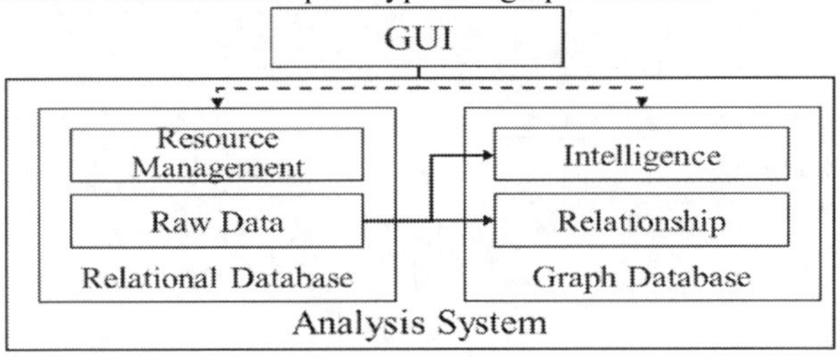

Figure 2. Hybrid architecture using a graph database

TABLE I. COMPONENTS OF A GRAPH DATABASE

Node		Relationship
Class	***Name***	
Resource	IP	C&C
	Domain	Create malware
	Hash	Defacing
Attribute	Account	Distribution
	Email	Download
	Filename	Filename
	FilePath	File Path
	Location	File String
	Process	Location
	Registry	Mapping
	String	Process
	Timestamp	Registrant
	URL	Registry
	URLPath	Landing

IV. CONCLUSION

With regard to utilization, we could create various intelligence types forecasting future cyber-crime from this system [5]. The importance of utilizing intelligence has been demonstrated by leading antivirus vendors. Before we enter into discussions on the detailed utilization of the system, we would like to stress that it is important to focus on the cyber incident report because the analysis system's output is nothing other than the intelligence that was carried out in the report. In this study, an efficient, accurate scheme was proposed to solve performance, which was derived by analyzing information in a relational database.

We have to establish a system for responding to cyber incidents because cyber incidents have escalated. Graph database is used for managing massive information like social network services. We can collect huge amounts of information about cyber incidents and construct the relationship between them. It is also a matter of increasing utilization using this system and making various intelligence types. This matter is a subject of further study. Therefore, future work should develop the intelligence analysis system and include verification utilization.

ACKNOWLEDGMENT

This work was supported by a grant from the Institute for Information & Communications Technology Promotion (IITP) funded by the Korean government's MSIP (no. B0101-16-0300, Development of Cyber Blackbox and Integrated Security Analysis Technology for Proactive and Reactive Cyber Incident Response).

REFERENCES

[1] G. Wangen, "The Role of Malware in Reported Cyber Espionage: A review of the Impact and Mechanism," Information, 6(2015), pp. 183-211, 2015.

[2] W. Kim, C. Park, S. Lee, and J Lim, "Methods for Classification and Attack Groups based on Framework of Cyber Defense Operations," KTCP, Vol.20 No.6(2014), pp. 317-328, 2014.

[3] C. Vicknair et al., "A comparison of a graph database and a relational database: a data provenance perspective," In proceedings of the 48th Annual South-east Regional Conference, ACM SE '10, pages 42:2-42:6, 2010.

[4] https://neo4j.com/developer/language-guides/ [accessed September 2016]

[5] H. Cho, S. Lee, B. Kim, Y. Shin, and T. Lee, "The study of prediction of same attack group by comparing similarity of domain, " Information and Communication Technology Convergence (ICTC), 2015 International Conference, pp.1220–1222, October 2015.

column	sample
sequence	463
registration	2016.5.15
index	50
collection	2015.11.11
detection	5258
domain	be*****den.co.kr
ip	115.68.*.*
protocol	http
url	http://be*****den.co.kr /common/js/tinyfader.js
type	landing_url
seed_path	/home/kisa/via/collect_ domain/

(a) Raw data(Landing sites)

idx_1	idx_2	relationship
68701	68702	mapping
68701	5257	landing
5257	5258	landing_time

<relationship>

resource_idx	value
68701	be*****den.co.kr
68702	115.68.*.*

attribute_idx	value
5257	http://be*****den.co.kr/ common/js/tinyfader.js
5258	2015.11.11

<resource/attribute>

(b) Management

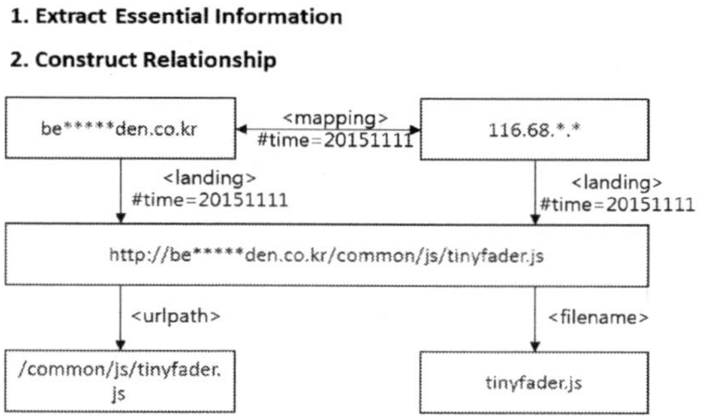

(c) Refined raw data in a graph database

Figure 3. Example of stored raw data in a relational and graph database

Dynamic QoS on SIP Sessions Using OpenFlow

Jérémy Pagé*, Charles Hubain† and Jean-Michel Dricot‡

OPERA Wireless Communications
Université libre de Bruxelles
Brussels, Belgium
Email: *jeremy.page@ulb.ac.be, †charles.hubain@ulb.ac.be, ‡jean-michel.dricot@ulb.ac.be

***Abstract*—With the increase in Internet bandwidth demand and emergence of new multimedia internet applications, new technologies are needed to guarantee the Quality of Service (QoS). Traditionally, QoS has been enforced using predefined Service Level Agreements (SLAs), which lack dynamic adaptability and flexibility. This article introduces an implementation leveraging the Software Defined Networking (SDN) protocol OpenFlow to dynamically adapt QoS to the network usage by analyzing Session Initiation Protocol (SIP) session negotiations. The implementation is verified on real world OpenFlow-enabled switches with different types of traffic QoS requirements.**

Keywords–SDN; OpenFlow; QoS; SIP; SDP.

I. Introduction

Over the last decade, with the increase of bandwidth demand, new multimedia internet applications have emerged such as, Voice over IP (VoIP), IP Television (IPTV), online gaming, etc. Those applications have strong requirements regarding the QoS in terms of bandwidth, latency, packet loss and jitter. To guarantee those requirements, predefined SLAs have traditionally been used but they lack the flexibility to adapt dynamically to the client needs. Besides those applications, the network environment can also have strong requirements, e.g., a medical-grade network regarding the transmission of delay-sensitive information [1], [2]. Indeed, when medical data or audio/video data transmission is required, the latency must be as low as possible and a bandwidth must be guaranteed.

In addition, the deployment of new network services in the operator networks comes at a high cost. Indeed the integration and operation typically come with separate hardware entities. Network Functions Virtualization (NFV) [3], [4] aims to address this problem by allowing to deploy network services onto virtualized industry servers, which can be located in data centers. Network functions can thus be deployed as virtualized instances without the need to install hardware equipment. By migrating the hardware to software, NFV is expected to lower not only the Capital Expenditure but also the Operational Expenditure [5]. The services can be deployed more flexibly and scaled up and down very quickly. As explained in [5], from an architecture perspective, NFV can be complementary to technologies, such as SDN and cloud computing.

Moreover, SDN aims to solve the lack of flexibility of the SLAs. SDN [6], [7] provides an abstraction between the data-plane forwarding (hardware) and the control-plane (software). It makes the control-plane programmable by a centralized SDN controller on a per data flow basis. The OpenFlow protocol [8] is an open standard implementation for the signaling between an SDN switch and an SDN controller.

Previous studies such as [5] has focused on the deployment of an Long-Term Evolution (LTE) Evolved Packet Core (EPC) system in an operator cloud environment with SDN as a network enabler. In the LTE EPC architecture, IP Multimedia Subsystem (IMS) is used for the VoIP and the SIP serves as the signaling protocol [9]. SIP is independent of the technologies chosen, and can be used regardless of IMS. Furthermore, SIP is the de facto standard for initializing multimedia communications between entities and, this protocol provides sufficient information to deduce QoS needs.

In a previous work [10], we demonstrated the integration of SDN and the 4G architecture towards 5G and we presented the benefits of SDN in the mobile environment in terms of performances and flexibility.

The paper is organized as follows. The next section presents the related works. Section III gives a short introduction to OpenFlow. Section IV describes the 5G architecture proposed in [10]. Section V introduces the protocols SIP and Session Description Protocol (SDP). Section VI explains how OpenFlow can be used to implement dynamic QoS. Section VII describes the implementation and verification that have been made over real world HP 2920 switches (implementing OpenFlow). The last section presents the conclusion and future works.

II. Related Work

Providing QoS for SIP-based applications started in 2002 [11]. The idea is to extend the SIP protocol to encapsulate the Common Open Policy Service (COPS) protocol, which could then be used in a DiffServ network. However it requires a complex network architecture and modifying existing SIP applications.

In 2006, the authors of [12] introduced an architecture for SIP-based QoS applications. This architecture combined both DiffServ and IntServ and generally works with standard SIP end systems.

In 2007, the authors of [13] proposed to use the SDP (included in some of the SIP messages) to negotiate SLAs. This has the advantage of requiring very limited modifications to existing applications but the authors did not expand on how the QoS would be enforced.

PolicyCop, a framework for autonomic QoS policy enforcement using SDN, was introduced in 2013 [14]. It uses OpenFlow to provide a dynamic, flexible, efficient and simpler alternative to DiffServ. Unfortunately, the implementation is not yet complete and the paper only presents link failure tests.

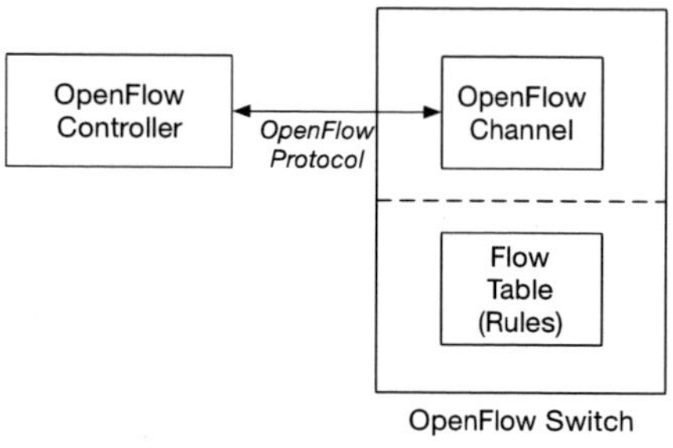

Figure 1. OpenFlow Controller and Switches

III. OpenFlow

As defined in the SDN architecture, OpenFlow separates the data-plane from the control-plane. The networking devices, i.e., the OpenFlow switches, form the data-plane where data packets flow according to rules (flows). Each rule is composed of matching parameters and a set of actions to execute when there is a match. Examples of matching parameters include: Internet Protocol (IP) address source/destination, Media Access Control (MAC) address source/destination, Transmission Control Protocol (TCP) or User Datagram Protocol (UDP) source/destination port. Examples of actions include: sending the packet on a specific port, changing some header fields of the packet.

Every switch is connected to the controller and communicates with the OpenFlow protocol (Figure 1). The OpenFlow controller can inject flows, i.e., rules, into the switches in order to define the routing of specific packets. When the switch receives a new flow, it adds it in its flow table. When an incoming packet arrives, the flow table of the switch is looked up to match the packet according to the flows. If there is a match, the set of actions defined by the flow is executed. If there is no match, the packet is sent to the controller for inspection. The controller can then decide which action to take (e.g., create a new flow, drop the packet, send the packet to a specific port) [15].

IV. Previous Work: 5G OpenFlow Integration

In a previous work, the integration of OpenFlow in the core network of the mobile architecture between the Evolved NodeB (eNodeB) and the Packet Data Network Gateway (P-GW) has been demonstrated [10]. As it can be observed in Figure 2, the proposed solution removes the Serving Gateway (S-GW) and introduces the OpenFlow Controller. Hence, allowing for a faster circuit-switched transport from the antenna to the core network. The control path from the Mobility Management Entity (MME) to the P-GW and the data path from the eNodeB to the P-GW is comprised of OpenFlow Switches as underlying infrastructure. These switches are controlled by and connected to the controller.

When a new User Equipment (UE) connects to the network, it sends an *Attach Request* to the MME through the eNodeB (the antenna). The MME authenticates the user using information from the Home Subscriber Server (HSS) (the user database) and retrieves which services it can access to, e.g., IMS for VoIP, Internet. The MME selects the P-GW for the corresponding service and forwards the request to it. The

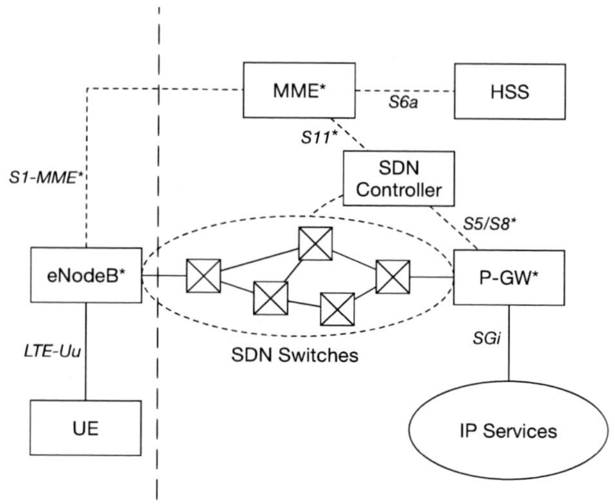

Figure 2. Proposed 5G Architecture [10]

controller is able to intercept and analyze the request in order to optimize the path and to proactively create the flows in the switches. These flows are created for the control path and for the data path. Each flow can have different QoS parameters attached to them, as it will be shown in the next sections, in order to satisfy some requirements. When the P-GW sends back a response, the flows are already created and the response is sent back to the UE, which is then successfully connected to the service.

V. SIP and SDP

The SIP [9] protocol is used to negotiate multimedia sessions between multiple clients. Figure 3 presents the SIP architecture comprising the SIP servers (*proxy* and *registrar*) and two UEs, Alice and Bob. First of all, the SIP clients need to register themselves to the registrar server. They send a `REGISTER` SIP request to their proxy which forwards it to the registrar. When a client is registered, it opens a multimedia session with another registered client by sending an `INVITE` SIP request to the proxy with the username of the other client.

The proxy behaves as an intermediary between the clients who do not know each others' IP addresses. It forwards the `INVITE` SIP request to the recipient. If the receiver accepts the session, i.e., responding with a `200 OK` SIP response, the session is established. Nevertheless, SIP is only providing the signaling and not the media transfer. When the session is established, the data path is going directly from end to end, not passing through the proxy. Real-time Transport Protocol (RTP) [16], for example, is a protocol used to exchange multimedia data. Figure 4 shows an example of the initiation and termination of a SIP session.

In order for RTP to transfer media from end to end, SDP [17] can be used to describe the media codecs supported by the clients and the connection parameters (IP addresses, port numbers, protocol). The SDP part is embedded in the `INVITE` request and in the `200 OK` corresponding response. The clients can send media streams from end to end as shown, but the server can also act as a media proxy. Figure 5 shows an

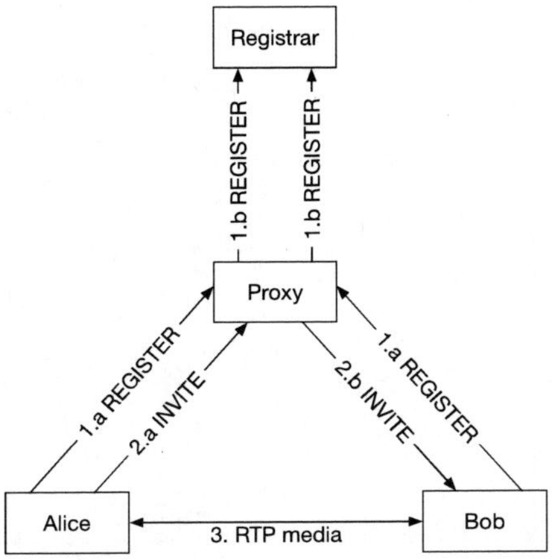

Figure 3. SIP Architecture

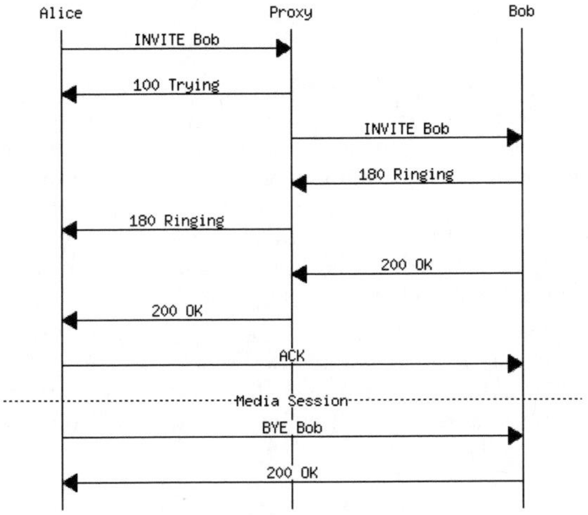

Figure 4. SIP Flow Example

example of a SIP `INVITE` message with a SDP part where the IP address is `192.0.1.100` and the port number is `49172`.

The session traffic between two clients is uniquely identified by combining the SDP information, which produces a pair of IP addresses, a pair of port numbers and a protocol.

VI. Dynamic QoS with OpenFlow

The flexibility of OpenFlow allows to dynamically attribute a specific QoS for incoming packets by creating flows with the attributed QoS. First, in order to intercept all the SIP packets in the controller, a flow is created in each switch where the matching is done on the port 5060 (the default SIP port) and the actions set is composed of one action: send the packet to the controller. If the switches are configured to send the packets to the controller when there is no match, this flow is optional because the default behavior of the switch would be to send the packet to the controller.

By intercepting all the SIP signaling, the controller is able to analyze their content and to attribute a QoS to each one of the sessions. This attribution is done by extracting

```
INVITE sip:bob@example.com SIP/2.0
Via: SIP/2.0/UDP client1.example.com:5060;branch=z9hG4bK74bf9
Max-Forwards: 70
From: Alice <sip:alice@example.com>;tag=9fxced76sl
To: Bob <sip:bob@example.com>
Call-ID: 3848276298220188511@example.com
CSeq: 1 INVITE
Contact: <sip:alice@client1.example.com;transport=udp>
Content-Type: application/sdp
Content-Length: 144

v=0
o=alice 2890844526 2890844526 IN IP4 client1.example.com
s=-
c=IN IP4 192.0.1.100
t=0 0
m=audio 49172 RTP/AVP 0
a=rtpmap:0 PCMU/8000
```

Figure 5. SIP Message Example with SDP Part

the IP address, port numbers and media parameters from the SDP parts of the SIP messages. Once the controller detects that a session has been established (a `200 OK` following an `INVITE`), it can enforce the attributed QoS for this session by creating flows in the switches along the path of this session. The matching part of the flows contains the IP addresses and port numbers extracted from the SDP part. The actions set of the flows contains an action attributing the QoS parameter and action outputting the packet to the right destination.

There are several possibilities to enforce QoS using OpenFlow. OpenFlow defines a specific action to enqueue packets on a specific output queue, guaranteeing a minimal bandwidth [15]. However its implementation is optional, and there is no mechanism to configure those queues with OpenFlow. The HP 2920-24G switch used for the verification does not implement the enqueue method defined in OpenFlow [18, p. 12]. A generic workaround has been implemented by the modification of the IP version 4 (IPv4) header fields to attribute a QoS class. Indeed, the cited switch is compliant with IEEE 802.1p [19, p. 14]. OpenFlow defines actions to set the IPv4 Type of Service (ToS) field, the Virtual Local Area Network (VLAN) Identifier (ID), or the VLAN Priority Code Point (PCP) [15].

On HP switches the VLAN PCP field is directly mapped to specific QoS output queues [20]. Changing it allows to give some packets a higher priority and thus enforce QoS. On other hardware, the method used to enforce a specific QoS must be adapted.

VII. Implementation and Verification

The verification architecture is presented in Figure 6 and can be described as follows. 3 HP 2920 switches are connected to an OpenFlow Controller running on a server (Ubuntu 14.04 LTS). Each one of the switches is also connected to a host computer (Ubuntu 14.04 LTS). The topology used can be extended to a more complex one, by including more switches and hosts. When the network grows, the question of the scalability can arise. According to [21], the scalability concerns are not unique to SDN and solutions exist. However, the scalability issues are still studied and are not trivial [22]. HyperFlow [23], e.g., is a distributed control plane for OpenFlow and provides scalability.

The verification procedure was conducted as follows. First, Host 2 connects to Host 1 and maximize the utilization of the

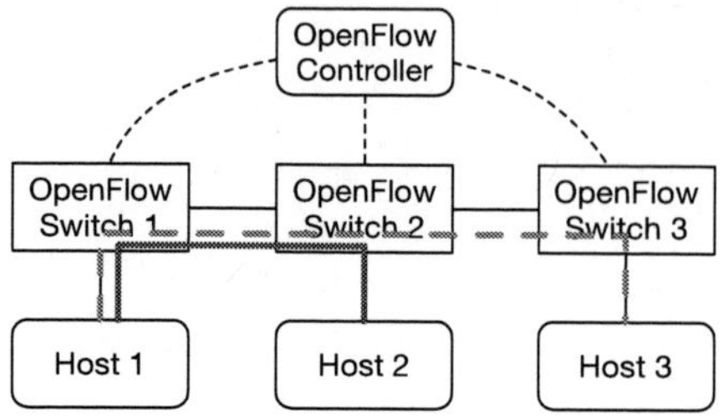

Figure 6. Verification Architecture

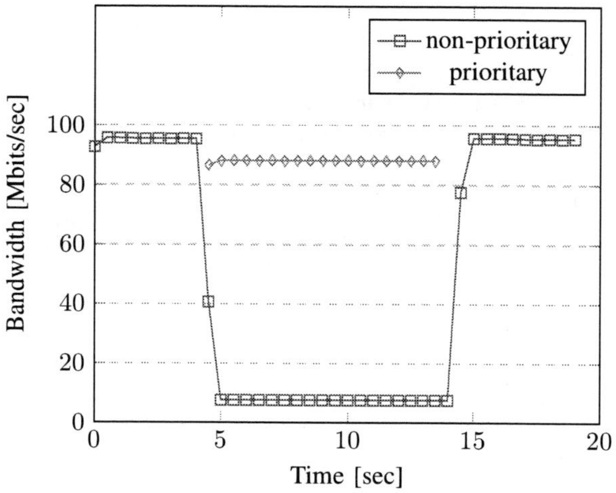

Figure 7. Bandwidth of a Priority and non-Priority UDP Traffic over Time

available bandwidth for a period of 20 seconds. During this period, some measurements are made on the bandwidth used and the jitter observed. After approximately 5 seconds, Host 3 connects to Host 1 and tries also to maximize the utilization of the bandwidth, but for a period of 10 seconds. The traffic generated by the Host 3 has priority over the traffic generated by the Host 2. The tool used to generate the traffic and to analyze the bandwidth and jitter is *iPerf* [24].

Figure 7 and 8 show the effect of such QoS implementation on the two UDP traffics that compete for the same 100 Mbps bandwidth. The results indicate that around 80% of the bandwidth is allocated to the priority traffic. Also the jitter, which is crucial to real-time multimedia applications, is significantly limited with respect to the non-priority traffic. This demonstrates that a line rate QoS using OpenFlow is possible on real world hardware.

When this dynamic QoS implementation is used in conjunction with the detection of new media traffic by analyzing the SIP signaling, the controller can enforce a specific QoS for new media sessions based on the SDP parameters.

VIII. Conclusion and Future Work

This article presents and verifies that SDN is an elegant solution to the QoS problem of modern internet multimedia applications. By analyzing on the fly the SIP signaling, the OpenFlow controller was able to dynamically enforce QoS over negotiated sessions. The integration of OpenFlow in the

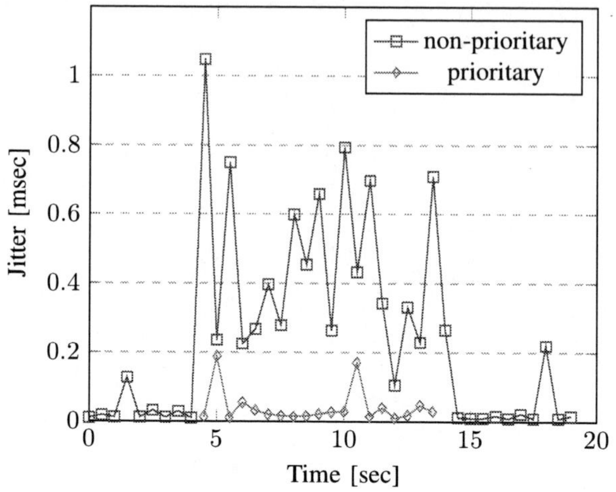

Figure 8. Jitter of a Priority and non-Priority UDP Traffic over Time

mobile architecture with a dynamic QoS for the SIP traffic towards IMS allows to be more proactive and flexible. Indeed, the approach is entirely software and the granularity is higher. The network can be programmed in software and the packets can be inspected until the fourth layer. Moreover line rate OpenFlow dynamic QoS performances were shown to be possible on real world hardware with results comparable to traditional static configurations.

Future work will focus on the integration of this implementation on a full-featured IMS platform (Voice over LTE (VoLTE)). Also, further tests will include various traffic and the proposed approach will be included with different kinds of protocols and networks.

Acknowledgment

This work is supported by a grant of Innoviris, the Brussels Institute for Research and Innovation.

References

[1] L. Skorin-Kapov and M. Matijasevic, "Analysis of QoS requirements for e-Health services and mapping to Evolved Packet System QoS classes," Int. J. Telemedicine Appl., vol. 2010, Jan. 2010, pp. 9:1–9:18.

[2] A. Zvikhachevskaya, G. Markarian, and L. Mihaylova, "Quality of service consideration for the wireless telemedicine and e-health services," in WCNC, 2009, pp. 3064–3069.

[3] SDN and OpenFlow World Congress, "Network Functions Virtualization," White Paper, Oct. 2012.

[4] H. Hawilo, A. Shami, M. Mirahmadi, and R. Asal, "NFV: state of the art, challenges, and implementation in next generation mobile networks (vEPC)," IEEE Network, vol. 28, no. 6, 2014, pp. 18–26.

[5] A. Basta, W. Kellerer, M. Hoffmann, K. Hoffmann, and E.-D. Schmidt, "A virtual SDN-enabled LTE EPC architecture: a case study for S-/P-Gateways functions," in 2013 IEEE SDN for Future Networks and Services (SDN4FNS), Nov. 2013, pp. 1–7.

[6] Open Networking Foundation, "Software-Defined Networking: the new norm for networks," ONF White Paper, Apr. 2012.

[7] B. A. A. Nunes, M. Mendonca, X.-N. Nguyen, K. Obraczka, and T. Turletti, "A survey of software-defined networking: Past, present, and future of programmable networks," IEEE Communications Surveys & Tutorials, vol. 16, no. 3, 2014, pp. 1617–1634.

[8] N. McKeown et al., "OpenFlow: enabling innovation in campus networks," ACM SIGCOMM Computer Communication Review, vol. 38, no. 2, Apr. 2008, pp. 69–74.

[9] J. Rosenberg et al., "SIP: session initiation protocol," Tech. Rep., 2002.

[10] J. Pagé and J.-M. Dricot, "Software-Defined Networking for low-latency 5G core network," in 2016 International Conference on Military Communications and Information Systems (ICMCIS). IEEE, May 2016.

[11] S. Salsano and L. Veltri, "QoS control by means of COPS to support SIP-based applications," IEEE Network, vol. 16, no. 2, 2002, pp. 27–33.

[12] E.-H. Cho, K.-S. Shin, and S.-J. Yoo, "SIP-based QoS support architecture and session management in a combined IntServ and DiffServ networks," Computer Communications, vol. 29, no. 15, 2006, pp. 2996–3009.

[13] H. Park, J. Yang, J. Choi, and H. Kim, "QoS negotiation for IPTV service using SIP," in The 9th International Conference on Advanced Communication Technology, vol. 2. IEEE, 2007, pp. 945–948.

[14] M. F. Bari, S. R. Chowdhury, R. Ahmed, and R. Boutaba, "PolicyCop: an autonomic QoS policy enforcement framework for software defined networks," in 2013 IEEE SDN for Future Networks and Services (SDN4FNS). IEEE, 2013, pp. 1–7.

[15] OpenFlow Switch Specification, "Version 1.0. 0 (Wire Protocol 0x01)." Open Networking Foundation, Dec. 2009.

[16] H. Schulzrinne, S. Casner, R. Frederick, and V. Jacobson, "RTP: A Transport Protocol for Real-Time Applications," RFC 3550 (INTERNET STANDARD), Internet Engineering Task Force, Jul. 2003, URL: http://www.ietf.org/rfc/rfc3550.txt [accessed: 2016-08-30].

[17] M. Handley and V. Jacobson, "Session Description Protocol," Apr. 1998.

[18] Hewlett Packard, "HP Switch Software OpenFlow administrator guide for K/KA/WB 15.17," Jun. 2015.

[19] ——, "HP 2920 Switch Series."

[20] ——, "HP Switch Software advanced traffic management guide WB.15.17," Jun. 2015.

[21] S. Yeganeh, A. Tootoonchian, and Y. Ganjali, "On scalability of software-defined networking," IEEE Communications Magazine, vol. 51, no. 2, 2013, pp. 136–141.

[22] B. J. van Asten, N. L. M. van Adrichem, and F. A. Kuipers, "Scalability and Resilience of Software-Defined Networking: an overview," CoRR, vol. abs/1408.6760, 2014.

[23] A. Tootoonchian and Y. Ganjali, "HyperFlow: A distributed control plane for OpenFlow," in Proceedings of the 2010 internet network management conference on Research on enterprise networking, 2010, p. 3.

[24] NLANR/DAST: iPerf - the network bandwidth measurement tool. URL: https://iperf.fr [accessed: 2016-08-30].

Machine Learning Techniques for Mobile Application Event Analysis

Ben Falchuk, Chris Mesterharm, Euthimios Panagos
Applied Communication Sciences (Vencore Labs)
Basking Ridge, NJ, USA
e-mail: {bfalchuk,jmesterharm,epanagos}@appcomsci.com

Shoshana Loeb
InterDigital Inc.
Wilmington, DE, USA
e-mail: Shoshana.Loeb@InterDigital.com

***Abstract*—As increasing amounts of economic, entertainment and social activities are occurring using native and web applications, it has become essential for developers to analyze user interactions in order to better understand their behavior and increase engagement and monetization. In this paper, we describe how JumpStart, a real-time event analytics service, utilizes machine learning techniques for empowering developers and businesses to both identify users exhibiting similar behavior and discover user interaction patterns that are strongly correlated with specific activities (e.g., purchases). Discovered interaction patterns can be used for enabling contextual real-time feedback via JumpStart's complex event pattern matching.**

Keywords - Machine Learning; Analytics; Big Data; Mobile Apps; Data Clustering;

I. INTRODUCTION

Organizations offering mobile applications of all kinds (e.g., games, social media, etc.) are presently interested in learning about how users interact with these applications for reasons that range from marketing and advertising to application improvements and user retention. The most common way to acquire these insights is through the collection and analysis of events corresponding to specific actions users take while using an application. Event collection is typically achieved by using a home-grown or third-party library (e.g., software development kit – SDK – such as those offered by Google, Facebook, and Yahoo) for instrumenting the application code to record information related to specific user actions (e.g., kill an opponent in a first-person shooter game). Recorded information is then periodically uploaded to a back-end system for processing and analysis.

Many of today's mobile event processing/analytics offerings expose computed statistical information relating to key performance indicators (KPI) (e.g., daily active and new users, day 1 retention, and total sessions) in the form of reports and visualizations using a small number of pre-defined events or event attributes. These same offerings may also expose limited querying interfaces for users to filter the collected event data or offer the ability to download the collected information for further analysis by business intelligence and data mining tools.

A major limitation of such offerings is that they lack automated techniques for discovering interesting event patterns in collected events. In addition, they are often limited in their ability to match and react to such event patterns in real time. (e.g., notify users about a YouTube video that offers hints on how to complete the current game level after they fail three times).

The JumpStart [1] real-time context-aware analytics service overcomes these shortcomings by offering an end-to-end solution that enables application developers to capture events (via a simple SDK), specify event patterns (via a web portal) that will be matched in real-time as events are streamed to the service, and associate specific information to be sent back to the application on event pattern matches. JumpStart employs machine learning techniques to automatically learn user behavior in the context of specific applications. Such deep analysis allows, for example, for the discovery of otherwise hard-to-detect issues that may be limiting user experience (e.g., specific levels in a gaming application may be far too hard for many users).

In this paper, we focus on JumpStart's machine learning component. In particular, we discuss how JumpStart applies supervised and unsupervised machine learning technique to application event streams for: (1) identifying users exhibiting similar application behavior and (2) discovering event patterns that are strongly correlated with specific user activities within an application. These techniques enable JumpStart customers (e.g., application developers and businesses) to understand and control many aspects of their application. For example, customers can specify event patterns that, when matched against received event streams, provide contextual information back to the application to: help users that are stuck at a particular place in a given game, select the next level in a game with multiple levels based on the difficulty level of the level and user skills, offer incentives for increasing monetization opportunities, etc.. Our mechanisms and syntax for the aforementioned returned contextual information (also referred to as triggered alerts) has previously been described in [2].

The remainder of the paper is structured as follows. In Section II, we briefly cover related work in the area of mobile application analytics. In Section III, we offer an overview of the JumpStart service architecture. In Section IV, we provide some details about the two example applications used in this paper during the discussion of the JumpStart machine learning techniques. In Section V, we discuss the JumpStart machine learning techniques and present some results for the two example applications. Finally, in Section VI, we conclude our work.

II. RELATED WORK

The past several years have seen a dramatic rise in big data, application (app) analytics, and ever-increasing sophistication in advertising and monetization [4]. Both startups and well established technology companies are in the game, including (but not limited to): Facebook, Flurry, Google, Amazon, Adobe, and Riot. Smaller startups for analytics include Localytics, Swrve, Countly, MixPanel, and Apptimize, to name only a few. Without this increasingly necessary new breed of tools, developers would have very limited insight into how users interact with their apps, especially standalone apps that do not depend on a backend server component (in the cloud or private data center).

Fundamental features shared by many of today's mobile analytics offerings include: SDKs for various platforms (Android, iOS, etc.), in-app event collection and warehousing, creation and analysis of app "funnels" consisting of sequences of key in-app events, event charting dashboards for various metrics (including KPI, retention, number of active users), analysis of user base demographics and personas, and push notifications. Furthermore, the very desirable ability to manage campaigns, such as A-B variants, is also rapidly becoming fundamental.

Although existing mobile analytics solutions can compute a large number of metrics, developers still bear the burden of understanding how specific application events (e.g., purchases) are correlated with user interactions prior to these events. Our work lifts this burden by employing machine learning techniques that learn event patterns that are: (1) common across many users, and (2) correlated with specific user actions. Developers can then register discovered patterns with JumpStart and associate specific information (i.e., actionable alerts) that is sent back to the app when these patterns are matched in near real time [2].

The two main machine learning techniques utilized by JumpStart are: Bayesian Rule Lists [6] and Falling Rule Lists [7]. These are machine learning algorithm for returning a classifier that can be easily interpreted by humans. This can be compared to techniques that learn a complex rule, such as [5]. Interpretability is an important constraint as we want a user of JumpStart to be able understand and modify these rules. We build on these algorithms in novel ways. The most interesting is a new clustering technique that uses Falling Rule Lists to do dynamic hierarchical clustering.

III. JUMPSTART OVERVIEW

JumpStart aims to be the first cross-platform solution to offer near real-time detection of user behavior patterns associated with past and current user interactions with mobile applications. User behavior pattern matches can trigger actionable alerts aimed to achieve specific goals, such as increased user retention and monetization. Our implementation uses the Esper pattern matching engine [3] and is cloud based to allow scalability for multiple applications and users. This allows devices to respond to user events that match patterns stored on the server with latencies based primarily on the quality of the network connection.

Fig. 1 shows the high-level architecture of JumpStart. Input and output adaptors are responsible for connecting to data sources or sinks and retrieving or storing/sending events. The analytics component is responsible for on-line and batch processing of events and computation of various metrics (e.g., daily active and new users, user retention, session and users per hour, event funnels of various lengths). The machine learning component, the main focus of this paper, is responsible for discovering correlations between events that reflect specific user interactions with an application utilizing supervised and unsupervised learning. The profile manager component is responsible for managing user profiles in terms of both statistical properties (e.g., session duration and event distributions) and user-specific event patterns discovered by machine learning. Finally, the real-time rules processor is carrying out real-time complex event processing and matching of event patterns, referred to as triggers in the remainder of the document.

As a simple example of JumpStart event collection, consider a game that has multiple levels (the basketball game described in Section IV). By recording events that correspond to level completion and failure, JumpStart can gauge the difficult of a level. A level that is easy to complete will require few attempts before success while a more difficult level might require many attempts.

Fig. 2 shows the ratio of the number of failures to the number of successes. While there are a range of opinions on how the game level difficulty should progress, it is without controversy that we do not want to advance to a new level that is considerably easier than the last level. At a minimum, the JumpStart framework gives us the analytics to determine if the order of levels is appropriate. If it is discovered that certain levels are too easy or hard, they can be removed, redesigned, or moved to a more appropriate location in the game, as the case may be.

Things get more interesting when we use the real-time nature of the JumpStart rules processor. With JumpStart we can detect how well a user is doing on a particular level by

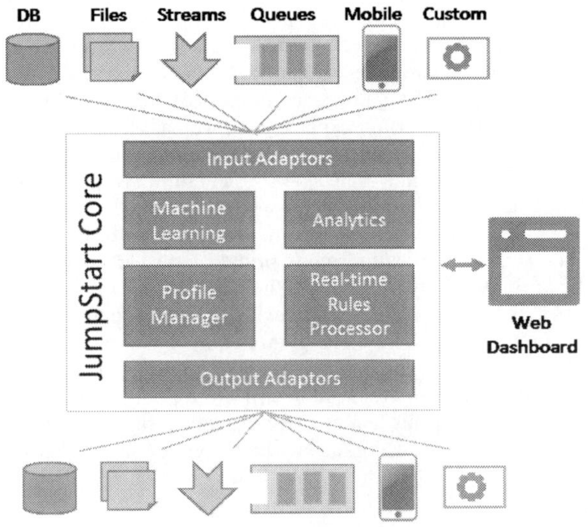

Figure 1. JumpStart high-level architecture

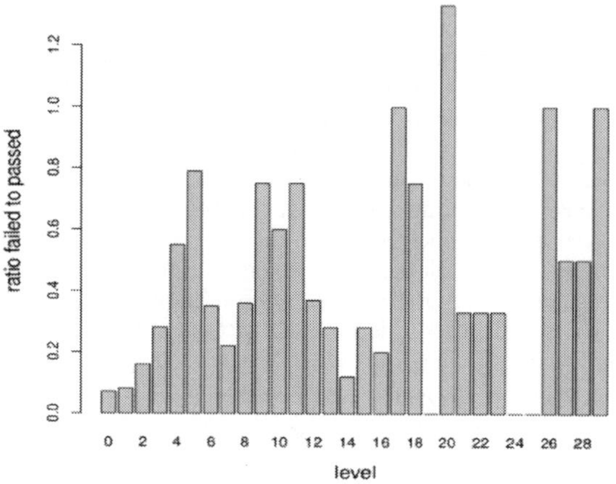

Figure 2. Basketball game level difficulty

comparing the level's outcome and time taken to those of the previous level via the appropriate event pattern. The output of the event pattern match can trigger a modification to the levels and even the creation of a non-linear path through the levels. This can reduce the churn of users who are bored by simple levels or frustrated by difficult levels. While some of this logic could be built into the application, using JumpStart is advantageous because:

1. Since it analyzes events from the entire user-base (not just the user in question), it can anticipate churn before it happens by, for example, clustering the user in with a "high churn" group.
2. It allows us to make modifications based on real user data as opposed to doing expensive customer trials that delay the release of the application and might be dated by the time the application is released.

IV. Event Generating Applications

In this paper, we give experimental results for two applications. The first application is a game where either a single player or two players can compete in a basketball shooting contest. The game is composed of thirty levels of varying difficulty. For our experiments, we have 7,395 users, 122 unique types of events, and more than 630,000 collected events. Example events include taking a shot, missing a shot, completing a level, failing a level, and completing a section of the tutorial. In this paper, we call this game **basketball**.

The second application sends printed letters to members of the military. Many members of the military are not allowed access to the internet and need to receive physical letters. This application allows users to easily and simply compose these letters. For our experiments, we have 3,400 users, 55 unique events, and more than 137,000 collected events. Example events include buying tokens to send letters, starting a new letter, typing a letter using the keyboard, and taking a picture to send with the letter. In this paper, we call this application **post office**.

We have also performed experiments on three other applications: a music application, an event scheduling application, and a novelty humor application (with more that 11 million events). We obtained similar results but do not have the space to include these additional experiments.

V. Machine Learning with Events

While analytics based on event data provides a useful tool for learning user behavior, machine learning techniques can often find non-obvious correlations that a human might miss. In this section, we give several techniques that find patterns that, while interesting on their own, can be used as a source of inspiration for creating event pattern expressions to be matched by JumpStart.

For the learning algorithms we are going to use, we need to represent a sequence of events as a fixed length $\{0, 1\}^n$ vector. We use the following mix of standard features.

- We take the last three events in the sequence and create a feature for every possible event type value (referred simply as event in the remainder of this paper). For example, if the last event is A, we create a binary feature A=1 to represent that the last feature is event A.
- We use a bag-of-words on the events in the sequence. We include single words and pairs. For example, if the events A and B occur consecutively in the event stream we create three binary features, A and B for the single events and A+B for the pair of consecutive events.
- We remove repeated consecutive events and represent them with special features that take into account the count. For example, if the event stream has 8 consecutive A events, we create features A, A>1, A>3, A>7. Notice that we create the features based on powers of 2.

In all cases, if a feature occurs more than once in an event sequence, we remove the repeats. In the following sections, we will occasionally add or remove features for specific learning problems.

A. Algorithms

We consider two algorithms for building understandable rules: the Bayesian Rule List (BRL) algorithm [6] and the Falling Rule List (FRL) algorithm [7]. Both algorithms return rules in the form of a decision list. A decision list is an ordered sequence of rules such that the first rule that is true makes the prediction. A rule is a conjunction of predicates that predicts a probability that the label is true. Fig. 3 gives an example of our notation.

```
rule 1 (90%)
    A+B
    C
rule 2 (5%)
    D=3
default (10%)
```

Figure 3. Decision list notation example

In this example, rule 1 has two predicates. First, the consecutive events A followed by B must occur somewhere in the sequence of events. Second the event C must occur somewhere in the sequence. If these two predicates are true, then the decision list gives 90% probability that the label is 1. If rule 1 fails, we check rule 2. In this example, rule 2 is true if event D is the third to last event in the sequence. If rule 2 is true, then the decision list predicts label 1 with 5% probability. The final rule is the default rule. If all the previous rules fail, we predict label 1 with 10% probability.

Both rule list algorithms are Bayesian algorithms that try to learn accurate - yet short - decision lists. The FRL algorithm has the extra constraint that a rule that is earlier in the list should have a higher probability of predicting the label than a rule that occurs later in the list. While this extra constraint can return a less accurate decision list, it makes the rules easier to interpret because many people will only consider the first few rules. A major competitor to these algorithms is decision trees. Experiments have found that the accuracy of the rule list algorithms is comparable to decision trees [8]. Decision lists also tend to be easier to understand because they are just a one sided subset of decision trees.

All experiments were performed using a single core of a 2011 vintage 2.4 GHz processor. The computational time for both algorithms, on the problems we studied, was on the order of a minute. While BRL does not scale as well on larger problems there is active research in improving its computational performance [9].

B. Supervised Learning

The first technique we cover is based on supervised learning. In supervised learning we have a set of objects, and we want to predict labels for these objects. For example, an object might be all the events in a session of a game and we want to predict if a user will make a purchase during the session. In order to learn a prediction model, we take a set of training data that consists of already labeled objects and use them to induce a classifier.

Typically, this classifier is used to predict labels for new objects. Instead we are focused on creating rules that describe the classifier and can be used to understand the data and generate triggers (e.g., register event patterns with the JumpStart rules processor). These rules can often reveal correlations that while reasonable in hindsight are difficult for humans to create by inspecting the data.

We perform three types of experiments based on events from the previously described post office application. The label for these experiments is based on a purchase event enabling the sending of future letters. For each experiment, we have a baseline level of performance based on this label. For example, out of the set of users we are considering say 25% make a purchase. Therefore, a rule that predicts a purchase with 25% probability is making a safe baseline prediction. Rules that have higher probability point to an informative situation where a purchase is more likely than the baseline. Rules that have a lower probability point to situations where a user is less likely to make a purchase. Note that cases at the baseline probability suggest that the user is "on the fence" with regard to a purchase.

A typical use of these algorithms is to run both the BRL and FRL multiple times to find interesting decision lists. In our experiments, we ran each algorithm twice (reporting here on only a subset of results; for the non-reported experiments, we get qualitatively similar results).

The first experiments are based on the initial 30 events generated by a user. Our goal is to predict if the user will eventually make a purchase. The baseline probability that a user makes a purchase is 31%. Fig. 4 gives the results of using FRL to generate a decision list.

```
rule 1 (60%)
        user_logged_in+compose_new_letter_screen
        launch_camera
rule 2 (37%)
        compose_letter_kb
default (7%)
```

Figure 4. FRL applied to **post office** for first 30 events

In this case, based on the first rule, if right after a user logs in to the application the user starts to compose a letter and at some point in these initial 30 events the user takes a picture then there is a 60% chance that the user will eventually make a purchase. If the first rule fails, then rule 2 is about equal to the baseline. However, if rule 2 also fails, then there is a good chance the user will never make a purchase. This suggests it is important to get a user actively creating a letter as soon as they start using the application.

The second experiments predict whether a user will make a purchase during a session based on the initial 15 events of the session. The baseline probability that a user makes a purchase is 25%. Fig. 5 gives the results of using BRL to generate a decision list.

```
rule 1 (2%)
        1=menu_opened
rule 2 (68%)
        letters_billing_appear
        user_info-user_logged_in
rule 3 (47%)
        launch_camera
rule 4 (11%)
        kin_pressed_from_menu+menu_closed
rule 5 (27%)
        compose_letter_kb
default (3%)
```

Figure 5. BRL applied to **post office** for first 15 events of session

Here we see that if a user opens a menu on the last event in our window of 15 events, he is unlikely to make a purchase. This rule might be a rare occurrence, but it suggests something that might need further study. (We also see this in some non-reported rule lists.) Next, we see that if a user does billing along with logging in right after the start of the session, then they are likely to make a purchase. If we reach rule 3, using the camera is likely to lead to a purchase as the user is probably creating pictures to send with the letters. Finally, if we get through all the rules then the user is extremely unlikely to make a purchase.

Figure 6. Sliding Window Example

The third experiment is based on a sliding window over the event sequence. The idea is that we want to make a timely prediction about whether a user is about to make a purchase. We use a window size of 15 events. We want advanced notice that the user is going to make a purchase so we don't look for purchase events right after the end of the window. Instead, we have a gap of 5 events. To give us more flexibility, we look for a purchase that occurs in the 5 events that follow the gap. Fig. 6 gives a graphical explanation based on window of size 5, a gap of size 3 and label of size 5. Because this instance generation technique creates a large number of instances that don't have a purchase in their label window, we de-skew the labels by randomly selecting negative instances to ensure that 10% of the instances have a purchase label. Fig. 7 gives the results of the FRL algorithm, but only reports the first five rules.

```
rule 1 (36%)
        new_recipient_next_pressed
        letters_new_next_pressed
rule 2 (28%)
        compose_new_letter_screen+compose_letter_kb
        launch_camera
rule 3 (26%)
        confirmation_for_purchase_letters
        compose_new_letter_screen+compose_letter_kb
rule 4 (20%)
        launch_camera+compose_letter_kb
        compose_new_letter_screen
rule 5 (19%)
        new_recepient+compose_letter_kb
        compose_letter_kb>1
```

Figure 7. FRL applied to **post office** with sliding window

All of these rules show that a user in the process of creating a letter has a higher probability of making a purchase. This is not surprising. However, it is interesting how the ordering of the rules can be interpreted as giving insight on the relative importance of the various actions.

What we are lacking with previous FRL example is the kind of actions lead to a user not making a purchase. This is a result of how FRL builds a decision list with the highest probabilities first. To study events that do not lead to a purchase, we flip the labels on the problem. This creates a decision list where the top rules are more likely to predict that the user does not make a purchase. Fig. 8 gives the first five rules generated by the FRL algorithm.

```
rule 1 (0%)
        menu_opened+units_pressed_from_menu
        units_pressed_from_menu
rule 2 (0%)
        2=menu_closed
        menu_opened
rule 3 (0%)
        1=menu_closed
        menu_closed
rule 4 (0%)
        1=menu_opened
rule 5 (0%)
        edit_profile_pressed_from_menu
        menu_closed+menu_opened
```

Figure 8. FRL applied to **post office** with sliding window and flipped labels

Here we observe interesting evidence that a user who uses the menu is unlikely to make a purchase in the near future. This matches our previous result dealing with sessions and suggests that any enticement for a user to make a purchase should wait until they are done using the menu.

C. Clustering

For many applications it is useful to organize similar users or sessions. We can automate this task by applying an unsupervised clustering algorithm. One problem with clustering is that it is difficult to understand the results. In this section we give results on using the FRL algorithm to better understand clusters and therefore help generate possible event patterns that can be used for generating actionable alerts.

The simplest form of our algorithm is easiest to explain with an example. Assume we create three clusters. We use these clusters to create three supervised learning problems. For each problem the instances in the cluster get a label of 1 while the instances in other clusters get a label of 0. Now we can apply FRL to learn a decision list that concisely describes each cluster. We use the FRL algorithm because we want our decision list to give preference to the high probability rules that describe what examples are in the cluster.

A further refinement of the algorithm is to add the ability to do dynamic hierarchical clustering. By this we mean that after the initial clustering one can use the insights provided by the rules returned to select clusters to expand. For example, assume we want to expand cluster B. We just rerun our simple algorithm to create a new clustering and new set of rules just using examples from cluster B. We can repeat this process to create a clustering tree with rules to explain the various clusters.

We believe our novel technique has many advantages over a traditional hierarchical clustering.

- The decision lists give an understanding of the various clusters. This includes how one cluster relates to another based on their ancestry.
- Instead of having to interpret a dendogram and picking an appropriate level of granularity, one can use our top down dynamic procedure to explore the data.
- The technique has a computational advantage in that we can decide to only explore the interesting part of the data to a depth that is informative.

Next, we give experiments for applying our clustering technique to the basketball data. Like many problems, the basketball data does not have an obvious label for supervised learning, so clustering is the logical approach. Note that clustering is also useful with problems amendable to supervised learning - such as the post office problem.

Our FRL based clustering code works with any clustering algorithm that returns a hard clustering. (A hard clustering is a clustering algorithm that assigns each example to one cluster.) We performed experiments with two clustering algorithms: k-means [10] and spectral clustering [11]. We found that, with our representation, k-means returned more meaningful clusters with the added bonus of being much faster; k-means only took a minute to build the clustering while spectral clustering took 30 minutes.

For our experiments, we use the same features as described in the start of Section V with the following modifications. First, we removed the features that represent the last three events in the sequence. These features are not needed as there is no special significance to the last events. Second, we added a feature called Short for any session that has less than four events. Based on an early analysis using our clustering technique, we found this useful to allow the clustering to identify the large number of short sessions in our data. Research shows that many users only try an application once before uninstalling potentially creating many short sessions.

Our experiments are based on clustering sessions. Using sessions can be useful for a range of applications. For example, one might want to understand users based on how they transition from various session types. For example, a user who continually returns to the tutorial might need extra assistance in using the app.

Fig. 9 show the results of generating two clusters for the basketball data. We have modified our decision list output to include information on the cluster and the number examples that are covered by the individual rules. As can be seen in the output, cluster 0 deals primarily with the game's tutorial while cluster 1 deals largely with the sessions that are very short.

```
Cluster 0 has 805 out of 2746 examples
  rule 1 (100%) 799 examples
        tutorial_sr_for_power_completed
        tutorial_drag_left_completed
  rule 2 (86%) 7 examples
        tutorial_sr_for_power
  default (0%) 1940 examples

Cluster 1 has 1941 out of 2746 examples
  rule 1 (100%) 1219
        Short
  rule 2 (95%) 194
        user_info+ pvp_pressed
  rule 3 (78%) 438
        user_info+story_mode_pressed
  rule 4 (47%) 104
        me_pressed
  default (18%) 791.0
```

Figure 9. Top level FRL clusters for **basketball**

Based on this analysis, we decided that cluster 0 is more interesting. We expand cluster 0 by creating two new clusters only using the examples from cluster 0. We show these decision lists in Fig. 10. Cluster 0-0 deals with the tutorial, but cluster 0-1 is interesting in that it is primarily deals with users who have started playing the game and completed some of the initial levels. These can be sessions where the user goes straight from the tutorial to playing the game.

VI. CONCLUSION

In this paper, we discussed the machine learning techniques used by the JumpStart real-time event analytics service in the context of two example mobile applications. JumpStart applies supervised and unsupervised machine learning techniques to application event streams for identifying users exhibiting similar application behavior and discovering event patterns that are strongly correlated with specific user activities within an application. In addition, we presented a novel approach that uses the Falling Rule List algorithm to concisely describe clusters generated by unsupervised machine learning algorithms. Cluster descriptions via decision lists enable hierarchical clustering by creating new clusters from existing ones.

Machine learning enables JumpStart customers to gain deep insights into how users interact with their applications and discover user behaviors that are correlated with specific application actions. These capabilities go far beyond the computed metrics and aggregate user actions offered by existing mobile analytics solutions.

```
Cluster 0-0 has 420 out of 805 examples
  rule 1 (87%) 79
        tutorial_sr_power+ tutorial_sr_power_completed
        missed_shot_0+tutorial_completed
  default (48%) 726

Cluster 0-1 has 385 out of 805 examples
  rule 1 (99%) 323
        missed_shot_1+shot_punk
        1_level_0_completed
  rule 2 (96%) 24
        1_level_1_completed
        shot_made
  rule 3 (39%) 103
        missed_shot_0+shot_punk
        tutorial_pull_back_to_aim_at_target
  default (0%) 355
```

Figure 10. Second level FRL clusters for **basketball**

REFERENCES

[1] InterDigital Inc., "JumpStart", [Online]. Available from: http://www.interdigital.com/jumpstart, accessed: 2016.08.26.

[2] B. Falchuk, K.C. Lee, S. Loeb, E. Panagos, and Z. Yao, "Just-in-time reconnaissance and assistance for video game streams and players", Proc. IEEE Consumer Communications and Networking Conference, Las Vegas, pp. 99-102, 2016.

[3] EsperTech Inc., "EsperTech event series intelligence". [Online] Available from: http://www.espertech.com, accessed: 2016.08.26.

[4] T. Leaver and M.A. Wilson (eds.), "Social, casual and mobile games: the changing gaming landscape," Bloomsbury Academic, New York, 2016.

[5] M.A. Alsheikh, D. Niyato, S. Lin, H. Tan, and Z. Han, "Mobile big data analytics using deep learning and apache spark, IEEE Network, 30(3), pp. 22-29, June 2016.

[6] B. Letham, C .Rudin, T.H. McCormick, and D. Madigan, "Interpretable classifiers using rules and Bayesian analysis: building a better stroke prediction model", Annals of Applied Statistics, 9(3), pp.1350-1371, 2015.

[7] F. Wang and C. Rudin, "Falling rule lists", *JMLR* Workshop and Conference Proceedings 38, pp. 1013-1022, 2015.

[8] J.R. Quinlan. "Induction of decision trees." Machine Learning Journal, 1(1) , pp. 81-106, March 1986.

[9] H. Yang, C. Rudin, and, M. Seltzer, "Scalable Bayesian rule lists", arXiv:1602.08610, 2016.

[10] E.W. Forgy, "Cluster analysis of multivariate data: efficiency versus interpretability of classifications", Biometrics, 21, pp. 768-769, 1965.

[11] A.Y. Ng, M.I. Jordan, and Y. Weiss, "On Spectral Clustering: analysis and an algorithm", Advances in Neural Information Processing Systems, pp. 849-856, 2001.

Development of an Energy Performance Assessment System for Existing Buildings

Youn-Kwae Jeong, Jong-Won Kim, Tae-Hyung Kim, Jong-Woo Choi, Hong-Soon Nam and Il-Woo Lee
ETRI (Electronics and Telecommunications Research Institute)
Daejeon, South Korea
ykjeong, jongwkim, taehyung, jwchoi89, hsnam, iwlee@etri.re.kr

***Abstract*—In this paper, we describe the development of an energy performance assessment system to evaluate the energy performance of existing buildings to deliver energy efficiency improvements by building remodeling. In consideration of the performance effect of building structure and operation, this system uses two kinds of building energy models, such as ISO 13790 and EN15232, to calculate the energy consumption of a building. In order to run an accurate building energy model, we use bill based energy consumption data and the Bayesian calibration method to find the current value of uncertainty parameters such as performance coefficient and deterioration coefficient of various building components. So, this system can accurately evaluate the energy performance of an existing building. Also, it can provide Energy Conservation Measures (ECM) for remodeling of existing buildings. The proposed system can be used as an effective and accurate energy performance assessment tool for improving energy efficiency of existing buildings through building remodeling.**

Keywords- building energy paerformance; assessment; buildung energy model; Bayesian calibration; ECM.

I. Introduction

Recently, the Korean government has announced it will reduce greenhouse gas emissions by 37% from the previous projected emission levels for 2030. It takes about 22% of national energy consumption in the building sector. Therefore, building remodeling strategies to improve the energy efficiency of buildings to cope with these requirements have been actively promoted. In Korea, there are official building energy simulation programs, such as ECO2, ECO2-OD (Office Design)[1], Building Energy Simulation for Seoul (BESS) that evaluate the energy performance and validate building energy efficiency rating of a new building. But now there is no tool to evaluate the energy performance of existing buildings. Therefore, a new way is needed to effectively determine the deterioration and performance degradation of building structures and equipment according to the aging of the building. Also, a way to determine the energy efficiency of the building in accordance with the operating method is needed. In this paper, we describe the functional element of the system and the energy performance evaluation model based on ISO13790[2] and EN15232[3] and the way to improve the accuracy of the model by using bill based energy consumption data of existing building and stochastic energy model calibration method. Finally, we show the comparison results between actual energy consumption and predicted energy consumption.

II. System Architecture

To evaluate the energy performance of existing buildings, it is very important to know how to effectively find the current value of unknown variable related to the performance of building components according to their age. We proposed three methods to effectively derive the coefficient of performance and deterioration, and to apply them to building energy model in calculating building energy consumption. First, we use the Bayesian calibration method, which is a stochastic energy calibration model that uses actual energy consumption data based on the bill. Second, we use the deterioration equation method that can predict the deterioration degree of building components according to their age. Third, we use the monitoring method to directly measure the actual value with respect to building components influencing the energy performance of buildings. Fig.1 shows the conceptual architecture of an energy performance assessment system for existing buildings.

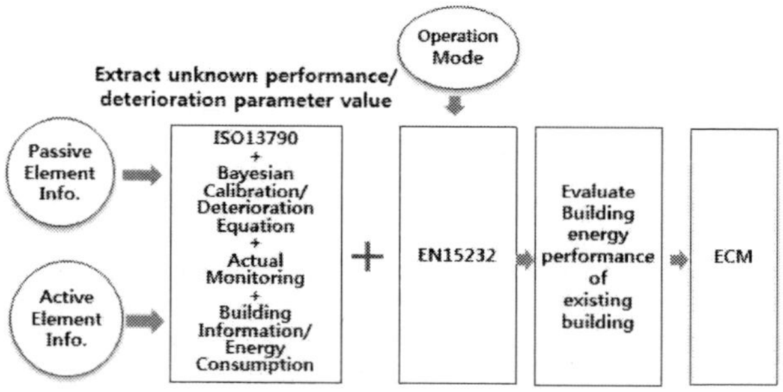

Figure 1. Conceptual architecture of an existing building energy performance assessment system

Fig.2 shows the functional architecture of the existing building energy performance assessment system. The system consists of 5 functions, namely, input file generation function, building model generation function, sensitivity analysis function, building energy model calibration function, and ECM generation and analysis function.

A. Input File Genergation

This function asks the user to input the attribute values of each building component such as envelope, heating, cooling, renewable energy, measured data, and operation mode etc. Also, it makes Excel-based building information and a list of input parameters with uncertainty and it selects probability distribution for these input variables. Excel-based building information consists of building attribute data (total floor area, floor number, location, etc.), envelope and thermal attribute data (azimuth area, u-value, etc.), buildings structure, building operation, building energy systems, renewable energy (solar, photovoltaic and wind power), Building Automation and Control System (BACS) information, weather data (monthly mean air temperature, wind speed, solar radiation data), monthly energy consumption data based on bill and energy source, the schedule data to calculate the monthly average indoor heat value, and etc.

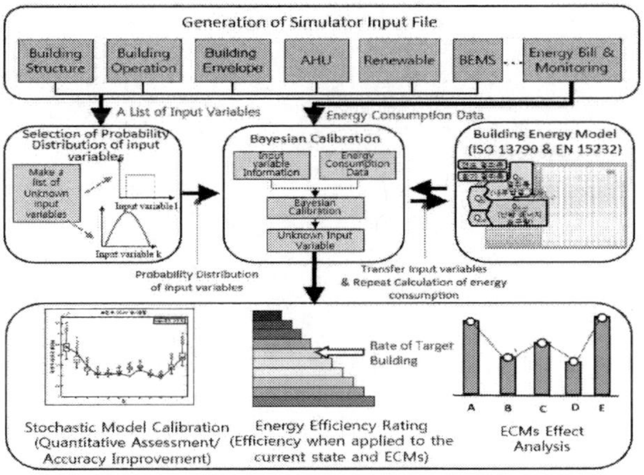

Figure 2. Functional architecture of an existing building energy performance assessment system

B. Building Energy Model Generation

This function creates a building energy model to calculate energy performance for existing buildings based on ISO13790 and EN15232 energy model. ISO13790 calculates the energy used by heating, cooling, hot water, lighting, ventilation. EN15232 rates the operation mode of BACS and applies efficiency coefficient according to the operation mode to ISO 13790 energy calculation.

C. Sensitivity Analysis

The sensitivity analysis is to identify the input variables that greatly influence energy consumption in the energy model. It is performed by Morris method to exclude input variables with low influence from Bayesian calibration.

D. Building Energy Model Calibration

This function performs calibration of input variables of the energy model by using the actual energy usage data of the analytic target building. It is performed in the building energy model calibration considering the inherent uncertainty of the unknown input parameters automatically generated building energy model. The unknown variables of building energy model are corrected by a stochastic model calibration scheme based on Bayesian theory. Bayesian calibration is a process that estimates the probability distribution of the calibrated input variables to make the predictive value of a building energy model similar to the actual building energy consumption. It uses the Metropolis-Hastings Markov Chain Monte Carlo (MCMC) sampling method.

E. ECM Generation and Economical Effect Analysis

This function is to predict the current value of an unknown variable with respect to each passive/active component of the building by using the calibrated building energy model as a base model. After that, it provides users with various ECMs for improving building energy performance. Users can select ECMs and it analyzes the energy and cost saving effects according to the user's selection of ECMs. It automatically provides the user with an optimal alternative in terms of the energy and cost saving effect. Finally, it reports energy consumption, energy reduction rate, CO_2 reduction, payback, etc.

III. Experimental Results

The developed prototype system was applied to three actual buildings in Seoul. The performance evaluation results are shown in Table I. This confirms excellent results in terms of energy calculation and error rate when compared to the ECO2-OD, which is used in conventional institutions.

TABLE I. EXPERMENTAL RESULTS APPLIED TO TESTBED BUILDINGS

	Building Name	*Actual Energy Consump. (KWh/m^2) 2013*	*ECO2-OD (KWh/m^2)*	*Developed Tool (KWh/m^2)*	*ECO2-OD Error rate (%)*	*System Error rate (%)*
1	*Credit Center*	233.3	214.8	229.8	8.0	1.5
2	*Hwain Building*	169	194.2	185.2	14.9	9.6
3	*Kaite Tower*	295	237.1	290.5	19.6	1.5

IV. Conclusion

In this paper, we described a new building energy performance assessment system to accurately evaluate the energy performance of existing buildings in Korea. This system can provide the user with ECMs and analyze the economic effect to retrofit existing building components. Experimental results verified that it is more accurate than the official building energy simulation program ECO2-OD. In addition, it has 1.5% error rate between the calculated energy consumption and actual energy consumption. So, it is expected that this system is a very useful building energy performance assessment system for building remodeling and building energy efficiency certification for existing buildings.

Acknowledgment

This work was supported by the Korea Institute of Energy Technology Evaluation and Planning (KETEP) and the Ministry of Trade, Industry & Energy (MOTIE) of the Republic of Korea (No. 20142010102370).

REFERENCES

[1] Korea Energy Agency. ECO2-OD. [Online]. Available from: http://www.kemco.or.kr/building/v2/bbs.asp?bid=data&sk=&kc=0&kt=ST&ks=ECO2%2DOD&pop=0&cp=1&act=view&bno=111 (2016.05.31)

[2] ISO 13790 (2008), Energy performance of buildings – Calculation of energy use for space heating and cooling

[3] EN 15232 (2012), Energy performance of buildings – Impact of Building Automation, Controls and Building Management

Economic Impact Analysis of Energy Conservation Measures for Building Remodeling

Hong-Soon Nam, Jin-Tae Kim, Tae-Hyung Kim, Youn-Kwae Jeong, Ii-Woo Lee
Energy IT Research Section
Electronics and Telecommunications Research Institute
Daejeon, Korea
e-mail: hsnam,jtkim,taehyung,ykjeong,ilwoo@etri.re.kr

Abstract— **This paper describes energy conservation measures (ECMs) for building energy efficiency improvement and presents a method and process of economic impact analysis of ECMs in terms of energy and cost savings. ECMs have various measures including operation and maintenance improvements, retrofit activities or renewable energy sources. Most of these measures need investment expense for installation or replacement of facilities. Thus, it is not easy for building owners and energy managers to figure out the detailed cost saving and the payback period. To analyze economic impacts, this paper simulates the energy and cost savings, greenhouse gas emission reduction and payback period and examines the simulation results to verify the effects of ECMs.**

***Keywords**- energy conservation measure; energy saving; energy efficiency improvement.*

I. INTRODUCTION

Buildings consume almost 35% of total energy in the world and building owners spend around 30% of their budget on energy [4][5]. Buildings take up a major share of world energy consumptions, hence energy savings in buildings can lead to both great cost savings and enormous greenhouse gas emission reductions. Much of this energy use can be safely reduced with proper energy conservation measures (ECMs). ECMs are to improve the energy efficiency of buildings including roof and windows, heating, ventilation, and air conditioning (HVAC), utility systems, and renewable energy systems. The aims of ECM are to reduce building energy consumptions to save energy cost, and mitigate the greenhouse gas emissions.

To reduce building energy consumptions in a cost-effective manner, ECMs have three main approaches : energy efficiency improvement, operating time reduction and renewable energy adoption. The energy efficiency improvement approach is to improve energy efficiency by installing new facilities, replacing or upgrading existing ones. The operating time reduction approach is to control the facilities by using monitoring and control including accurate set points and occupancy monitoring. The other approach introduces renewable energy sources like solar, natural gas and wind energy, which substitute for conventional energy resulting in energy cost saving and greenhouse gas emissions reduction.

However, it is not easy for building owners and energy managers to estimate the economic benefits of ECM before implementation and to evaluate actual energy savings after implementation. Recent researches in the field of energy efficiency focus on simulation tools based on database [1-4] and standards [6]-[8]. This paper presents a method and process to analyze the economic impacts of ECM such as energy and cost savings, CO2 emission reduction and payback period. In this paper, we first present how to analyze the economic impacts of ECM in Section II. Afterwards, we describe an economic analysis tool to calculate the economic impacts and discuss how to use the analysis results in Section III. Finally we conclude this paper in Section IV.

II. ECONOMIC IMPACT ANALYSIS

Economic impact analysis is necessary for building owners and energy managers to evaluate the benefits of ECM, which is one of the most important issues before and after ECMs implementations. The benefits of ECMs need to be analyzed in terms of energy saving and non-energy savings including CO2 reduction. Thus, the energy and cost savings, CO2 reduction and payback period need to be analyzed in ECM planning phase and evaluation phase after implementation.

A. Energy Saving

Energy saving is determined by comparing energy uses before and after ECM implementation. To estimate energy saving, baseline energy E_{base} is defined as the amount of the energy that would be consumed without ECM implementation and post installation energy E_{post} as the estimated or measured energy use after the implementation [5-7]. Then, the energy saving E_{save} is given by summation of monthly energy savings as follow.

$$E_{save} = (E_{base} \pm E_{adj}) - E_{post} \tag{1}$$

where, adjustments E_{adj} compensate for the condition changes in weather, occupancy, or other factors between the baseline and performance periods.

On the other hand, the energy saving of each ECM can also be estimated. We describe three kinds of ECMs as examples: outer wall, variable air volume (VAV), and solar energy. Table I presents symbols and units of variables related to the ECMs.

TABLE I. SYMBOLS AND UNITS OF VARIABLES

Symbol	Description	Unit
A	outer wall area	m^2
$t_{oper,m}$	operating time in month	hour
$T_{diff,m}$	temperature differences between outdoor and indoor in month	K
$U_{w,pre}$, $U_{w,post}$	thermal transmittance of outer wall	$W/(m^2K)$
P	power consumption	W
N	number of devices	
η	efficiency	

i) Efficiency improvement

Consider an ECM to improve the thermal transmittance of outer wall and refer to the variables in Table I. Then, the estimated annual energy saving of the ECM is obtained by

$$\hat{E}_{save,wall} = \sum_{m=1}^{12}(U_{w,pre} - U_{w,post})A\hat{T}_{diff,m}\hat{t}_{oper,m} \quad (2)$$

where $\hat{T}_{diff,m}$ and $\hat{t}_{oper,m}$ are the estimated mean temperature differences between indoor and outdoor in month and the estimated mean operating time per month, respectively.

ii) Operating time improvement

Consider an ECM to replace high efficient fans of a variable air volume (VAV) system. Then the operating time can be reduced from $t_{oper,pre,m}$ to $t_{oper,post,m}$. Then the estimated energy saving can be obtained by

$$\hat{E}_{save,fan} = \sum_{m=1}^{12}(t_{oper,pre,m} - \hat{t}_{oper,post,m})NP_{fan}\eta_{post} \quad (3)$$

where η_{post} and N represent the efficiency and the number of fans, respectively.

iii) Renewable energy

Consider an ECM to introduce solar photovoltaic energy, which generates electricity directly from sunlight via an electronic process. The savings are given by

$$E_{save,pv} = \sum_{m=1}^{12} P_{pv}\hat{t}_{oper,m} \,. \quad (4)$$

Assuming that a project has N ECMs, then the total annual energy savings can be obtained by summation of energy savings of each measure, as follows

$$\hat{E}_{save} = \sum_{i=1}^{N}\hat{E}_{save,i} \,. \quad (5)$$

The estimated energy saving $\hat{E}_{save}$ in (5) and the saving E_{save} (1) are logically same.

On the other hand, from the energy saving in (5), cost saving and CO2 reduction can be obtained by considering the associated energy source such as electricity, natural gas and solar energy.

B. Payback Period

Cost saving can be calculated from the energy savings in (5). Let C_{save} and $C_{project}$ be annual cost saving of a project and project expense, respectively. Then the payback period is given by

$$\hat{P}_{payback} = \frac{C_{project}}{\hat{C}_{save}} \quad (4)$$

where, $\hat{C}_{save}$ can be calculated from $\hat{E}_{save}$.

III. SIMULATION

A. Enoomic Analysis Tool

To examine the economic impacts of ECM, we set up an economic analysis tool as shown in Fig. 1. The tool consists of input block, output block, database and ECM impact analysis block. The input block is to enter information on the building to be analyzed including building attributes, energy use and monitoring-based commissioning (MBCx). The baseline energy is determined from the energy use, which is usually performed on an annual basis. The database consists of the information on ECMs, weather, energy price, measurement and verification (M&V) results, etc.

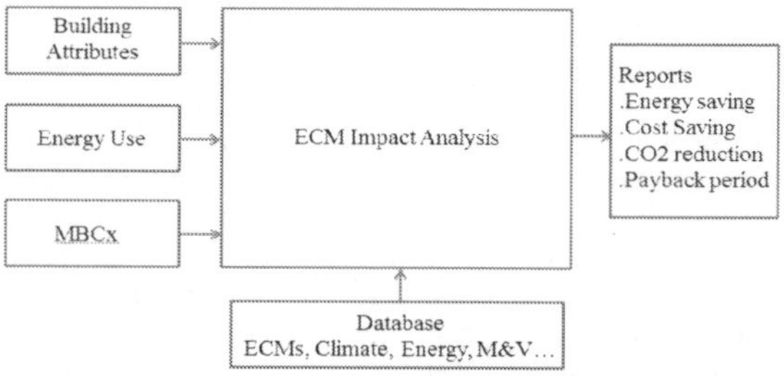

Figure 1. Architecture of economic analysis tool

The analysis block calculates the economic impacts including energy and cost savings, CO2 reduction and payback period. The output block then displays, saves, or prints out the analysis results.

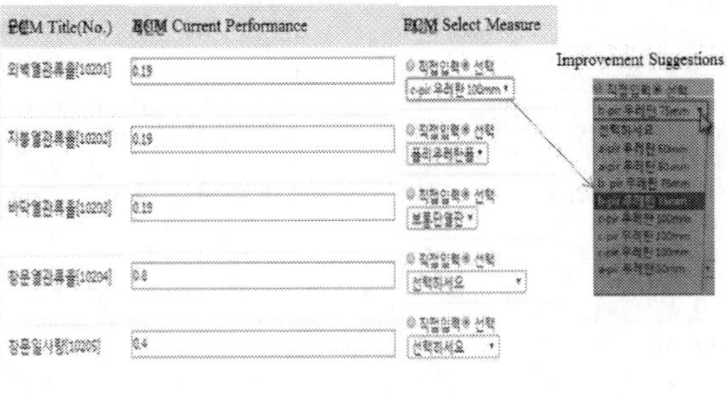

Figure 2. Combo box for detailed measure selection

Fig. 2 shows an example of detailed measure selection of ECM. The tool prepares a lot of typical measures in the ECM database for building owners and energy managers to simply select detailed measures and analyze their economic impacts.

B. Simulation Results

We carried out some simulations to examine the economic impacts of ECM. Simulation results can be represented in various forms. Fig. 3 shows the energy saving by comparing post installation energy and adjusted baseline energy. We assumed the baseline energy as the monthly energy use in the last year and the adjusted baseline energy is increased by almost 2.5 % every year after implementation. The post installation energy is obtained by subtracting the estimated energy saving from the adjusted baseline energy in planning phase or obtained by measurement after implementation.

Table II summarizes the annual economic impact analysis results of ECM, which represents energy and cost savings, CO2 reduction, and payback period. It can help the building owners and energy managers determine appropriate ECMs and implementation schedule.

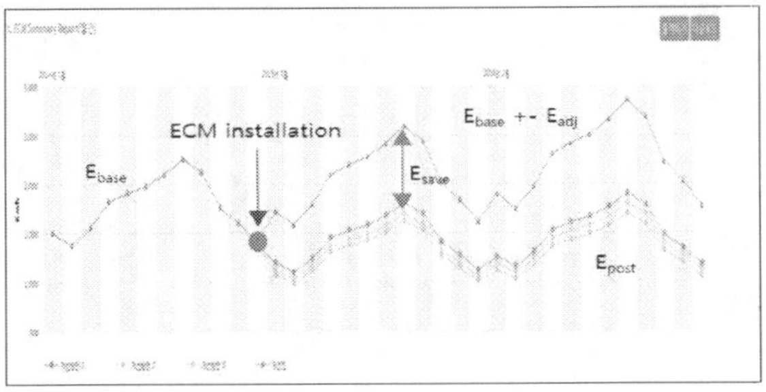

Figure 3. Energy saving impacts by implementing ECMs

TABLE II. ANNUAL ECONOMIC IMPACT ANALYSIS RESULTS

	items	before	N+1 년	N+2 년	N+3 년
baseline energy	energy use(MWh)	1,341	1,374	1,376	1,403
	energy cost($)	116,667	119,538	119,712	122,061
post-installation energy	energy use (MWh)	1,341	1,305	1,307	1,333
	savings(MWh)	-	69	69	70
	CO2reduction(kg)		29,256	29,256	29,680
	Saving ratio (%)	-	5.02	5.01	5.0
	energy cost($)	116,667	113,535	113,709	115,971
	cost savings($)	-	6,003	6,003	6,090
	implementation cost	-	18,969		
	payback period	-	3.16		

Energy cost =87$/MWh, CO2 Emission = 0.424 kg/kWh

Table III shows the monthly energy savings in the first year. Much of energy is used in winter and summer. From the table, we can estimate the effect of user habitat, weather, building use and occupancy and need to examine the efficiency of HVAC and thermal transmittance of the outer wall and roof. Fig. 4 shows the monthly energy consumption categories in the first year after implementation. From the figure, we can see which categories consume how much energy and which categories should be improved.

The economic impacts can be examined through M&V activities that are to verify operation of the installed equipment and systems.

TABLE III. MONTHLY ECONOMIC IMPACT ANALYSIS RESULTS

Month	Baseline (kWh)	Post-installation (kWh)	Energy Saving (kWh)
Jan	136,566	129,564	7,002
Feb	130,523	125,205	5,318
Mar	109,173	106,391	2,782
Apr	105,384	103,453	1,931
May	103,514	101,435	2,079
Jun	110,404	106,810	3,594
Jul	112,839	109,398	3,441
Aug	129,309	124,639	4,670
Sep	107,012	105,602	1,410
Oct	88,700	88,573	127
Nov	98,939	98,493	446
Dec	109,283	105,328	3,955
Total	1,341,646	1,304,891	36,755

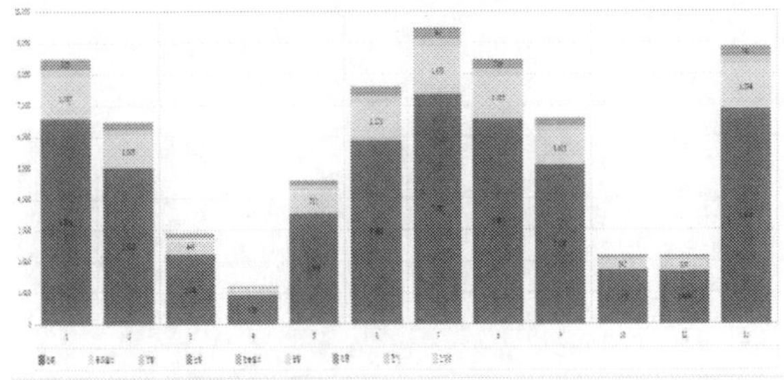

Figure 4. Energy consumption categories per month in the first year after implementation

IV. Conclusions

In this paper, a method and process to analyze economic impacts of ECM have been presented, which can help build owners, energy managers and facility managers plan ECM strategy. ECMs can save building energy so that building owners can reduce building energy cost and mitigate greenhouse gas emission. For building owners, the economic impact analysis is one of the most important issues since they spend around 30% of their budget on energy. However, it is difficult for a non-expert to select proper ECMs for one's buildings and to estimate economic benefits of ECMs. By proper ECMs much of building energy can be reduced, which leads to not only great cost saving but also enormous greenhouse gas reduction.

To analyze economic impacts, this paper set up an economic analysis tool and carried out simulations on energy and cost savings, CO2 emission reduction and payback period. The analysis results can be used for planning and evaluating ECM implementation. The energy saving is determined by comparing baseline energy and post installation energy. In ECM planning phase, it needs to estimate post installment energy by using an appropriate algorithm to calculate energy saving of each ECM. After implementation, baseline energy is adjusted to compensate for the condition changes including weather, occupancy and activities and the impacts of ECM can be examined through M&V activities.

Further studies are needed to establish a reliable database for ECMs and verify the economic impact analysis results of various buildings.

Acknowledgment

This work was supported by the Korea Institute of Energy Technology Evaluation and Planning(KETEP) and the Ministry of Trade, Industry & Energy(MOTIE) of the Republic of Korea (No. 20152010103180)

References

[1] S. H. Lee, T. Hong, and M. A. Piette, "Review of existing energy retrofit tools," LBNL, July 2014. [Online]. Avialable from: http://eetd.lbl.gov/publications/ 2016.06.13.

[2] B. R. Champion and S. A. Gabriel, "An improved strategic decision-making model for energy conservation measures," Energy Strategy Reviews 6 (2015), pp. 92-108, 2015.

[3] S. H. Lee, T. Hong, G. Sawaya, Y. Chen, and M. A. Piette, "A Database of Energy Efficiency Performance to Accelerate Energy Retrofitting of Commercial Buildings," LBNL, May 2015. [Online]. avialable from: http://eetd.lbl.gov/publications/ 2016.06.13.

[4] Y.-k. Juan, P. Gao, and J. Wang. " A hybrid decision support system for sustainable office building renovation and energy performance improvement," Energy and Buildings, pp. 290–297, 2010

[5] L. Pérez-Lombard , J. Ortiz, and C. Pout, "A review on buildings energy consumption information," Energy and Buildings, Vol. 40, Issue 3, pp.394–398, 2008

[6] Technavio, "Global Building Energy Software Market," 2015.

[7] ISO 13790 (2008), "Energy performance of buildings – Calculation of energy use for space heating and cooling," 2008.

[8] US DoE, "Energy Efficiency Program Impact Evaluation Guide," 2012. [Online]. avialable from: https://www4.eere.energy.gov/ 2016.06.13.

[9] US DoE, "M&V Guidelines: MeasurementAnd Verification for Performance-Based Contracts Version4.0, "Federal Energy Management Program.(2015). [Online]. Available from: www1.eere.energy.gov/femp/, 2016.06.13.

Leveraging Low-Power Hardware to Model-Aided Support of Production Automation Systems (Case Study Pilot for Underground Mine Ventilation)

Alexey Cheptsov

High Performance Computing Center Stuttgart,

University of Stuttgart

Stuttgart, Germany

e-mail: cheptsov@hlrs.de

***Abstract*—Modeling and Simulation are well-established techniques used in science and technology for prediction, analysis, and evaluation of properties of various complex dynamic systems. The actual trend in the simulation technology is the integration of models into the production automation and control systems, which aims to ensure a higher level of control and a better quality of the decisions made. The model-aided support is of a substantial importance for security-critical systems, such as underground mine ventilation networks, in which the risk of a spontaneous explosion of hazardous gases (like methane) is very high and might cause an enormous damage to human and technical resources. We discuss a possible approach to perform simulation closely to the controlled objects by leveraging low-power, embedded hardware.**

Keywords-Modeling; Simulation; Embedded Hardware;Automated Control Systems; PHANTOM.

I. INTRODUCTION

The high complexity of dynamic processes and their analysis methods require high-performance hardware. In case of big systems, such as the targeted ventilation networks, the use of supercomputers is necessary. However, there are cases in which the simulation should be performed close to the controlled object (an element of the ventilation system). For example, this is required when an emergency situation has happened and the air distribution is being manually controlled by an underground rescue team, e.g. according to a special emergency response plan. In that case, the availability of a simulation platform that would be capable of predicting the development of the air- and gas-dynamic situation based on the current conditions will be of a great advantage and will contribute to the quickest solving of the encountered problem. The goal of this research is to elaborate new concepts for the development of a portable simulation platform to be used in a productional technological environment. The platform should provide support to automated control systems for the case of unexpected events that cannot be handled by the native control systems due to their limited functionality, see Fig. 1. The modelling environment should be designed in a service-oriented way in order to ensure interoperation with the high-performance computing infrastructures whenever a better quality of results is needed.

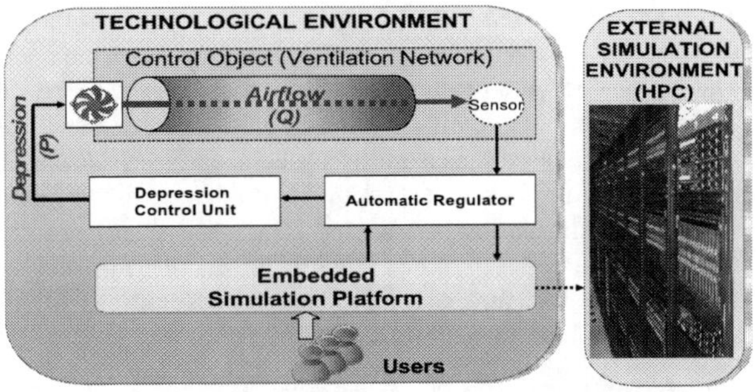

Figure 1. Reconfigurable application example

II. ENVISIONED APPROACH

The use of conventional hardware (Fig. 2a) in conditions of security-critical technological objects is often impossible due to factors like excessive dustiness, humidity, vibration, etc. The energy-efficiency requirements put another strict limitation on the hardware that is allowed to be used. The embedded hardware (Fig. 2b), on the contrary to conventional one, might meet those requirements of the use in the technological environment much better. However, the performance of the embedded systems is lower than of the conventional ones, which requires a trade-off between the required quality and performance of the simulation algorithms on one hand and the capabilities of the hardware platform on the other hand.

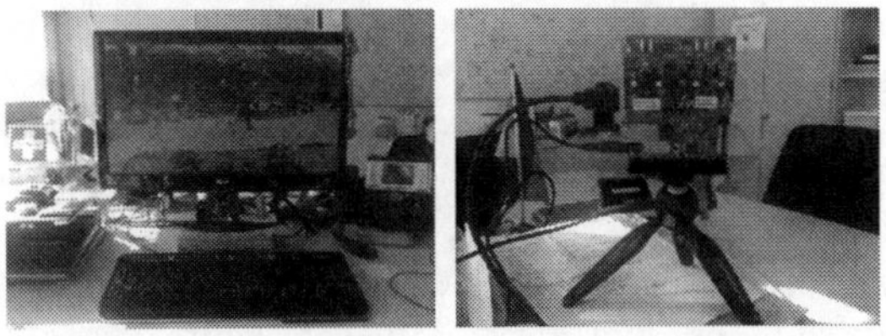

a) b)

Figure 2. Hardware platforms for simulation: a) commodity, b) specialized (Movidius' Myriad-2 [5].

The well-established simulation software packages like OpenFOAM [3] are prevalently designed for the conventional (x86 and x64) hardware. The broad spectrum of the embedded hardware platforms (from high-bandwidth microprocessors to SoCs) that is capable of use in industrial conditions as well as their adherence to the RISC (Reduced Instruction Set Computing) CPU architectures prevents the portability of the simulation software to the "light-weighted" hardware.

Cloud computing – the IT organization strategy that was widely established in 2000's – pushed the modeling and simulation community to reconsider their software development approaches towards their brighter service-orientation. The technological foundation for the development of simulation software in a decentralised way has been established, which allows the software components to become interoperable on heterogeneous hardware platforms. Service-oriented development in the form of "microservices" (small interoperable components that implement a specific part of the modeling algorithm, see an example in Fig. 3) seems extremely promising for the next-generation simulation platforms. This, however, requires new approaches to the organization of middleware frameworks for the development and execution of the service-oriented modeling software.

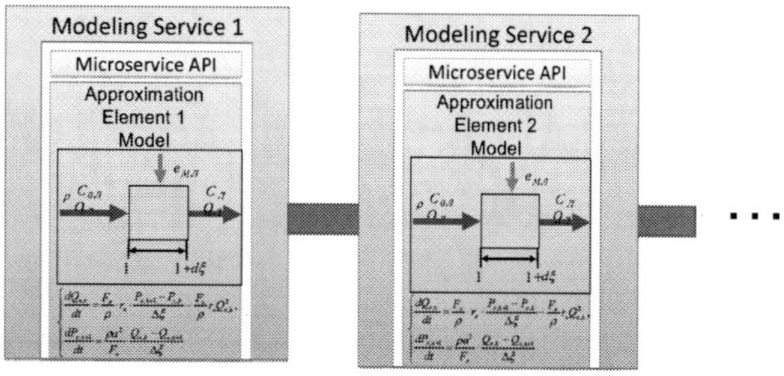

Figure 3. Example of a microservice-oriented simulation framework

III. MAIN ACTIONS FOR FUTURE WORK

The microservice-based approach allows a transition of the already known component-based simulation techniques (e.g. as proposed by Matlab and Simulink [4]) into a modern technological platform, leveraging the advances of the service-oriented Cloud technologies. The challenge of the low-power hardware support is to be tackled by the software compilation and execution technologies developed within PHANTOM [3] – an EU-funded project started in December 2015.

Our goal is to elaborate a **methodology for the development of portable, efficient, and scalable component-based simulation software based on a microservice architecture**. The methodology will be implemented in a software platform for model-aided support of the security-critical technological processes.

We are going to reimplement the available modeling algorithms with the framework we are proposing and evaluate the effects of porting to low-power embedded hardware in terms of performance and power consumption.

REFERENCES

[1] Basics of the underground mine ventilation. Available at: https://en.wikipedia.org/wiki/Underground_mine_ventilation [Retrieved: May,2016]

[2] OpenFOAM simulation package website. Available at: http://www.openfoam.com/ [Retrieved: May,2016]

[3] PHANTOM project website. Available at: http://www.phantom-project.org [Retrieved: May,2016]

[4] Introduction to MATLAB Functional Blocks. Available at: http://de.mathworks.com/help/simulink/ug/what-is-a-matlab-function-block.html?s_tid=gn_loc_drop [Retrieved: May,2016]

[5] Movidius description. Available at: http://www.movidius.com/solutions/vision-processing-unit [Retrieved: May,2016]

How is Big Data Transforming Operations Models in the Automotive Industry: A Preliminary Investigation

Gary Graham
Leeds University Business School
Leeds, United Kingdom
e-mail: g.graham@leeds.ac.uk

Bethany Tew
Leeds University Business School
Leeds, United Kingdom
e-mail: bn15bjt@leeds.ac.uk

Royston Meriton
Leeds University Business School
Leeds, United Kingdom
e-mail: r.meriton@leeds.ac.uk

Patrick Hennelly
Institute for Manufacturing, University of Cambridge,
Cambridge, United Kingdom
e-mail: pah70@cam.ac.uk

***Abstract* - Over the years, traditional car makers have evolved into efficient systems integrators dominating the industry through their size and power. However, with the rise of big data technology the operational landscape is rapidly changing with the emergence of the "connected" car. The automotive incumbents will have to harness the opportunities of big data, if they are to remain competitive and deal with the threats posed by the rise of new connected entrants (i.e. Tesla). These new entrants unlike the incumbents have configured their operational capabilities to fully exploit big data and service delivery rather than production efficiency. They are creating experience, infotainment and customized dimensions of strategic advantage. Therefore the purpose of this paper is to explore how "Big Data" will inform the shape and configuration of future operations models and connected car services in the automotive sector. It uses a secondary case study research design. The cases are used to explore the characteristics of the resources and processes used in three big data operations models based on a connected car framework.**

Keywords - big data; automotive industry; business model; operations model; connective capability

I. INTRODUCTION

As today's consumers are surrounded by connected devices, such as smartphones and tablets, the idea of connected cars is gaining in popularity. It is estimated that by 2025, all new passenger vehicles will be connected [2][4]. Yet, the connected car represents a major disruption to the automotive industry's traditional value creation model. A connected car can be defined as: "*a car that is equipped with Internet access, and usually also with a wireless local area network. This allows the car to share internet access with other devices both inside as well as outside the vehicle*"[1]. These services are made possible by a firm's capacity to capture and leverage high volumes of structurally diverse and high-speed data ("*big data*") generated by the sensors and embedded electronics of connected devices.

Two main service segments can be clearly distinguished in the growing connected car market: i. integrated product-services (to enhance the driver experience) and; ii. mobility services (to offer alternative modes of transportation from traditional private car ownership). Furthermore, moving into the service economy opens new streams of revenue for traditional manufacturers [6] and big data will enable superior value creation based on closer customer intimacy. However it also opens up the automotive industry to competitors from outside their traditional industry channel who are more proficient than incumbents at leveraging big data. In an industry unchanged in decades, these new entrants are finding ways to innovate and meet diverse customer needs for more information and mobility services, configuring their business and operating models around big data.

This work will help to identify from an operations perspective how big data is re-shaping the provision of products and services in the automotive industry, as it evolves towards further connectivity and autonomous driving. Whilst different models continue to co-exist, it is important for incumbents to understand how emerging operations models are configured compared to traditional models so that they can be proactive rather than reactive to the big data-driven disruption of the automotive industry. Big data is commonly hailed as the next frontier for productivity, innovation and competition [3]. As a complex and multi-faceted concept, it impacts on many things in different ways. Therefore, to narrow the scope of the study, big data is considered in terms of how it impacts on the way in which resources and processes are managed within an operation. This is justified because the way in which resources and processes in an operation are managed has a strategic impact on the organization [3]. It is therefore valuable to look at the configuration of emerging operations models to explore the impact of big data.

As operations models are dynamic and fast-changing, the overall objective is to identify the characteristics of the emerging big data-enabled operations models in the automotive industry. To our knowledge, this topic has not yet been theoretically studied from an operations perspective and there is a need for work to fill this research gap. A conceptual framework of emerging big data-connected operations for the automotive industry is developed, based on the literature, and the underpinning concepts are examined through theory-guided case study analysis.

II. THEORETICAL FRAMEWORK

While moving to a consumer-centric service approach based on big data has economic benefits, there are operations challenges. The main challenge for incumbents is a shift in the nature of value. Operations models must be able to process information and customers more than raw materials. The basis for all connected car services is information. With customer value based on intangible services, each stage of the transformation process is different; resource inputs and process outputs have perishable value if not captured and consumed in time. The transformation process is shaped by new constraints, including a company's capacity to capture, analyze and leverage real-time big data in the operations model [7]. The characteristics of the operation's resources, processes and capabilities are described in Figure 1. The dotted line illustrates the scope of analysis in the case studies. In contrast to traditional operations models that predominantly process materials, emerging operations models in the automotive industry process information (big data) and customers. It is therefore proposed that big data and customers are the dominant transformed resources, while the dominant transforming resources comprise big data analytics (to extract insights from the real-time data captured) and vehicles (to physically transport the customers).

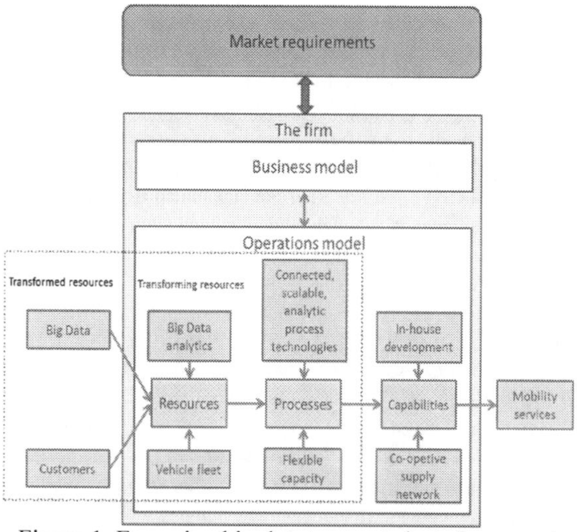

Figure 1: Emerging big data-connected car framework

III. RESEARCH METHOD

A multiple case study design was chosen to strengthen conclusions drawn from the cases and to increase external validity [8]. Three secondary cases were purposefully chosen according to the logic of theoretical sampling. That is, cases were selected based on the likelihood that they would critically challenge the predicted theoretical findings. This helps to confirm or advance the theoretical model. All the case studies were chosen according to their varying degrees of reliance on big data. As such, big data is the primary input into the operations model. That is, all services in the cases delivered to customers rely on real-time information extracted from big data. The first two cases Uber and Drive Now provide ride-hailing and car sharing services; the third case Tesla offers over-the-air software updates for its customers and customized services from: product design, through to purchase, product performance monitoring and after sales support. As their products diverge from the traditional offerings of the automotive industry, their operations models constitute "emerging" operations models.

IV. FINDINGS

Uber and DriveNow are examples of pure mobility services. Tesla is an example of a company using big data to deliver services related to its manufactured product, namely the owned electric vehicle. Despite these differences, several trends emerged across the three case studies. The operations outputs vary across the case studies. However, when compared to traditional operations models delivering a focused product, these emerging operations models have been designed to deliver a multi-variant consumer experience. For example, the operations outputs for Uber and DriveNow are to meet an immediate and real-time demand for flexible transport in urban environments.

In the case of Tesla, the service operations output is multi-faceted because Tesla provides a service offering based on a product, namely the vehicle that is sold to a customer. Tesla's service uses big data to understand, maintain and also improve vehicle functionality in line with customer expectations. It maintains vehicle functionality by collecting diagnostic data on individual vehicles, and improves vehicle functionality by aggregating driving data to understand driving conditions and vehicle performance, optimal locations are for charging stations. In terms of outputs that are software-based, such as those mentioned in the case studies, they are not constrained by time and space in the same way as tangible outputs. Updates to the service can easily be applied without physical presence or a mutually agreed time. One particularly noticeable trend across all case studies is therefore that of producing minimum viable products. This means that instead of delivering perfected products and services to customers, the company determines what is the minimum viable level for the service to work, produces that and then tweaks and perfects it based on how it is used and perceived by customers. It illustrates the importance of on-going relationships with customers, rather than ending the interaction at the point of sale.

The concept of allowing customers to use unfinished products is novel in the automotive industry. With feedback loops and real-time monitoring enabled by big data, the customer becomes part of the operations improvement process. It enables companies eventually to deliver exactly what the customers want. Tesla is a key example of this. Its major software updates (new, improved features) are released on a yearly basis, while minor updates (bug fixes) are released on average every month.

The hardware suite required for semi-autonomous driving (named "Autopilot") has been fitted into Tesla's vehicles since 2014. It includes forward-facing camera and radar, 12 long-range 360-degree ultrasonic sensors, GPS and electric braking system. Whenever vehicles are in manual mode, Tesla crowd-sources the fleet's driving data. Using so-called "fleet learning technology", Tesla uses these datasets to train its driving algorithms which ultimately are what drives the car when in Autopilot. The first version of Autopilot was released by OTA software update in 2015, and is still in beta mode today. This means that it is the driver's responsibility to remain alert at all times. While Autopilot is engaged, signals are sent back to the Tesla HQ server whenever a driver intervenes (i.e., by adjusting the steering wheel or braking) or resumes control. Based on these aggregated driving datasets, Tesla identifies where problem areas are and is able to investigate and improve the software. As the fleet learns, improvements can be noticed in days.

Uber is another example of a company producing minimum viable products. Its underlying system architecture was developed by many teams in any way possible as it rapidly expanded in the first five years. The result was a mixture of architectures and as it developed and customers made known their preferences, new system architecture was developed to support new service features. DriveNow was established as a separate entity from its parents company BMW to benefit from the agility of a start-up. It encourages customer feedback and adapts its operations model to suit.

Across all case studies, customers are the predominant transformed resource. This is in contrast to traditional operations models which focus on transforming materials into a product. Moreover, all services delivered to customers in these emerging operations models rely on real-time information extracted from big data. Although there are differences between the models as to what information is collected and analyzed, GPS positioning is captured in all models. Not only does this help riders and drivers locate each other / a suitable vehicle, but the GPS data generated from usage also helps companies to understand customers' popular routes and improve service provision.

While in traditional operations models, big data is used to enhance visibility over existing processes, in emerging operations models big data is one of the primary inputs enabling the provision of the service. Because of this the service operations of the case studies rely more heavily on intangible inputs, namely information. The value of such information is specific to time and space and if it is not captured, it is lost.

In every case, the operations model is configured to provide a flexible and convenient service. Inherent in the provision of services is fluctuating demand [5]. With big data, the companies in the case studies are able to monitor supply and demand in real-time and even to identify challenges ahead of time. They configure their capacity to accommodate a certain level of demand fluctuation, but importantly they also directly manage capacity by influencing the levels of supply and/or demand. The intangibility of services means that they cannot be easily stored [5] and therefore customers are less likely to be willing to wait for services than they are for a finished product.

For Uber, flexible capacity is achieved by not employing its drivers or owning a fleet of vehicles. Demand and supply are managed by surge pricing. For DriveNow, service capacity is constrained by the size and functionality of the fleet; if customers do not find a car available in a suitably close location, the service is of no value. Flexible service provision is therefore enabled by deploying a large fleet and a small team of service agents who check tyre pressures, clean the cars and move them to more popular locations if necessary.

Supply and demand are managed through incentives for customers to park in optimal locations and fixed pricing. For Tesla's service delivery, flexible capacity is configured by designing the vehicle from the ground up to ensure that features can be updated safely via software updates over time. However, Tesla also has to manage the constraints of producing hard products vehicles and is constrained in the usual way for the manufacturing side of its product-service.

Tesla vehicles contain over 3,000 purchased parts sourced globally from over 350 suppliers. Tesla's supply chain is a "unique hybrid of the traditional automotive and high tech industries" which means its pace is faster than traditional automotive supply chains. If suppliers cannot keep pace, software development and manufacturing is brought in-house.

While other automakers plan their production layout to keep it the same for several years to minimize costs, Tesla's production engineers move machines around frequently as a learning exercise. The company uses Tableau visualization software to monitor its production lines minute-by-minute. In terms of its supercharger network capacity, Tesla decides where to locate capacity by collecting and analyzing driving data from its fleet. It takes into account route patterns and local driving conditions. Each supercharger station is itself connected to the Tesla network, both for monitoring and maintenance purposes, but also to let customers know availability via Tesla's vehicle Navigation system.

By design, all the case studies have a reliance on connectivity. Without connectivity in the process technologies, the big data cannot be created and captured. Tesla has the most advanced configuration for connectivity as its vehicles have been designed from the ground up for connectivity. This enables OTA software updates for all functional features of the car. The hard asset requirements of the vehicle and the production efficiencies mastered by incumbents mean that few new entrants could offer a viable competitive threat to incumbent automakers in the traditional arena.

However, in the new market, new entrants are using big data to innovate entirely new operations models to deliver new products and services based on a closer understanding of customer's on-going needs. They are defining the strategic agenda for capturing, analyzing and leveraging big data in their operations models. Free from the organizational structures and investor commitments of the traditional players, the new players are better able to address fluctuating demand in the service area.

V. CONCLUSION AND FUTURE RESEARCH

Our paper explored how big data could enable the development of new operations models in the automotive sector and also suggested how these models could be evaluated across thematic categories of resources, processes and capabilities. Further it aimed at setting out a new research agenda that fuses and crosses the boundaries of operations management and big data technology. As the prominence of big data continues to develop and stakeholder groups become increasingly knowledgeable and engaged, there is considerable incentive for operations managers across industry sectors to consider the opportunities and challenges facing their processes and people, as well as the tools and frameworks they deploy for strategic and operational decision making.

The opportunities are not only in improving efficiency and effectiveness of their existing operations, but also in transforming their operations models, and in some cases, developing radically different new ones. They must become more customer-centric and service driven in this big data age. The automotive industry has evolved from Ford, to the TPS and post-Fordism, but now in the second decade of the twenty first century it is information and service not production driving the operations model. This is information driven automotive sector characterized by low inventory, customization, dissolvable supply chains, leasing, joint automotive/ICT ventures, Silicon Valley driven product R and D, the delivery of shared services and pooled capacity.

For organizations developing new operations models, the challenge is to build on and leverage the new digitized infrastructures emerging with smart and intelligent cities, in order to connect physical goods, services, and people (offline), with real-time data driven processes (online), in seamless O2O (online-to-online) operations. This requires a re-design of long run operational competencies and capabilities in order to respond to the rapidly changing city environments.

Despite the importance of operations management to big data implementation for both practitioners and researchers, we have yet to see a systematic framework for analyzing and cataloguing emerging operations models. As such, our conceptual framework makes an initial contribution to operations management theory in the big data context. This research only used three 'theory-guided' cases studies to illustrate the big data transformation of operations models. Therefore much more in-depth analysis and more detailed models are clearly needed to assist in the implementation of big data initiatives and facilitate new innovations in operation management. Some of the changes that operations and their connected supply chains face are revolutionary, and this requires careful consideration from both a practical and theoretical point of view.

REFERENCES

[1] Bayerische Motoren Werke AG, 2016. Press release. https://www.press.bmwgroup.com/global/article/detail/T0258269EN/bmw-group-driving-the-transformation-of-individual-mobility-with-its-strategy-number-one-next.

[2] Gissler, A. 2015. Connected vehicle: succeeding with a disruptive technology. Accenture strategy. [Accessed 11 August, 2016]. Available from: https://www.accenture.com/us-en/insight-connected-vehicle

[3] Manyika J., Chui, M., Brown, B., Bughin, J., Dobbs, R., Rosburg, C. and Hung Byers, A. 2011. Big data: The next frontier for innovation, competition, and productivity. McKinsey & Company: McKinsey Global Institute.

[4] Mayer-Schönberger, V., and K. Cukier. 2013. Big Data. A revolution that will transform how we live, work and think. London: John Murray Publishing.

[5] Sasser, W. 1976. Match supply and demand in service industries. Harvard Business Review. [Online]. [Accessed 7 July, 2016]. Available from: https://hbr.org/1976/11/match-supply-and-demand-in-service-industries

[6] Slack, N. 2005. Operations strategy: Will it ever realize its potential? GESTÃO & PRODUÇÃO. 12(3), pp.323-332.

[7] Slack, N. and M. Lewis. 2011. Operations Strategy. 3rd ed. London: FT Prentice Hall.

[8] Yin, R. 2014. Case study research: design and methods. Fifth edition. Thousand Oaks: Sage.

Big Data Analytics and Firm Productivity

Liang Guo, Mingtao Fu
NEOMA Business School
Mont Saint Aignan, France
e-mail: Liang.guo@neoma-bs.fr;
fu.mingtao.14@neoma-bs.com

Ruodan Lu
Cambridge University, UK
e-mail: Rl508@cam.ac.uk

***Abstract*—Increasing productivity is a key task for contemporary firms. Although big data analytics has been generally viewed as an effective advanced information processing tool that enables firms to better cope with business operation, thus holding the potential to boost firm productivity, evidence to support this view is lacking in the literature. Equipped with the theory of organizational information processing and resource-based view, we hypothesize that big data analytics systems (BDAS) can help improve productivity and this contribution is influenced by the firm's BDAS capability. These hypotheses are supported with a sample of 45 Chinese retailers over 2012-2014 using Data Envelopment Analysis and Malmquist Productivity Index. This study extends our understanding of the business value of IT by shedding light on the productivity benefit of big data investment. We also underline that for firms that have already implemented BDAS, a greater effort seems necessary to build predictive and prescriptive analytics capability.**

Keywords-big data analytics; retailing; China.

I. Introduction

Today's fast-moving, complex world of increasingly connected people and connected things that are creating vast new digital footprints require enterprises to constantly make sense of this big and fast-moving data and to gain real-time access to powerful insights and deliver them at the point of action [1]. Big data, defined as a holistic analytical approach to manage, process and analyse 5Vs (i.e., volume, variety, velocity, veracity and value, see [2]), is regarded as a powerful weapon to obtain actionable insights for sustained value delivery, to create business disruptions, and to establish competitive advantages [3].

However, such presumption confronts with scare empirical evidence. Recently, skepticism has emerged about the true business value of big data analytics. Given that the implementation of big data requires huge physical and human capital investment, the stake of embracing big data for a company is quite high. Big data may lead to big disappointment. Prior studies find that IT implementation is inherently risky and post-implementation may also be fail.

Although related strand of studies has focused on the nexus of IT investment and firm performance in general, there is not virtually any research that has quantified the performance impact of big data analytics system (BDAS). By performance, we refer to a firm's productivity, also called operation efficiency (i.e. using less input to achieve the same output or using the same input to achieve more output), one of the most important performance measures. [4] find that there is a significant contribution of IT to total factor productivity for the US economy in 2000-2004. However, there are relatively few studies addressing IT' s impact on productivity at firm level [5] and among the existing works, most of them focus on the association between productivity and either firm's IT investment Little attention has been paid to whether the use of specific IT system (say, BDAS) is associated with a firm's productivity.

Therefore, identify the true impact of BDAS on firm productivity, if any, would thus provide strong implications for both academic research and practice. In this study, we intend to fill in the void by examining whether BDAS boosts a retail firm's productivity. Grounded in the theory of organizational information processing [6] and resource-based view [7], we sought to theorize the business impact of BDAS. Productivity is commonly measured with Data Envelopment Analysis (DEA), a non-parametric approach to the empirical estimation of production function and with Malmquist Productivity Index (MPI), a special method of time series analysis in DEA [8]. Using a sample of 45 Chinese publically listed retailers, we intend to empirically answer two research questions: 1) what is the impact of BDAS on firm productivity? And 2) how does the impact of BDAS on firm productivity, if any, vary with the capability of BDAS? Our findings support the claim of BDAS's business value and its contribution increases with the firm's capability of BDAS.

In Section 2 we will review relevant literature and propose two hypotheses. We will test the hypotheses in Section 3 and discuss our findings in Section 4.

II. Literature Review and Hypotheses

From the late 2000s, the term business analytics has gained prominence over the previously dominant business intelligence principles, by stressing more on the analytical capabilities it offers. In this sense, business analytics refers to the process of transforming data into actions through analysis and gaining insights in the context of organizational decision making and problem solving. Big data analytics resorts to the use of data warehouse, information technology, statistical analysis, and computational intelligence models to help managers gain improved insights about their business operations and make better, fact-based decisions. The contextual application of analytical methods to analyse data sets that are very large in size and complex in terms of their sources and of the level of unstructuredness has led to the growth of big data analytics. It aids to better data analytics that can decipher and understand patterns from the business situations based on the data collected from diverse sources with the aim to predict future outcomes purely based on analytical frameworks. The unique features of big data analytics include the use of advanced data collection, data visualization technologies, feature extraction, and artificial intelligence technologies, which largely increment the speed of mining and analysis of previously ignored unstructured data that reside in disparate sources and different formats.

Big data analytics differs from traditional data processing architectures in terms of the speed of decision making, processing complexity, type and volume of data being analysed. The data sources are unstructured in form and rely on newer forms of business analytics like web analytics, click stream analytics and visual analytics that use advanced modelling methods. In general, we argue that big data analytics assist in decision making in the following ways: descriptive, predictive, and prescriptive analytics.

Descriptive analytics is the most common form of business analytics employed by firms to understand the historical business performance and derive useful wisdom as past performance summary. The analytics can be visualized using charts and figures. Its aim is to condense vast chunks of data and decipher useful information from the same. In this sense, it serves as a valuable information reduction technique. Descriptive analytics can be used to drill-down reports to decipher the association between, for instance, an advertising campaign and the product performance through patterns or trends on the basis of historical data. Descriptive analytics, however, cannot be used to test causality.

Predictive analytics analyses past historical performance to forecast future situations by identifying patterns of knowledge based on a variety of statistical tools. For instance, the use of past historical data of a particular advertising campaign to extrapolate the expected response of a new product launch campaign or predict the demand of a seasonal product based on the past years' data. The efficiency of predictive analytics lies in its ability of revealing causality that cannot be undertaken from descriptive analysis. The use of big data comes handy in adding diversity to data sources to reveal more detailed and to elaborate patterns and in modelling complex data originating from different, in-compatible data sources like text, speech, video, and photos.

Prescriptive analytics is a relatively new stream of business analytics that extends beyond descriptive and predictive analytics, by prescribing multiple solutions for future situations and the likely impact of each solution. This form of analytics is also based on a collection of business rules, algorithms, relying on statistical machine learning and simulation-optimization modelling procedures. The difference between predictive and prescriptive analytics lies in the outcome of each option that is offered by the latter method. This is incorporated as a feedback loop to track the impact of each forecasted solution in different what-if scenarios. And finally, based on probabilistic modelling, the most optimal solution is recommended. Some of the leading applications of prescriptive analytics include optimization models in field of operations, marketing, and finance to identify the best alternatives to minimize or maximize some objective. For instance, its applications in operations management include multiple scenario generation balancing the production planning based on different demand estimates to maximize revenue or natural disaster based recovery options.

The contribution of IT to business performance has been studies from two theoretical perspectives [9]. On the one hand, the theory of organizational information processing [6] suggests that IT systems enable improved information processing and managerial decision making so that a firm can better handle uncertainty, thus achieve better performance. On the other hand, IT is regarded as a kind of key resources for achieving business success and a power tool to help firms gain competitive advantage by altering the competitive forces that collectively determine industry profitability. This study is motivated by these two prior theoretical considerations to examine whether and how BDA influences firm's performance in general and productivity in particular. Answering this question fills a gap in the literature on the possible big business value of BDA.

Prior studies have indicated high level of business risk derived from dynamism and complexity decreases firm productivity. To boost a firm's productivity, managers should lower their business uncertainties by frequently processing a greater deal of information and by making better decisions. TOIP attributes part of firm's risk to the accuracy of information and manager's capability in information processing about uncertainty in the business environment. TOIP proponents argue that IT provides a technological basis for collecting and sharing information from different sources, for integrating business processes and for coordinates decisions makings and actions within and across organizational boundaries. This information processing effect is especially true, when a firm faces high environmental uncertainty and often needs to deal with a large amount of complex information [9]. Prior studies found empirical evidences that support TOIP, indicating improvements in information quality and visibility for decision makers reduce business risk and improve business performance.

We draw upon TOIP to theorize BDA's productivity benefits. Through the automation, optimization and transparentization effects, BDA equips managers with applications that are able to amass and apply information in ways in which upends customer expectations and optimized business operations to unprecedented degrees. In essence, BDA mitigates risks and boosts operational efficiency:

H1: An increase in firm productivity is associated with the implementation of BDA.

In line with TOIP, we suggest that the practice of a broad scope of BDA (i.e. more BDA applications) enhances a firm's information analytics quality and leads to more efficient operations. The practice of a broad scope of BDA allows firms to take the questions that traditional analytics is answering to the next level, moving from a retrospective set of answers to a set of answers focused on predicting performance and prescribing specific actions or recommendations. It is reasonable to believe, as TOIP suggests, a firm's operations will be more efficient thanks to the improvement of information processing capability and quality.

What is more, the analytics expertise and experience accumulated from practicing multiple types of BDA applications form a bundle of strategically important resources ranging from IT hardware assets, BDA human resources, and intangible social-technical resources. RBV theorists assert that firm's key and unique resources are of four properties--- value, rarity, inimitability and non-substitutability (VRIN) so that a firm's performance depends on management's capability to search for the best usage of these resources. IT-related resources have long be regarded as VRIN, which are firm specific and cannot easily be traded or transferred. Following the IT-RBV perspectives, we argue that a board scope of BDA helps firms to form valuable resources. Like most IT skills, expertise with different analytics applications can only be built through learning by doing practices and by creating the synergies between human and IT-assets. These synergistic intangible resources are value-creating, allowing an organization to capitalize strategic opportunities or diverge from potential threats. BDA professionals who master multiple types of BDA usually possess rare qualities that are much in demand, difficult and expensive to hire and given the very competitive market for their services, difficult to retain. This BDA human capital is rare resources for a firm, as there are not a lot of people with their combination of scientific background and computational and analytical skills.

Likewise, analytics skill shortage makes BDA human capital difficult to be easily imitated by competitors. More importantly, combining big data hardware and skill sets to create an enterprise-specific BDA infrastructure can be inimitable, because creating such synergy requires carefully melding IT and organizational resources to fit firm needs and business priorities. Finally, BDA expertise can be viewed as a social-technical synergy of tacit and explicit operations policies and practices within a firm. It is the result of the long-term, enterprise-wide integration of various BDA applications, business processes, human capital and continuous learning and innovation. BDA expertise is then difficult to substitute, because it is scarce, specialized, and appropriable. And given that data are woven into every sector and function in modern economy, much of advanced business decision making simply could not take place without BDA. There is then virtually no substitutable technology that can bring large pools of data, analyze to discern patterns, and optimize decisions.

Therefore, we argue that combining with organizational expertise gain from the practice of a broad scope of BDA is a source of competitive advantages, enhancing productivity and creating significant value by making better quality of decisions and optimized operations.

H2: An increase in firm productivity is associated with the practice of a broad scope of BDA.

III. Empirical Study

A. Sample

We tested these two hypotheses with a sample set of China's publically listed retail firms. The reasons that we chose the retail industry are because this is an industry with a long history of investing and implementing data-intensive IT systems (e.g. POS, ERP, CRM and consumer panel studies) and retailers usually demand a clear justification for the return on IT investment. We chose China's retail sector because of its enormous market size. The total sales of consumer goods in China in 2014 reached USD 4,099.906 billion, representing a growth of 12% [10]. Our final sample included 45 firms. We collected their financial data from their IPO prospectus and annual reports over 2012-2014.

B. Analyses and Results

Productivity is measured by DEA and MPI [8]. we took number of employee (hereafter A), management & administration expenses (B), marketing expenses (C), cost of sales (D), and inventory (E) as inputs and net revenues (hereafter 1), gross profits (2), net income (3) and market capitalization (4) as outputs. The productivity index was calculated with the averages of these inputs and outputs over 2012-2014. We decomposed the MPI into two components—technology change (i.e. technology frontier shift) and technology efficiency change (i.e. a measured of the diffusion of the best-practice technology in the sector). Then, we first calculated MPI, technology change and technical efficiency change with the Model ABCDE123 (i.e. number of employee, management & administration expenses, marketing expenses, cost of sales, and inventory as inputs and net revenues, gross profits, and net income as outputs) for the period 2012-2013 and 2013-2014 respectively. Then, we took the geometric mean of these two periods as the measures.

We measured whether a firm has implemented BDAS based on the answers of our interviews. BDAS Capability is measured with the Big Data and Analytics Maturity Model [11]. We developed a scoreboard of BDAS capability, which contains 16 dichotomous items (1 for have implemented a particular BDAS application in question, 0 for otherwise). The sum of these 16 items was used as the measure of a firm's BDAS capability.

(a) Descriptive Analytics Applications:

1. Big data analytics infrastructure platform such as Hadoop, No SQL Database and/or Massively Parallel Processing Databases

2. Data visualization applications or any business intelligence platforms for integrating and visualizing data from multiple sources, taking the raw data and presenting it in complex, multi-dimensional visual formats (e.g. reports and dashboards) to illuminate the information

(b) Predictive Analytics Applications:

3. Basic unsupervised machine learning clustering applications, such as k-means and A Priori association analysis

4. Basic supervised machine learning classification applications, such as, k-Nearest Neighbours and decision trees

5. Regression-based supervised machine learning applications, such as, linear regression, logistic regression, generalized linear models and the exponential family
6. Bayes statistics and kernel-based supervised machine learning applications, such as naïve Bayes, graphical models, support vector machines and Gaussian process
7. Latent variable-based machine learning applications, such as mixture models, the EM algorithm, principal component analysis, singular value decomposition
8. Advanced unsupervised machine learning applications, such as ANN, auto-encoder and deep learning
9. Reinforcement machine learning applications, such as Markov decision and MCMC
10. Time series and forecasting applications
11. Natural language processing applications
12. Computer vision applications

(c) Prescriptive Analytics Applications:

13. Linear optimization and sensitivity analysis applications
14. Network analysis applications
15. Nonlinear optimization applications
16. Simulation-based decision making applications

25 out of 45 retailers have scored 100 in full Model ABCDE1234. Among these 25, there are 14 retails that have implemented BDAS. Retailers that have implemented BDAS clearly achieved better productivity than their counterparts that have not in most DEA models, supporting H1.

We then followed [8] to conduct PCA on these 30 DEA models in order to theorize the impact of BDAS on productivity in a parsimonious way and to reveal the similarities and differences that exist between firms in terms of the 30 DEA models in a two-dimensional plot. The first principal component accounts for 44.37% of the total variance while the second for 34.62% (i.e. in total 78.99%). Most models are loaded on Component 1, which can be associated with an overall measure of efficiency. We labelled the second component as "Management & Administration, Inventory and Marketing Efficiency"(see Table 1).

We then calculated the weighted average of two components for each retailer by multiplying the factor loading of each DEA model on its productivity score. We plotted each firm on a two-dimension figure with the first component as the X-axis and the second component as the Y-axis (See Fig. 1). It seems that most BDAS retailers achieved high overall efficiency and scattered along the X-axis while those non-BDAS retailers achieved relatively high efficiency on management and administrative expense, marketing expense and inventory management and scattered along the Y-axis. We conducted an ANOVA analysis by comparing two components between two groups. The results suggest that the overall productivity (i.e. Component 1) of the BDAS retailers outperforms that of those without BDAS (F-score=9.228, p<0.01). However, there is no significant difference on Component 2 (F-score=0.118, p=0.67). Finally, we aggregated the scores of 30 DEA models into one factor and the result of the ANOVA analysis of this aggregated factor indicates that retailers with BDAS are at an advantage in achieving higher efficiency score (F-score=9.823, p<0.01).

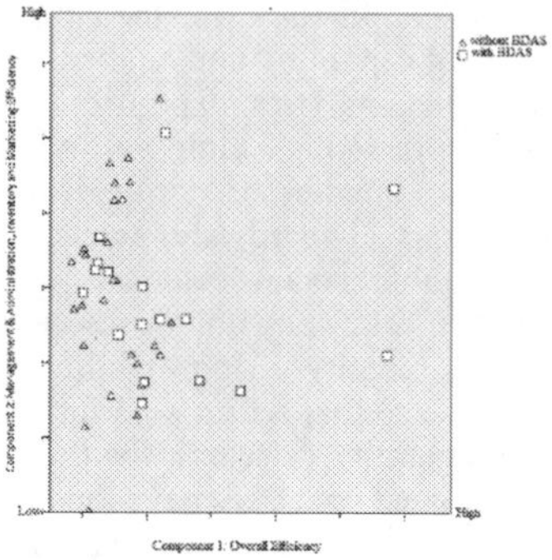

Figure 1: Visualization of DEA Results on Two Principal Components

The MPI analysis shows that 23 out of 40 retailers have experienced productivity progress during 2012-2014. Among these 23, 11 are retails that have implemented BDAS. Company 29, who has implemented BDAS, has registered the highest improvement in MPI (1.442). It can be seen that the progress of MPI for this company was contributed by a significant increase in technology change (1.345) and in technical efficiency change (1.072). Company 39, who also has equipped BDAS, has experienced the largest increase on technology change (1.17). But its decrease in technical efficiency change (0.894) implies that this retailer has failed to conduct proper investment in organizational factors in accordance with its operation. The results of ANOVA analyses showed that on average, retailers with BDAS achieved better MPI (F-score=5.427,p<0.05) and technology change (F-score=4.780, p<0.05) than those without BDAS. But there is no significant difference in technical efficiency change. However, technical efficiency change is a measure of the deviations from the best practice frontier with the sample and it is not directly related to BDAS. So we can safely conclude that H1 is also supported by the MPI analyses.

Finally, we then tested H2 by calculating the Spearman correlation coefficients between BDAS capability score with the aggregated DEA efficiency score and the MPI. Both are statically significant (0.689, p<0.01 for DEA and 0.359, p<0.05 for MPI). The relationships between these three measures were visualized by plotting a bubble chat (Figure 2), in which the aggregated DEA is the X-axis, the MPI is the Y-axis and BDAS capability as bubble size. In Table 2, it is clear that retailers with high BDAS capability score concentrate around the upper-right corner, which means they achieve both high DEA and MPI scores. H2 is supported.

IV. DISCUSSION AND CONCLUSION

In this study, we theorize how BDAS can help improve firm productivity through the automation and optimization effects. For the first time in the literature, our study empirically examines whether the implementation of BDAS has a significant impact on firm' s productivity and whether this contribution is influenced by the firm's BDAS capability. Our findings provide solid evidence that permits an accurate appraisal of the impact of BDAS on firm productivity.

There is a general consensus that the spectacular popularity of BDAS in the past few years has opened up new opportunities for firms to re-engineering business processes and to improve their operation efficiencies. Under this context, the analysis of BDAS's effects on firm productivity has been the subject of great attention. Our study complement to the long strand of research that has examined IT's business value in general by revealing the productivity improvement benefits derived from BDAS. Our findings are in line with TOIP and RBV theory, implying that the big data analytics capability of an IT system helps firms develop key and unique resources and then better coordinate and resolve environmental uncertainty.

Our findings are robust as our measure of productivity is calculated with 30 different combinations of multiple/single inputs and outputs DEA models. In addition, our analyses using the MPI approach provides in-depth information on whether BDAS triggers a firm's technology change, which provides managerial implications on what kind of weakness in terms of productivity they should watch out for and remedy. As technology progress is one of the most important factors for future retailing, implementing effectively new technologies like BDAS can help give business an edge in the market place.

Our study made another contribution by developing a measure of BDAS capability. Our findings suggest that only when the implementation of predictive as well as prescriptive big data analytics completed, the benefits from adopting big data start to surface. Descriptive analytics or business intelligence solutions have traditionally required a static, low-dimensional data model for operational reporting. These solutions often are incapable to use streaming data that can provide operational intelligence. However, the emergence of multi-channel selling and fulfilment has increased the need for dynamic, high-dimensional data analytics to process streaming and massive datasets. Predictive and prescriptive analytics businesses can gain new operational insights by taking advantage of the unique capabilities of BDAS and by using the right model to process large volumes of unstructured as well as structured data.

Our study provides strong managerial implications. One of highly productive firm in our sample has successfully deciphered the code of "Big Data Value". With its website and mobile app clickstream data, this retailer can predict the sales of its cash cow products, as well as determine the price range and features that most customers want. Based on the patterns of clicks, it can also determine the popularity of a new product. Another sample firm massively collects social login data (e.g. size of friends on social networks, frequency of posting, number of likes received) of its on-line shoppers and combines with shopping history data. The retailer is able to successfully optimize its retargeting advertising on its website and mobile app while real-time pricing their products according to the utility value that the purchase may generate based on the preferences of the consumers.

Finally, our study has some limitations. Firstly, it does not account for the effect of market power imperative, as the competitive strategy perspective suggests. Future research should extend our study by taking retail industry structure into account. Secondly, although we used market capitalization as an output, our study does not consider a firm's short-term stock market performance. One way to extend our research is to study what is the stock market reaction to a firm's BDAS investment announcement. Third, our measure of BDAS capability is mainly based on self-reported data. We were unable to investigate the quality of each firm's actual usage of the system. In-depth case study or longitudinal field research should be carried out to shed more light on how firms employ BDAS in a greater detail. Last but not least, our research is mainly took a technology-centric view on BDAS. It would be necessary in future works to examine how organization should change to accommodate automated and advanced analytics technology in order to improve firm's performance.

REFERENCE

[1] Capgemini, "Big & Fast Data: The Rise of Insight-Driven Business," Capgemini, Paris: Capgemini, 2015.

[2] S. F. Wamba, S. Akter, A. Edwards, G. Chopin, and D. Gnanzou, "How 'big data'can make big impact: Findings from a systematic review and a longitudinal case study," Int. J. Prod. Econ., vol. 165, pp. 234–246, 2015.

[3] Forbs, "Data Analytics Dominates Enterprises' Spending Plans For 2015," Retrieved: 2016.09.

[4] D. W. Jorgenson, M. S. Ho, and K. J. Stiroh, "A retrospective look at the US productivity growth resurgence," J. Econ. Perspect., vol. 22, no. 1, pp. 3–24, 2008.

[5] C. Q. Romero and D. R. Rodríguez, "E-commerce and efficiency at the firm level," Int. J. Prod. Econ., vol. 126, no. 2, pp. 299–305, 2010.

[6] J. R. Galbraith, "Organization design: An information processing view," Interfaces, vol. 4, no. 3, pp. 28–36, 1974.

[7] J. Barney, "Firm resources and sustained competitive advantage," J. Manage., vol. 17, no. 1, pp. 99–120, 1991.

[8] C. Serrano-Cinca, Y. Fuertes-Callén, and Cecilio Mar-Molinero, "Measuring DEA efficiency in Internet companies," Decis. Support Syst., vol. 38, no. 4, pp. 557–573, 2005.

[9] F. Tian and S. X. Xu, "How Do Enterprise Resource Planning Systems Affect Firm Risk? Post-Implementation Impact," Mis Q., vol. 39, no. 1, pp. 39–60, 2015.

[10] Deloitte, "China Power of Retailing 2015," Retrieved: 2016.09.

[11] Oracle, "An Architect's Guide to Big Data," Retrieved: 2016.09.

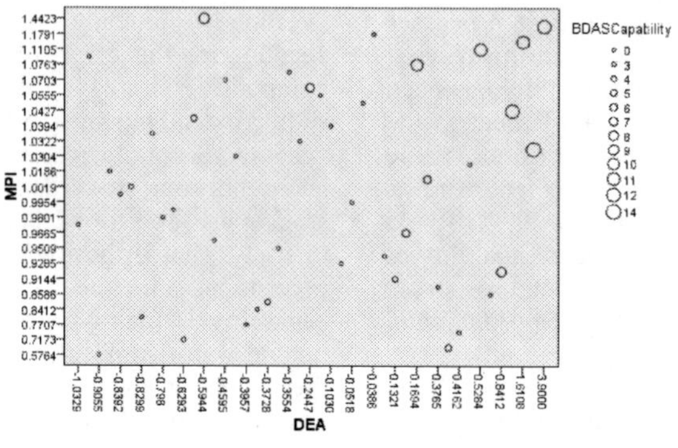

Figure 2: The Visualization of the Correlation between DEA, MPI and BDAS Capability

TABLE I: FACTOR LOADING OF 30 DEA MODELS ON TWO PRINCIPAL COMPONENTS

Model	*Component 1*	*Component 2*
ABCDE1234	0.394	
ABCDE1	0.383	
ABCDE2	0.644	
ABCDE3	0.814	
ABCDE4	0.787	
A1234	0.769	
A1	0.336	
A2	0.805	
A3	0.914	
A4	0.821	
B1234		0.679
B1		0.689
B2		0.769
B3	0.644	
B4	0.752	
C1234	0.58	
C1		-0.696
C2	0.836	
C3	0.874	
C4	0.733	
D1234	0.871	
D1	0.868	
D2	0.868	
D3	0.894	
D4	0.763	
E1234	0.52	
E1		0.454
E2		0.609
E3	0.741	
E4	0.685	

TABLE II: MPI OF 45 FIRMS

Firm ID	*BDAS(1=with)*	*MALMQUIST INDEX*	*TECHNICAL CHANGE*	*EFFICIENCY CHANGE*
1	0	0.824	1.006	0.819
2	1	0.914	1.012	0.903
3	0	0.841	0.993	0.848
4	0	0.859	0.979	0.877
5	1	1.068	0.964	1.108
6	1	1.031	1.031	1
7	1	1.076	1.022	1.053
8	1	0.717	0.932	0.77
9	1	0.843	0.855	0.986
10	0	0.98	0.983	0.598
11	0	0.866	0.977	0.887
12	0	1.056	0.986	1.071
13	0	1.019	0.987	1.032
14	1	1.041	0.95	1.096
15	0	0.98	0.98	1
16	1	1.002	1.002	1
17	0	0.771	0.771	1
18	0	1.039	0.986	1.054
19	0	1.085	1.02	1.063
20	0	0.576	0.576	1
21	0	1.039	1.021	1.017
22	0	0.998	0.942	1.059
23	0	0.928	0.928	1
24	0	1.03	0.975	1.057
25	0	0.995	1.019	0.977
26	0	1.07	1.002	1.068
27	0	1.071	1.043	1.027
28	0	1.032	1.017	1.015
29	1	1.442	1.072	1.345
30	1	0.698	0.879	0.794
31	1	0.967	0.932	1.037
32	0	1.179	1.081	1.09
33	0	1.028	0.971	1.059
34	0	0.718	1.007	0.713
35	1	1.004	1.028	0.976
36	0	0.951	1.074	0.886
37	1	1.148	1.016	1.13
38	1	1.11	1.028	1.08
39	1	1.043	1.167	0.894
40	1	0.919	1.076	0.855
41	1	1.194	0.904	1.321
42	0	0.987	1.013	0.975
43	0	0.95	1.018	0.933
44	0	1.049	1.059	0.99
45	0	0.961	0.961	1

Reconfiguring Composite Signature Labels over Optical MPLS Network Codecs to Secure Data Packets Routing

Jen-Fa Huang*, Kai-Sheng Chen, and Ting-Ju Su

Advanced Optoelectronic Technology Center, Institute of Computer and Communications Engineering, Department of Electrical Engineering, National Cheng Kung University, Taiwan.
Tel.: +886-6-2757575 ext. 62370; *Fax*: +886-6-234-5482;
E-mail: huajf@ee.ncku.edu.tw, q38024016@mail.ncku.edu.tw, Q36034497@mail.ncku.edu.tw

***Abstract*—This paper proposes a network security scheme in which optical network coders/decoders (codecs) reconfigure signature label codes to enhance system confidentiality for optical multi-protocol label switching (OMPLS) transmissions. In the proposed codec labels reconfiguration, we structure composite signatures from maximal-length sequence (M-sequence) codes to identify both data packet labels and network node codecs. Each core node can dynamically change its signature label to combat eavesdroppers for a reliable data packets routing. The results verify that the proposed approach via signature labels reconfiguration is effective against eavesdropping.**

Keywords-Composite signature key, Maximal-length sequence (M-sequence) codes, Network confidentiality.

I. Introduction

Optical Multi-Protocol Label Switching (OMPLS) is a swiftly emerging technology that plays a significant role in next generation networks by delivering quality of service (QoS) and traffic engineering features. Interest in OMPLS has been steadily growing in recent decades. One of the most promising advances in packet-switching systems in recent years has been the development of MPLS, where the separation of routing and forwarding procedures enables high-speed optical packet transmission [1]. Great processing delays can be shortened at each node due to the avoidance of label de-composition in the network layer. In other words, OMPLS simplifies the forwarding function of routers. Without abandoning the basics of IP network, OMPLS is considered an extension protocol because it provides a more flexible and efficient packet switching.

Within the OMPLS network, signature labels assignment and decomposition on data packets can follow from Optical Code-Division Multiple-Access (OCDMA) techniques. Orthogonal coding labels can stack on data packets and correlate with the corresponding label codes at each successive routing node. However, weaknesses, including susceptibility to eavesdropping, have recently been reported in OCDMA [2][3] and hence in OMPLS systems. As respectively noted by Prucnal [4] and Shake [5], OCDMA techniques suffer from inherent security disadvantages in the signature decoding. In each routing node, an eavesdropper can use a simple energy detector to detect whether energy is present or not. In such cases, there is no routing security at all because the energy detector output contains the user's data stream. In addition, an OMPLS encoder uses the same fixed code repeatedly over a large number of bits. Consequently, an eavesdropper equipped with a sophisticated detector on the data node may be able to tap into the network and recover specific code, if he/she can obtain a sufficient signal-to-noise ratio (SNR). Thus, to ensure network routing confidentiality when designing physical transport layer, enhanced security mechanisms must incorporate appropriate signature codecs to enhance secure packets routing over OMPLS networks.

Data network confidentiality can be enhanced by methods based on optical signal processing. The three main approaches are: increasing code-space size [5], reducing subscriber transceiver power, and frequently changing signature code [6]. By employing the third approach, it is difficult for eavesdroppers to keep up with the speed when the code is changed. Thus, the code cannot be descrambled by simply detecting the channel waveform. In addition, multiple-access interference (MAI) limits the number of users simultaneously accessing the system. The most significant advantage of composite M-sequences is its cyclic property. Other characteristics include achieving enhanced communication with data security mechanisms, increasing system capacity by adding additional users to the same channel and eliminating MAI.

In this paper, we adapt a dynamically reconfigurable mechanism over the spectral-amplitude coding scheme of OMPLS to counter eavesdropping. We compose relatively prime-length M-sequence codes into sets of complex codes that govern reconfigurable network codecs by changing signature codes. Furthermore, we structure codec pairs based on arrayed-waveguide gratings (AWGs), along with the corresponding reconfiguration switches, to implement complex signature coding in the proposed network. By exploiting linear cyclic, periodic, and virtually orthogonal characteristics of M-sequence codes, we exemplify signature reconfiguration over AWG-based network codecs in this work.

The remainder of this paper is organized as follows. Section II briefly outlines the dynamic reconfiguration scheme consisting of the proposed composite signatures. Section III describes how the reconfigurable scheme operates to prevent eavesdroppers from solving the user's code, resulting in improved security. Section IV explains the perspectives on eavesdropper before and after reconfigurations. Finally, Section V summarizes and presents our conclusions.

II. STRUCTURING COMPOSITE SIGNATURE CODECS FOR OPTICAL-MPLS NETWORK

Label stacking is used in MPLS systems by attaching one or more labels to a single packet to support hierarchical addressing, reducing the number of labels detected at each node. The core nodes only need to check an optical label matching to their label set to determine whether the packet should be forwarded or not. They do not need to remove the previous labels and swap a new one. It avoids the function of optical swapping at the expense of having a large number of stacked labels.

In the proposed MPLS network, the labels are encoded by spectral-amplitude-coding (SAC) because it has consentience with label stacking, fast recognition, and low system cost. Due to its inherent nature, all SAC labels occupy the same optical band, regardless of the wavelength used for the optical payload in our system. The payload is coded by a laser whose spectrum is outside the band of labels. Thus, label and payload can be combined as an optical packet and be transmitted simultaneously. Figure 1 shows such a scheme of an optical packet with label stacking.

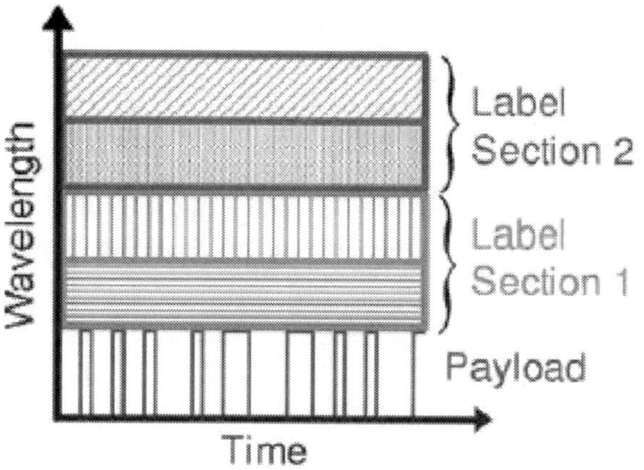

Fig. 1. Optical packet with stacked SAC labels.

As shown in Figure 2, the MPLS network is composed of many different types of nodes. According to the role of the label switching router (LSR) in the MPLS network, they can be divided into three different kinds: Ingress node, Core node, and Egress node. Figure 2 shows the optical packet switching in the MPLS network. There are six nodes in total, (*A*, *B*, *C*, *D*) are the core nodes and (*E*, *F*) are edge nodes. The label switching path (LSP) of this packet is assumed to be *E* (Ingress)-*A*-*D*-*F* (Egress). Later, we will verify the situation of the composite label code packet that we propose.

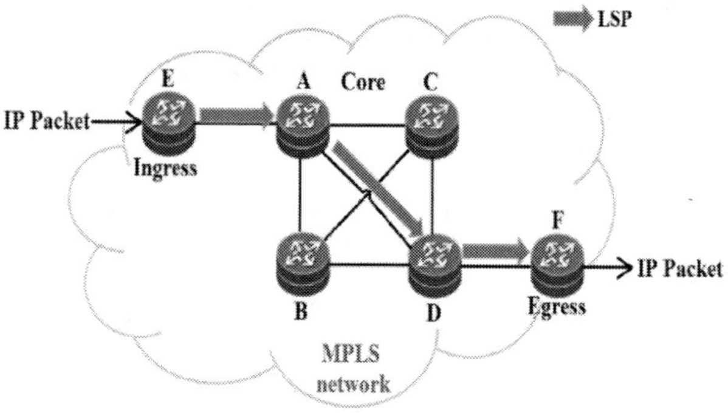

Fig. 2. The diagram of label switching in MPLS network.

In the proposed network, the reconfiguration has two mechanisms. The first one is, each core node changes its label at a fixed frequency by cyclic shifting signature code. This scheme is based on the assumption that the upper layers of the network effectively detect the threat of eavesdropping. The other way is, the reconfiguration command changes the signature code to a new one at the transceiver. If a tapper attacks the network frequently, the changing time becomes short, making the optical switch operate faster to reconfigure the code so that the tapping process is blocked. On the other hand, if the network is mostly in a secure environment, the frequency of signature code changing is lowered. The detailed design of the specifications for the central controller is very complex and beyond the scope of this paper. In this paper, we use the first mechanism.

III. SUMMED SPECTRL LABELS ON RECONFIGURATIONS

At the ingress node, composite SAC-labels are implemented by two AWGs, two multiplexers, one BLS, and several optical switches, as shown in Figure 3. By using the cyclic properties of AWG routers and M-sequence codes, the codecs pair can encode/decode multiple labels simultaneously. Thus, all labels share the same hardware for the coding process. A modulo-2 operation combines M-sequences from two AWGs into a composite code. Optical switches are used for selecting composite codes for label stacking, in accordance with the number of pass nodes determined by label switching path (LSP). The optical modulator is used to modulate the payload bits onto the optical coded carrier. The Mach-Zehnder modulator (MZM) modulates the payload bits onto the coded optical carrier. Then, the SAC labels are combined with the payload bits to form a packet.

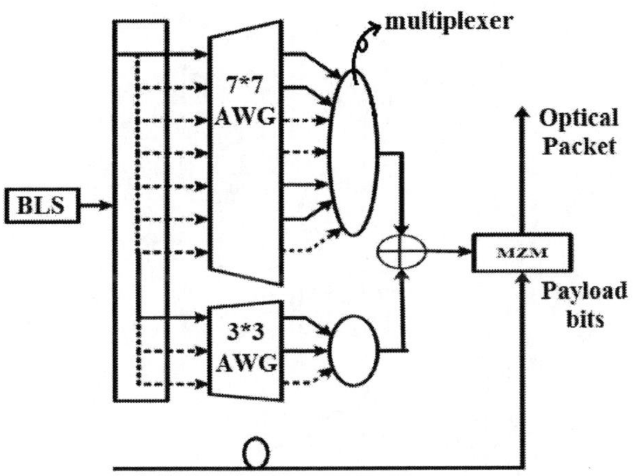

Fig. 3. The mechanism of labels encoding.

In the discussed composite label signatures reconfiguration, the core node will change the label dynamically. Let us consider an example optical-MPLS network with three nodes to illustrate composite signature codes reconfiguration. The three nodes are node #A, #D, and #F. We represent the operation of the network codecs prior to and subsequest to code reconfiguration using numerical coding data. Reconfiguration switches will switch on corresponding M-sequence codes to compose a set of composite signature codes. The setup for packets with SAC labels is illustrated in Figure 4. In our illustration, we select a 3×3 AWG and a 7×7 AWG for nodes to compose their label codes.

By combining each of the upper codes (T^0C_1, T^1C_1 and T^2C_1) in Table I (a) with the 1st lower code $T^0\boldsymbol{C}_2$ in Table I (b), we can get a subset label codes $T^iC_1 \oplus T^0\boldsymbol{C}_2$, i=0, 1, 2. Similarly, we can combine each of the upper codes with the 2nd lower code $T^1\boldsymbol{C}_2$ to get another subset label codes $T^iC_1 \oplus T^1\boldsymbol{C}_2$, i=0, 1, 2. In this way, we can combine each of the upper M-sequence codes T^iC_1 in Table I (a), i=0, 1, 2, with either of the lower M-sequence codes $T^j\boldsymbol{C}_2$ in Table I (b), j=0, 1, …, 6, to get the subset composite label codes $T^iC_1 \oplus T^j\boldsymbol{C}_2$ in Table I (c). We can have 7 yards groups in total, and each group can provide 3 label codes for the network labels assignment.

From the point of view of eavesdroppers, if a M-sequence code $T^i\boldsymbol{C}_1$ of period length n_1=3 (Table I (a)) is adopted in the network, the eavesdropper will have a 1/3 probability of detecting the signature code correctly. On the other hand, if an M-sequence code $T^j\boldsymbol{C}_2$ of period length n_2=7 (Table I (b)) is utilized, the eavesdropper will have a 1/7 probability of correctly detecting the signature code. However, if a composite code $\boldsymbol{S}^{(i,j)} = T^i\boldsymbol{C}_1 \oplus T^j\boldsymbol{C}_2$ of period length n=21 is used (Table I(c)), the probability of interception by the eavesdropper can be lowered to 1/21. This makes the eavesdropping more difficult and causes the eavesdropper to spend more time trying to guess the correct code.

TABLE I. STRUCTURING COMPOSITE SIGNATURE $\boldsymbol{S}^{(i,j)}(X)$ FROM M-SEQUENCES $T^i\boldsymbol{C}_1(X)$ AND $T^j\boldsymbol{C}_2(X)$. (a). 7 BLOCKS OF $T^i\boldsymbol{C}_1(X)$ SEQUENCES; (b). 3 BLOCKS OF $T^j\boldsymbol{C}_2(X)$ SEQUENCES; (c). COMPOSITE SIGNATURES $\boldsymbol{S}^{(i,j)}(X) = T^i\boldsymbol{C}_1(X) \oplus T^j\boldsymbol{C}_2(X)$.

(a).

C_1	110	110	110	110	110	110	110
TC_1	011	011	011	011	011	011	011
T^2C_1	101	101	101	101	101	101	101

(b).

C_2	1110010	1110010	1110010
TC_2	0111001	0111001	0111001
T^2C_2	1011100	1011100	1011100
T^3C_2	0101110	0101110	0101110
T^4C_2	0010111	0010111	0010111
T^5C_2	1001011	1001011	1001011
T^6C_2	1100101	1100101	1100101

(c).

Node #A

$C_1 \oplus C_2$	001111101010011000100
$TC_1 \oplus C_2$	100010000111110101001
$T^2C_1 \oplus C_2$	010100110001000011111

Node #D

$C_1 \oplus T^3C_2$	100001111101010011000
$TC_1 \oplus T^3C_2$	001100010000111110101
$T^2C_1 \oplus T^3C_2$	111010100110001000011

Node#F

$C_1 \oplus T^5C_2$	010011000100001111101
$TC_1 \oplus T^5C_2$	111110101001100010000
$T^2C_1 \oplus T^5C_2$	001000011111010100110

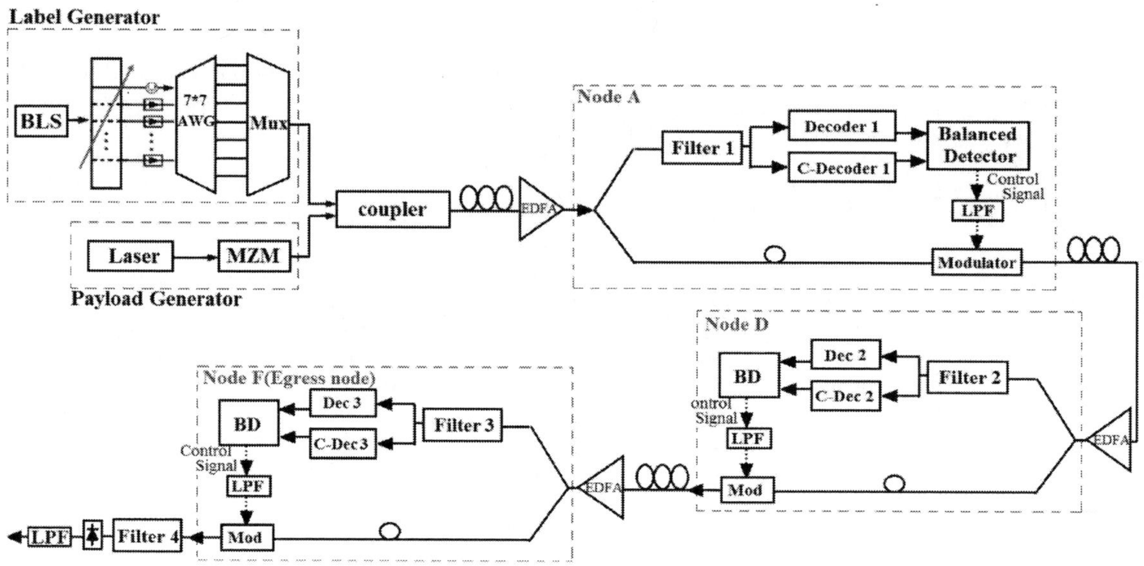

Fig. 4. Schematic optical-MPLS network with reconfigurable composite signature codecs.

Before signature reconfiguration, we suppose that the composite code for the node #A is combined from M-sequence codes $\boldsymbol{C}_1(\mathrm{X})$ = (110, …) and $\boldsymbol{C}_2(\mathrm{X})$ = (1110010, …):

$$\boldsymbol{S}_1^{(0,0)}(X) = T^0\boldsymbol{C}_1(X) \oplus T^0\boldsymbol{C}_2(X)$$
$$= (001\ 111\ 101\ 010\ 011\ 000\ 100).$$

As for the node #D, we suppose that the composite code is combined from M-sequence codes $T^1\boldsymbol{C}_1(\mathrm{X})$ = (011, …) and $T^3\boldsymbol{C}_2(\mathrm{X})$ = (0101110, …):

$$\boldsymbol{S}_2^{(1,3)}(X) = T^1\boldsymbol{C}_1(X) \oplus T^3\boldsymbol{C}_2(X)$$
$$= (001\ 100\ 010\ 000\ 111\ 110\ 101).$$

Further, we suppose the composite signature code for node #F is constructed from M-sequence codes $T^1\boldsymbol{C}_1(\mathrm{X})$ = (011, …) and $T^5\boldsymbol{C}_2(\mathrm{X})$ = (1001011, …):

$$\boldsymbol{S}_3^{(1,5)}(X) = T^1\boldsymbol{C}_1(X) \oplus T^5\boldsymbol{C}_2(X)$$
$$= (111\ 110\ 101\ 001\ 100\ 010\ 000).$$

The stacked label prior to signature reconfiguration thus takes the form $\boldsymbol{Y}_{(\mathrm{pri})}(X) = \boldsymbol{S}_1^{(0,0)}(X) + \boldsymbol{S}_2^{(1,3)}(X) + \boldsymbol{S}_3^{(1,5)}(X)$, the label coded signature chips will combine together to result in a label stack signal prior to signature reconfiguration:

$$\boldsymbol{Y}_{(\mathrm{pri})}(X) = \boldsymbol{S}_1^{(0,0)}(X) + \boldsymbol{S}_2^{(1,3)}(X) + \boldsymbol{S}_3^{(1,5)}(X)$$
$$= (001\ 111\ 101\ 010\ 011\ 000\ 100)$$
$$+ (001\ 100\ 010\ 000\ 111\ 110\ 101)$$
$$+ (111\ 110\ 101\ 001\ 100\ 010\ 000)$$
$$= (113\ 321\ 212\ 011\ 222\ 120\ 201).$$

Subsequest to signature reconfiguration, each core node changes its label by state shifting of the signature code. The resulted label codes allocated for each routing node are then stacked over the newly generated data packets. Other possible combinations of logic "ON" and logic "OFF" information on stacked label decoding can be similarly deduced.

IV. Perspectives On Eavesdropper Before And After Reconfigurations

The objective of secure OMPLS routing is to ensure that an unauthorized individual does not gain access to data in the network. We assume that an eavesdropper is technologically intelligent with knowledge about signals being transmitted in the network (i.e., the architecture of the network, types of signals, data rates, encoding rules, structure of codes, etc.). In other words, the eavesdropper is supposed to know everything about the network operations and signatures coding scheme except for the specific signature key in the network node.

Figure 5 depicts a general configuration of OMPLS label decoder at each routing node. A pair of AWGs with signature label $\boldsymbol{S}_u^{(i,j)}$ and complementary key $\underline{\boldsymbol{S}}_u^{(i,j)}$ is adopted here for the u-th receiver decoder. The stacked label $\boldsymbol{Y}$ from the optical fiber channel is directed to the (i+1)-th and the (j+1)-th input ports of the 3x3 and 7x7 AWG decoders. Then the label is decoded by executing balanced detection of correlation subtraction. Only when the label code of the incoming packet matches that of the core node, a "matched" indication signal is generated, and the modulator stays in an "ON" state. In contrast, when the packet label does not match that allocated in the passing node, no matched indication signal exists, and the modulator stays in an "OFF" state.

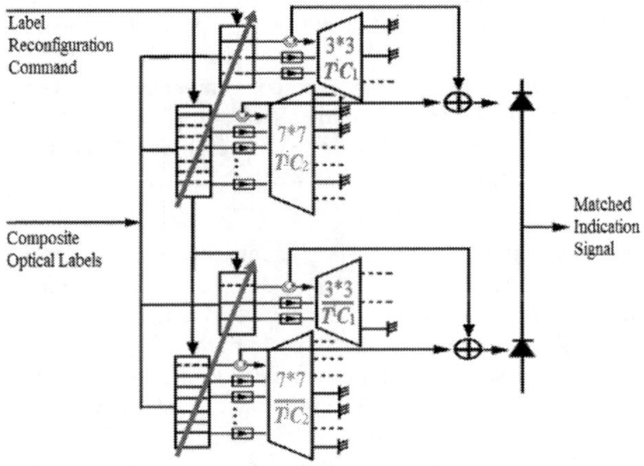

Fig. 5. Composite signature decoder with complementary subtraction scheme.

In the illustrative OMPLS data packets routing, an eavesdropper is supposed to tap on node #D. As we have mentioned, the eavesdropper may bear the same decoder structure as those in the tapped routing nodes, but with different signature label codes. Since an eavesdropper is assumed to tap on node #D, both node #D and eavesdropper will bear the same label code $\boldsymbol{S}_2^{(1,3)}$ = (001 100 010 000 111 110 101) just prior to signature reconfiguration. Correlation outputs on node #D and also on eavesdropper before signature reconfiguration will be

$$\boldsymbol{Y}_{(\mathrm{pri})} \times \boldsymbol{S}_2^{(1,3)} = (003\ 300\ 010\ 000\ 222\ 120\ 201)$$
$$\boldsymbol{Y}_{(\mathrm{pri})} \times \underline{\boldsymbol{S}}_2^{(1,3)} = (110\ 021\ 202\ 011\ 000\ 000\ 000).$$

The above correlation magnitudes on the upper and the lower photodiodes of balanced decoder will subtract to result in a net photo-energy of $|\boldsymbol{Y}_{(\mathrm{pri})}\boldsymbol{S}_2^{(1,3)}| - |\boldsymbol{Y}_{(\mathrm{pri})}\underline{\boldsymbol{S}}_2^{(1,3)}|$ = 19-11 = 8 units, indicating a label switching state of 'ON' and is able to route the packet data into eavesdropper.

The network will dynamically reconfigure signature labels allocated to each routing node, either by local node codecs or globally-controlled state machine. Let us examine the situation on labels decoding after signature reconfiguration. With reference to Table I(c), assume that node #A changes its signature label from $\boldsymbol{S}_1^{(0,0)}$ to $\boldsymbol{S}_1^{(1,0)}$, node #D changes from $\boldsymbol{S}_2^{(1,3)}$ to $\boldsymbol{S}_2^{(2,3)}$ and node #F changes from $\boldsymbol{S}_3^{(1,5)}$ to $\boldsymbol{S}_3^{(0,5)}$. We therefore have a stacked label signal after signature reconfiguration:

$$\boldsymbol{Y}_{(\mathrm{pst})}(X) = \boldsymbol{S}_1^{(1,0)}(X) + \boldsymbol{S}_2^{(2,3)}(X) + \boldsymbol{S}_3^{(0,5)}(X)$$
$$= (221\ 031\ 100\ 321\ 112\ 212\ 113).$$

This reconfigured and stacked label signal then cascade with payload data to route the resulted data packets to the corresponding nodes in the network.

Figure 6 depicts schematic diagram on data packets routing to node #D while an eavesdropper taps there to "steal" the information that is sent to the node. Since node #D can duly reconfigure its label code dynamically, node #D can correctly decode the information sent into node #D. However, the eavesdropper would not know the change of label code and would not decode information correctly while it still uses "old key" on the decoded summed signal spectra.

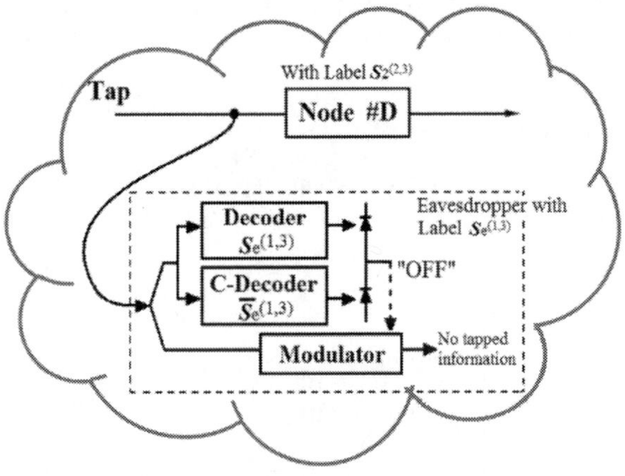

Fig. 6. Schematic of eavesdropper tapping on Node #D.

Specifically, for node #D with new label code $\boldsymbol{S}_2^{(2,3)}$ = (111 010 100 110 001 000 011) and the newly stacked label $\boldsymbol{Y}_{(\mathrm{pst})}$ = (221 031 100 321 112 212 113), correlation output energies obtained at the decoding side for node #D are

$$\boldsymbol{Y}_{(\mathrm{pst})} \times \boldsymbol{S}_2^{(2,3)} = (221\ 030\ 100\ 321\ 002\ 000\ 013),$$
$$\boldsymbol{Y}_{(\mathrm{pst})} \times \underline{\boldsymbol{S}}_2^{(2,3)} = (000\ 001\ 000\ 001\ 110\ 212\ 100).$$

The above correlation magnitudes will subtract at the balanced photo-detector in the node #D to result in a net photo-energy of $|\boldsymbol{Y}_{(\mathrm{pst})}\boldsymbol{S}_2^{(2,3)}| - |\boldsymbol{Y}_{(\mathrm{pst})}\underline{\boldsymbol{S}}_2^{(2,3)}|$ = 21-10 = 11 units, indicating a label switching state of 'ON' and is able to route the packet data into node #D.

Nevertheless, even after label signature reconfiguration, the eavesdropper remains with its prior label code $\boldsymbol{S}_e^{(1,3)} = \boldsymbol{S}_2^{(1,3)}$ = (001 100 010 000 111 110 101). Correlation with the received stacked label $\boldsymbol{Y}_{(\mathrm{pst})}$ at the photodiodes will result in detected output energy for the eavesdropper;

$$\boldsymbol{Y}_{(\mathrm{pst})} \times \boldsymbol{S}_e^{(1,3)} = (001\ 000\ 000\ 000\ 112\ 210\ 103),$$
$$\boldsymbol{Y}_{(\mathrm{pst})} \times \underline{\boldsymbol{S}}_e^{(1,3)} = (220\ 031\ 100\ 321\ 000\ 002\ 010).$$

Correlation subtraction at the balanced photo-detector in the eavesdropper will result in a net photo-energy of $|\boldsymbol{Y}_{(pst)}\boldsymbol{S}_e^{(1,3)}| - |\boldsymbol{Y}_{(pst)}\underline{\boldsymbol{S}}_e^{(1,3)}| = 12\text{-}18 = -6$ units, indicating a label switching state of 'OFF' and is unable to route the packet data to the eavesdropper.

Table II summarizes the numerical results on the decoded subtracted correlation for node #D and the eavesdropper, subsequent to signature reconfiguration. It is clear that, if the label code is not changed, the eavesdropper who detects the label code assigned for the corresponding transceiver user can easily detect the information for that user. That is the reason we employ a dynamic code reconfigurations scheme to change labels allocated to the nodes.

TABLE II. EAVEDROPPER'SPERSPECTIVES CONSEQUENT TO SIGNATURE RECONFIGURATION

	Correlation subtraction	Subtracted correlation energy
For Node #D	$\boldsymbol{Y}_{(pst)}\times\boldsymbol{S}_2^{(2,3)}$ = (221 030 100 321 002 000 013) $\boldsymbol{Y}_{(pst)}\times\underline{\boldsymbol{S}}_2^{(2,3)}$ = (000 001 000 001 110 212 100)	$\|\boldsymbol{Y}_{(pst)}\boldsymbol{S}_2^{(2,3)}\| - \|\boldsymbol{Y}_{(pst)}\underline{\boldsymbol{S}}_2^{(2,3)}\|$ = 21-10 = 11 ➔ Label 'ON'
For Eavesdropper tapped at #D	$\boldsymbol{Y}_{(pst)}\times\boldsymbol{S}_e^{(1,3)}$ = (001 000 000 000 112 210 103) $\boldsymbol{Y}_{(pst)}\times\underline{\boldsymbol{S}}_e^{(1,3)}$ = (220 031 100 321 000 002 010)	$\|\boldsymbol{Y}_{(pst)}\boldsymbol{S}_e^{(1,3)}\| - \|\boldsymbol{Y}_{(pst)}\underline{\boldsymbol{S}}_e^{(1,3)}\|$ = 12-18 = -6 ➔Label 'OFF'

The dynamic code reconfiguration mechanism significantly reduces the probability of correct information being obtained by attackers via interception, and hence significantly enhances system confidentiality. By changing the label code of the nodes, the eavesdroppers have less chance of intercepting the correct code. Simulation results show that the degree of network security is significantly improved when dynamic signatures reconfiguration are implemented over the composite M-sequence codes.

V. CONCLUSIONS

In this paper, we proposed a scheme based on reconfigurable signatures to combat eavesdropping in optical-MPLS networks. In the proposed scheme, each user is randomly assigned one set of prime-lengths M-sequence codes, and then these signature codes get dynamically reconfigured to enhance network confidentiality. Each core node changes its label at a fixed frequency by cyclic shifting one or two chips of signature code to change the code sets assigned for each node to enhance confidentiality.

When the number of signature codes increases, detection of the unique user code by an eavesdropper becomes more difficult; thus, network confidentiality is significantly increased. The most important feature is the signature codes reconfiguration mechanism that thwarts an eavesdropper's code detection attack. Further work is required in order to implement fast optical switching and to get lower SNR transmissions. Nevertheless, the proposed scheme can considerably improve simple composite coding techniques to provide superior security.

REFERENCES

[1] M.J. O'Mahony, D. Simeonidou, D.K. Hunter, and A. Tzanakaki, "The application of optical packet switching in future communication networks," *IEEE Commun. Mag.*, vol. 39, no. 3, pp. 128–135, Mar. 2001.

[2] B.B. Wu and E.E. Narimanov, "A method for secure communications over a public fiber-optical network," *Optics Express*, vol. 14, no. 9, pp. 3738-3751, May 2006.

[3] J.F. Huang, S.H. Meng, and Y.C. Lin, "Securing optical Code-Division Multiple-Access Networks with a Post-Switching Coding Scheme of Signature Reconfiguration," *Optical Engineering*, vol. 53(11), pp. 116101-1 ~ 116101-11, Nov. 2014.

[4] P.R. Prucnal, M.P. Fok, Y. Deng, and Z. Wang, "Physical layer security in fiber-optic networks using optical signal processing," in *Optical Transmission Systems, Switching, and Subsystems VII*, edited by Dominique Chiaroni, Proc. of SPIE-OSA-IEEE Asia Communications and Photonics, 2009.

[5] T.H. Shake, "Security performance of optical CDMA against eavesdropping," *J. Lightwave Technol.*, vol. 23, no. 2, pp. 655–670, Feb. 2005.

[6] M.L.F. Abbade, L.A. Fossaluzza Jr., C.A. Messani, G.M. Taniguti, E.A.M. Fagotto, and I.E. Fonseca, "All-Optical Cryptography through Spectral Amplitude and Delay Encoding," *Journal of Microwaves, Optoelectronics and Electromagnetic Applications*, vol.12, no.2, São Caetano do Sul, Dec. 2013.

Biploar Optical Labeling with Spectral Amplitude Coding Scheme for Packet Switching over GMPLS Network

Kai-Sheng Chen[1], Jen-Fa Huang[3]
Institute of Computer and Communication Engineering,
Department of Electrical Engineering
National Chen Kung University
Tainan, Taiwan
[1]Q38024016@mail.ncku.edu.tw
[3]huajf@ee.ncku.edu.tw

Chao-Ching Yang[2]
Department of Electro-Optical Engineering
Kun Shan University
Tainan, Taiwan
ccyang@mail.ksu.edu.tw

***Abstract*—Generalized multi-protocol label switching (GMPLS) is a promising technique to implement all-optical core networks. In this paper, we propose a new optical code labeling (OCL) based on optical code- division multiple access (OCDMA) techniques for packet switching. To improve the efficiency of label-recognition and network throughput, bipolar label coding is employed in the proposed scheme. Label switching capabilities in packet loss probability (PLP) is greatly enhanced since our proposal enlarges the Hamming distance of the star diagram of the decoded label signals. The proposed label mapping mechanism is achieved through spectral amplitude coding (SAC) in the physical layer. In performance analysis, we present a numerical simulation of PLP to quantify the switching efficiency. Results show the proposed bipolar coding technique reduces PLP in switching process, resulting in an extension of label switching path (LSP) in GMPLS core network.**

Keywords-generalized multi-protocol label switching (GMPLS); optical code labeling (OCL); spectral amplitude coding (SAC); optical code-division multiple access (OCDMA).

I. Introduction

From its combination with the existing Internet Protocol (IP) layer and the control paradigm over multiple routing domains, one can realize the maturity in Generalized Multi-Protocol Label Switching (GMPLS) in practical application and deployment [1]. After being standardized by Internet Engineering Task Force (IETF), great effort in investigating the inter-operable GMPLS network has been taken by numerous researchers. Much attention to GMPLS protocols comes from the integration across network layers [2]. This advantage is a fundamental principle of designing a reliable system and reduces the complexity in network control for operators.

Optical Code Labeling (OCL), mapping the packet address onto the label through optically encoding, is proposed as a labeling procedure in GMPLS networks [3]. This labeling scheme is modified from a multiplexing technique known as Optical Code-Division Multiple Access (OCDMA). Optical code is used as a label to switch different data flows to the desired path without Optical-to-Electrical (O/E) conversion [4]. Spectral Amplitude Coding (SAC) system has a cost-effective de/encoder due to the rapid development of filter components [5], such as Array Waveguide Grating (AWG) and Fiber Bragged Grating (FBG). Furthermore, the code chips are encoded on the spectrum slices, without compressing the time waveform. The electronic devices in the codec could operate at a low speed of bit-rate instead of high chip-rate. Meanwhile, coded signals from different users can be transmitted over the same wavelength band without the impact of Multiple Access Interference (MAI). From above reasons, we adapt the SAC codec for the label generating and processing units in GMPLS network.

In this paper, we modify the node structure in GMPLS so that it could fit for the proposed bipolar OCL. With the moderate complexity of node architecture, label space is enlarged while keeping the short processing time. Compared to On-Off Keying (OOK), the packet is switched in a more secure environment since label of each packet is represented by one of two distinct codes, according to the payload bit [6]. Another advantage of bipolar OCL is a higher measured Signal-to-Noise Ratio (SNR) at the decoder end, due to the larger Hamming distance between levels of bit "0" and "1". Therefore, the system performance has a huge advance in Packet Loss Probability (PLP), achieving a longer transmission distance in Label Switching Path (LSP).

This paper is divided into five main sections. Section I provides some background information about GMPLS network and the label generating and processing schemes for packet switching. Section II outline the design of the proposed bipolar OCL scheme in GMPLS network. Section III describes the architecture of Edge Node (EN) and Core Node (CN) with the function of bipolar OCL. Sections IV presents the system performance analysis and shows the improving results of PLP. Finally, section V draws the conclusion.

II. Bipolar OCL Scheme in GMPLS Networks

We present an edge-core-edge transmission in GMPLS network with the proposed labeling scheme. Hadamard codes are used as optical labels for the network, to achieve all optical switching by constructing the code switching layer among network nodes. Hadamard codes, obtained by selecting the rows of Hadamard matrix as code vectors, were originally used for Two-Code Keying (TCK) in SAC-OCDMA systems to enhance system performance [7]. In that scheme, user sends Hadamard code vector C_m for data bit "1" and its complement $\overline{C}_m$ for bit "0". The correlation properties of Hadamard codes are [7]:

$$C_m \odot C_n = \begin{cases} N/2, & m = n \\ N/4, & m \neq n \end{cases} \quad (1)$$

$$C_m \odot \overline{C}_n = \begin{cases} 0, & m = n \\ N/4, & m \neq n \end{cases} \quad (2)$$

where the symbol $\odot$ is the dot-product operator and N is the code length. Based on the following two properties, Hadamard codes can be adapted for TCK without the MAI by performing the correlation subtractions:

$$C_m \odot C_n - C_m \odot \overline{C}_n = \begin{cases} N/2, & m = n \\ 0, & m \neq n \end{cases} \quad (3)$$

$$\overline{C}_m \odot C_n - \overline{C}_m \odot \overline{C}_n = \begin{cases} -N/2, & m = n \\ 0, & m \neq n \end{cases} \quad (4)$$

Adapting bipolar OCL for packet switching increases the efficiency of packet processing, with a moderate degree of complexity at CN. To append optical labels on a packet, edge node (EN) performs label mapping and generating. Each path connected between nodes is assigned two code labels, a Hadamard code, and its complement, as shown in Fig. 1. For instance, the path between CN1 and CN2 corresponds to code C_1 and $\overline{C}_1$. The reason for this assignment is to support bipolar OCL, as well as to expand the label space. Figure 1 also shows the demonstration of label stacking. The data flow along LSP of (CN1-CN2-CN3) is switched by CNs according to the two-level label, C_1 and C_2. Edge node EN1 performs the integration of distinct code labels before the packet traffics the node-to-node path.

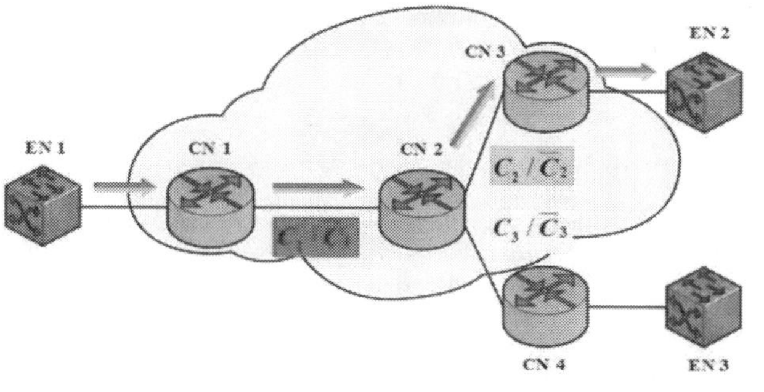

Figure 1. Node-to-node transmission in GMPLS with bipolar OCL.

The LSP in Fig. 1 includes two path segments of codes $C_1/\overline{C}_1$ and $C_2/\overline{C}_2$. Table I illustrates the bipolar OCL scheme with Hadamard coded label of length 4. For payload bit "1", C_1 and C_2, matching wavelength bins of (λ_1, 0, λ_3, 0) and (λ_1, λ_2, 0, 0) are selected. On the other hand, for the case of bit "0", the edge node transmits $\overline{C}_1$ = (0, λ_2, 0, λ_4) and $\overline{C}_2$ = (0, 0, λ_3, λ_4) to the network. Since all labels are spectrally coded on the same wavelength band λ_1~λ_4, the combined signal is the summation of the coded spectrum, S_1 = (2 λ_1, λ_2, λ_3, 0) for bit "1" and S_0 = (0, λ_2, λ_3, 2λ_4) for bit "0". Table II shows the packet switching process at CN1 and CN2. The label summation of S is correlated with C_1 and $\overline{C}_1$, indicating the path between CN1 and CN2. The result of correlation subtraction for bit "1" is 2-unit power, and CN1 establishes a link to CN2 as a part of LSP. At CN2, the correlated results for bit "1" with C_2 and C_3 are 2 and 0-unit power, respectively. Thus, CN2 switches the packet to CN3 along the path matching C_2. Note that for bit "0," the CN does not set up any connection due to the negative correlation value, and the packet is blocked for a bit interval.

TABLE I. BIPOLAR LABEL STACKIGN FOR LSP OF CN1-CN2-CN3.

Path Segment	Hadamard Code Vector	Spectral Label for Bit "1"	Spectral Label for Bit "0"
CN1-CN2	C_1= (1,0,1,0)	(λ_1, 0, λ_3, 0)	(0,λ_2, 0, λ_4)
CN2-CN3	C_1= (1,1,0,0)	(λ_1, λ_2, 0, 0)	(0, 0, λ_3,λ_4)
CN2-CN4	C_1= (1,0,0,1)	(0, 0, 0, 0)	(0, 0, 0, 0)
Summed Label Stack		(2 λ_1,λ_2,λ_3,0)	(0, λ_2, λ_3, 2λ_4)

TABLE II. PACKET SWITCHING PROCESSES AT CN1 AND CN2.

Node No.	Correlation Subtraction for Bit "1"	Correlation Subtraction for Bit "0"
CN1	$S_1 \odot C_1 - S_1 \odot \overline{C}_1$ =| (2,0,1,0) | - | (0,1,0,0) | = 2	$S_0 \odot C_1 - S_0 \odot \overline{C}_1$ =| (0,0,1,0) | - | (0,1,0,2) | = -2
CN2	$S_1 \odot C_2 - S_1 \odot \overline{C}_2$ =| (2,1,0,0) | - | (0,0,1,0) | = 2	$S_0 \odot C_2 - S_0 \odot \overline{C}_2$ =| (0,1,0,0) | - | (0,0,1,2) | = -2
	$S_1 \odot C_3 - S_1 \odot \overline{C}_3$ =| (2,0,0,0) | - | (0,1,1,0) | = 0	$S_0 \odot C_2 - S_0 \odot \overline{C}_2$ =| (0,0,0,2) | - | (0,1,1,0) | = 0

III. DESCRIPTION OF NODE STRUCTURE WITH BCL FUNCTION

To make fully switching, there are N pieces of encoders for bipolar OCL in an EN, where N is the total path number in the network, as shown in Fig. 2. Broadband Light Source (BLS), which connects to an optical switch, is used as the encoder's input. The header processor sets up the connection between BLS and OCL encoder by firstly analyzing packet destination and deriving a specific LSP. Then, a control signal closes the switches linking to the corresponding label generators. Each OCL unit has two outputs: spectrally Hadamard coded signal C_m and its complement. The outputs of optical codes and their complementary codes from different encoders are combined respectively by power combiners. An optical switch selects the one of the two summed signals based on data bit "0" or "1". The chosen one is further sent into a fiber.

CN executes the opposite decoding operation and switches packet to the proper path. In a CN, there are M pieces of OCL decoders similar to the encoders in edge node, where M is the number of output paths, as shown in Fig. 3. At first, a part of the incoming signal is split for label recognizing using a 1 by 2 power splitter. The tapped signal is distributed into different OCL decoders using a 1 by M power splitter. The outputs of decoders control the switching state of the M by M optical cross bar, which establishes a connection to the output path corresponding to the incoming label.

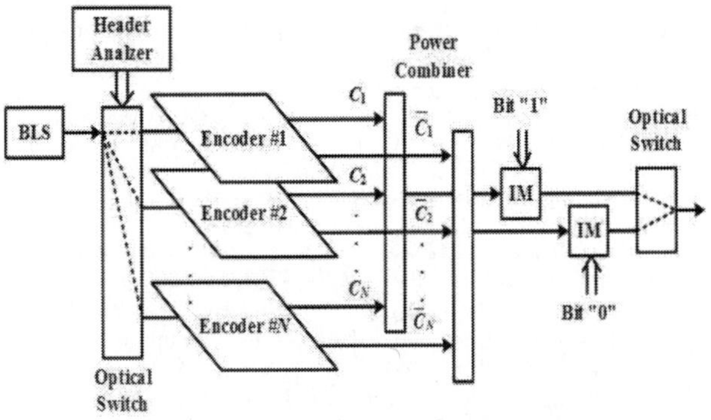

Figure 2. Architecture of EN with bipolar OCL.

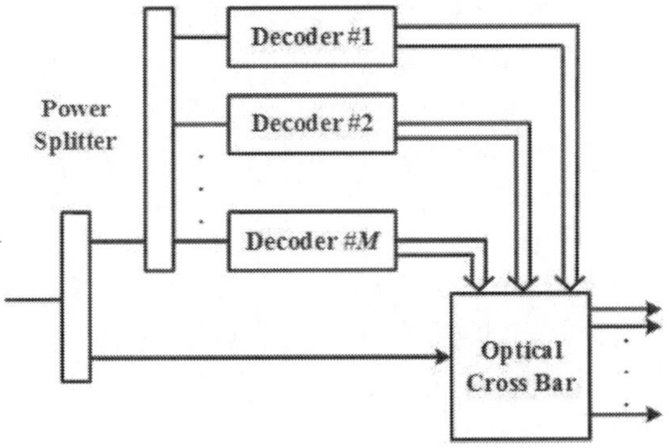

Figure 3. Architecture of CN with bipolar OCL.

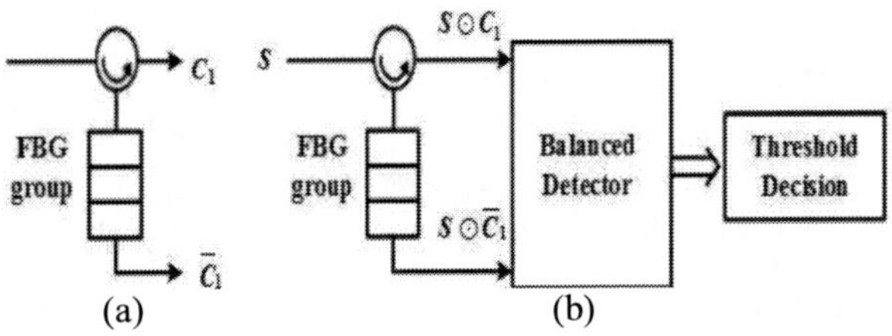

Figure 4. (a) FBG encoder for label generating; (b) FBG decoder for label recognizing.

Spectrally Hadamard-coded signal with length N and code weight $N/2$ is formed by a series of wavelength bins that match code chip "1" at the output of OCL encoder, as shown in Fig. 4(a). The coded label is generated from a group of $N/2$ copies of FBGs in the encoder. To transfer payload bit "1" or "0" into wavelength bins, the FBG-based encoder performs optical encoding by reflecting and transmitting wavelength bins. The FBG-based decoder, as shown in Fig. 4(b), rejects other uncorrelated labels or MAI and makes sure that the correlated one can be successfully recovered to the original data bit. Following the decoder is a balanced detector (BD), which outputs zero power if the summed signals do not include the matching label. To determine the initial payload bit, a quantizer restores the signals by threshold decision.

IV. PERFORMANCE ANALYSIS AND SIMULATION RESULT

In order to express the switching benefit of the proposed OCL, SNR shown at the label decoder is analyzed to quantify the system performance. We use the assumption for BLS characteristics and the mathematical deduction [8] to firstly derive the photocurrent, which is expressed as

$$I = RP_{sr} / 2 \tag{5}$$

where P_{sr} is the received power at decoder and R is the responsivity of the photo-diode in the BD. Phase intensity noise and thermal noise are main degrading factor of SAC systems [9]. This paper only considers Phase Intensity Induced Noise (PIIN) since it is the dominant noise when optical signal is converted to electrical domain. The variance of PIIN is denoted as

$$\sigma^2 = R^2 P_{sr}^2 BK(K+1) / 2v \tag{6}$$

where B is the electrical noise bandwidth, v is the spectral width of BLS and K is the number of stacked labels. By using Gaussian approximation, the PLPs of bipolar and unipolar label, PLP_b and PLP_a are expressed as:

$$PLP_b = \frac{1}{\sqrt{2\pi}\sigma}\left\{\frac{1}{2}\int_{-\infty}^{0}\exp\left[\frac{-(x-I)^2}{2\sigma^2}\right]dx + \frac{1}{2}\int_{0}^{\infty}\exp\left[\frac{-(x+I)^2}{2\sigma^2}\right]dx\right\} \tag{7}$$

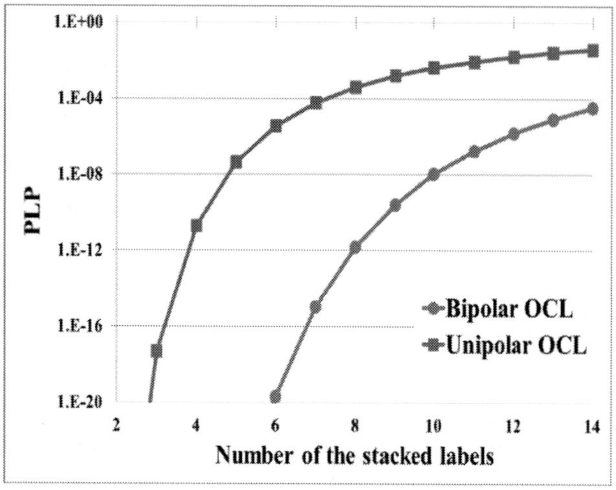

Figure 5. PLP comparison for the proposed bipolar OCL and the conventional unipolar OCL.

$$\mathrm{PLP}_{\mathrm{a}} = \frac{1}{\sqrt{2\pi}\sigma}\frac{1}{2}\int_{-\infty}^{I/2} \exp\left[\frac{-(x-I)^2}{2\sigma^2}\right]dx \tag{8}$$

The spectral width of BLS is 4.5THz and the electrical noise bandwidth is 10GHz. We use the Hadamard coded labels of $N = 16$ for simulation. In Fig. 5, packet with the proposed label performs better PLP than the one with the unipolar label. Under small number of the stacked labels, both types have relatively good results keeping the PLP under 10^{-9}. However, PIIN increasing with the label number degrades the system performance, when the number of stacked labels is large. For the bipolar label code, despite a larger PIIN variance, it still has a higher SNR value due to the doubled signal power. The stacked label number for bipolar OCL is 2 times of the other under PLP = 10^{-9}. This implies more labels can be attached to a single packet, resulting in an extension of LSP.

V. Conclusions

In this paper, we propose a bipolar OCL scheme in GMPLS network that enhances the switching efficiency by enlarging Hamming distance on the star diagram of the decoded labels. Reducing the PLP during label-recognizing procedure is a critical issue in GMPLS since it increases the distance of LSP in all-optical switching. The bipolar labeling is implemented based on the correlation and orthogonal properties of Hadamard codes. We adapt the FBG-based codec of OCDMA technique for modifying the node structure. A numerical simulation is conducted for the proposed scheming, proving the stacked label number is increased by utilizing the proposed bipolar label.

References

[1] W. Imajuku et al., "A multi-area MPLS/GMPLS interoperability trial over ROADM/OXC network," IEEE Commun. Mag., vol. 47, no. 2, pp. 168-175, Feb. 2009.

[2] K. Shiomoto et al., "Use of addresses in generalized multiprotocol label switching (GMPLS) networks," IETF RFC 4990. 2007.

[3] A. Banerjee, J. Drake, J. P. Lang, and B.Turner, "Generalized multiprotocol label switching: An overview of routing and management enhancements," IEEE Commun. Mag., vol. 39, no. 7, pp. 144-151, Aug. 2001.

[4] T. Khattab and H.Alnuweiri, "Optical CDMA for all-optical sub-wavelength switching in core GMPLS networks," IEEE J. Sel. Areas Commun., vol. 25, no. 5 pp. 905-921, May 2007.

[5] Z. A. El-Sahn et al., "Experimental demonstration of a SAC-OCDMA PON with burst-mode reception: Local versus centralized sources," J. Lightw. Technol., vol. 26, no. 10, pp. 1192-1203, Jun. 2008.

[6] C. C. Yang, J. F. Huang, H. H. Chang, and K. S. Chen, "Radio transmissions over residue-stuffed-QC-coded optical CDMA network," IEEE Commun. Lett., vol. 18, no. 2 pp. 329- 331, Feb. 2014.

[7] J. F. Huang, C. C. Yang, and S. P. Tseng, "Complementary Walsh-Hadamard coded optical CDMA coder/decoders structured over arrayed-waveguide grating routers," Optics Commun., vol. 229, no. 1-6, pp. 241-248, Jan. 2004.

[8] C. C. Yang, "Compact optical CDMA passive optical network with differentiated service," IEEE Trans. Commun., vol. 27, no. 8, pp. 2408-2409, Aug. 2009.

[9] M. M. Rad, L. A. Rusch, and J. Y. Chouinard, "Performance degradation of source matching in optical CDMA due to source coherence effects," IEEE Trans. Commun., vol. 57, no. 6, pp. 1776-1783, Jun. 2009.

Design and Development of a Large-scale Network Testbed on a Research and Education Network

Chu-Sing Yang, Pang-Wei Tsai, Jen-Fa Huang
Institute of Computer and Communication Engineering,
Department of Electrical Engineering
National Cheng Kung University (NCKU)
Tainan City, Taiwan
{csyang, pwtsai, huajf}@ee.ncku.edu.tw

Te-Lung Liu
National Center for High-Performance Computing
National Applied Research Laboratories (NARLabs)
Tainan City, Taiwan
tlliu@narlabs.org.tw

***Abstract*—As the Internet continues to grow in width and depth, its very architecture presents challenges when it comes to implementing innovations. For testing new developments, networking developers need an environment for evaluating their ideology and practicality. The testing environment is required to emulate a production network, and it also has to operate in the private area without real-world interference. Under these circumstances, the network testbed provides such a platform for the developers. This paper presents the TaiWan Advanced Research and Education Network testbed, a large-scale, as well as multi-layer network testbed, constructed for network research, and designed to orchestrate and aggregate resources of different testbed sites for supporting the conduction of experiments. The paper aims to share the building experience of this network testbed, introducing the key development points and future work.**

Keywords-Network Testbed; Virtualization; SDN; Cloud; Resource Control.

I. Introduction

The Internet has become a critical infrastructure in modern society [1] even though its design choices could not be used to anticipate the current needs [2]. While the scope of the Internet continues to grow at a fast pace, its architecture makes implementing innovations difficult. Therefore, before new approaches and concepts can be implemented to the actual global network, they need to be evaluated in a bench-scale environment first. A testbed enables new technologies to be tested experimentally with realistic and reproductive scenarios. Thus, network developers are able to verify their new ideas without the fear of interfering with the real environment. For the reasons above, recently, many institutes [3][4][5] have been designing and developing testbeds to satisfy research requirements.

Since the Software-Defined Networking (SDN) [6] has been proposed to improve the programmability of network architecture, it is commonly applied in network provision. There are also several testbed projects using SDN in their designs. For example, the Global Environment for Network Innovations (GENI) [7], is supported by National Science Foundation of the United States, and RISE [8] is a large-scale testbed with nation-wide network infrastructure for research and academic use. Furthermore, OFELIA [9] project financially supported by European Union is a testbed which using SDN to integrate various sites as a large-scale network testbed in Europe. OF@TEIN [10] is another project to utilize production network to constructed a collaborated testbed with cloud services and SDN techniques. The common point of these network testbeds is that they integrate underlay infrastructure, access networks and computing resources for supporting testbed purposes, providing such a platform to explore new network inventions for network researchers.

In Taiwan, the TaiWan Advanced Research and Education Network (TWAREN) [11] operated by the National Center for High-performance Computing (NCHC) [12] is an academic network in Taiwan, providing variety services and applications for research and education purposes. In order to support more advanced experiment of the Future Internet researches, a plan of building a SDN-enabled testbed on TWAREN has been proposed. The design goal of the testbed is to extend the software-defined controllability into TWAREN. By doing this, the testbed users are able to have more flexibility on conducting their experiments. This testbed is also designed to aggregate geographically distributed resources from different providers, and testbed users are able to use the cloud resources of participated providers in distributed testbed sites. To manage these resources, a resource control software is also developed. The design goal of this testbed is to provide a flexible environment to sustain innovative researches of Taiwan's academic and research institutes.

While the testbed is still under verification and improvement, in this paper, we present our experience for building this SDN network testbed on TWAREN (i.e., TWAREN testbed), and several on-going progress steps are also introduced. The remainder of this paper is organized as follows. The background and related work are introduced in Section 2. The concerns, design and development issues are described in Section 3. The initial performance measurement is presented in Section 4. Finally, the conclusions and future work are provided in Section 5.

II. Background and Related Work

A. Software-Defined Networking

With the advancement of network technologies, many ideas and implementations have sprouted in recent years. However, due to the architecture of the legacy network, new innovation may be limited by existing policies and rules. The SDN is recognized as a new architecture to enhancing the network programmability for fulfilling requirements. Two of the most significant characteristics of SDN is the centralized control and softwarized management. By using the SDN controller, network devices are able to change behaviors according to upper layer instructions. Nowadays, the most well-known SDN protocol is OpenFlow [13]. It is a SDN solution to improve the controllability and scalability on network provision. In an OpenFlow network, there are three basic components: switch, controller and application. The switch is used to handle traffic transmission, and controller is responsible for managing the switch operation. The application is able to tell the controller what is the required network behavior for the upper layer.

In the beginning, the SDN research was focusing mainly on layer 2 and layer 3 networks [6]. However, to enhance the network control ability, there is a trend to extend the controllability into underlay network. For example, Mambretti et al. [14] proposed their research about using an experimental control-plane architecture to achieve Light-path provisioning dynamically. Filer et al. [15] also introduced their experience on observing network infrastructure in a cloud system, discussing the impact of elasticity on network capacity and flexibility. Moreover, Channegowda et al. [16] made a discussion on their OpenFlow testbed, which is allowing seamless operation across heterogeneous optical and packet transport domains. Larrabeiti et al. [17] also presented their research of building a large-scale network testbed with both packet-switched and circuit-switched services. As described above, it can be found that the software-defined mechanism is becoming more and more popular in network design, development and implementation in network innovation.

B. SDN-enable Network and Testbed Development

For conducting a large-scale network experiment, the main problem is to access the required resources for building the testing environment. Therefore, many large-scale network researches are often supported by network operation institutes or enterprises. Following are the three typical instances:

- **Internet2 and GENI Testbeds:** GENI is a project to build a national resource control framework and provide a testing environment for experiments and verifications [3]. The testbed network of GENI is based on the Internet 2 [18] backbone. Internet 2 provides GENI testbeds with a multi-layer resources including optical facility, layer 2 service and IP route. By deploying computing resources and network control systems [19] [20], GENI testbeds have an open, large-scale, realistic network environment for researchers to evaluate their ideas and explore network research.
- **JGN and RISE Testbed:** The Japan Gigabit Network (JGN) [21] is a nationwide network supported by the National Institute of Information and Communication Technology in Japan. The Research Infrastructure for large-scale network Experiments (RISE) testbed is using this network infrastructure to virtualize the physical network as logical network for experimental purposes [8]. By assigning a number of logical networks called Existing Virtual Networks (EVNs) for creating private experiment networks, the testbed users of RISE are able to operate their desirable topologies in parallel and reduce the time spent in the experiment deployments.
- **TEIN and OF@TEIN Testbed:** The Trans-Eurasia Information Network (TEIN) is a network which connects more than fifty countries in Europe and Asia [22]. TEIN plays an important role of inter-continental traffic exchanges among Europe and Asia countries, and it is also actively being used for international joint researches and education purposes. The OpenFlow at TEIN (OF@TEIN) collaboration community was established in 2012, and its career is to carry out the SDN research issues. The OF@TEIN testbed [10] is using distributed architecture, deploying testbed sites at the domestic collaborators, and making site-to-site connection through the TEIN.

C. Research and Education Network in Taiwan

The TWAREN was initiated to construct a fundamental network for research and education in Taiwan. The infrastructure of TWAREN backbone consists of four core nodes. All these nodes are connected with spare dark fibers for redundancy. There are also many GigaPOPs (Point of Presence) located at regional network centers. These GigaPOPs are the communicating entities among the TWAREN backbone and local networks. In initialization, most GigaPoPs are using dark fibers with SDH technique to connect to the core nodes [23]. By using SDH, the TWAREN Optical network is able to divide multiple light-paths between two GIgaPOPs for different purposes. For upper layer connection, the GigaPoPs provide layer 2 entrance to stitch the network. By using this infrastructure, TWAREN facility provides various kinds of networking services [23]. For example, the TANet is a logical network based on TWAREN backbone. It is used to serve the academic institutes for network access. For another, TWAREN VPLS VPN is a network service to establishing point-to-point connections among branches of research institutes. The proposed testbed in this paper also uses this method to create logical and isolated networks to support user experiments.

III. System Design

In this section, we present our experience on building a large-scale, as well as multi-layer network testbed on

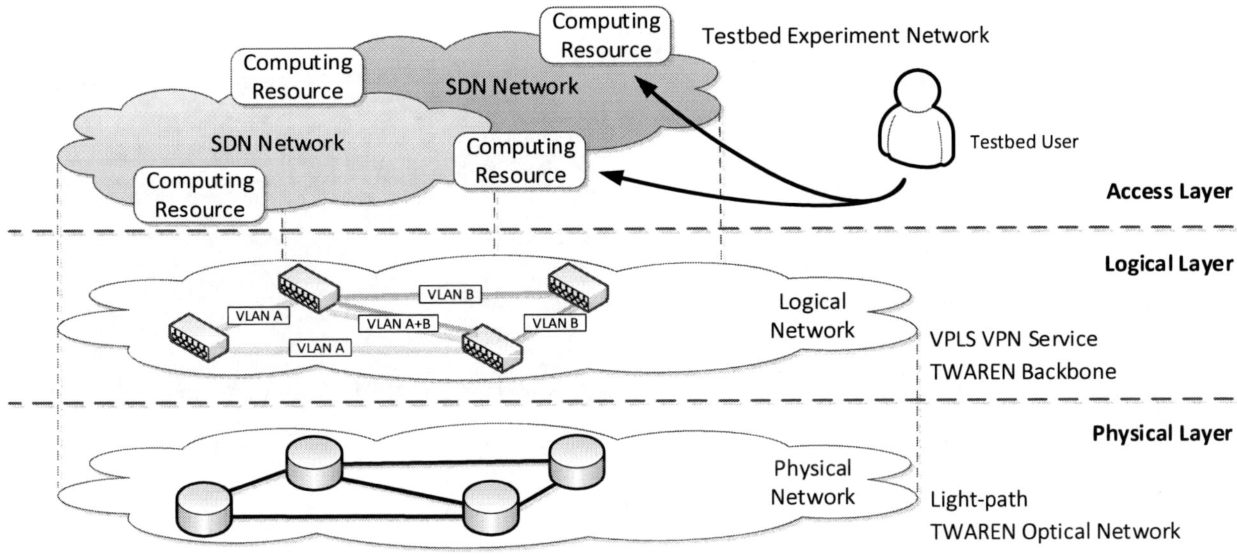

Figure 1. The architecture overview of TWAREN testbed.

TWAREN. The introduction includes concerns, system architecture, and system deployment. Several key development issues in testbed construction are also discussed.

A. Testbed Architecture

To explain the TWAREN testbed design, the overview of the TWAREN testbed is shown in Fig. 1. The testbed system can be categorized in three parts: the physical layer, the logical layer and the access layer.

- **Physical Layer:** The physical layer is provisioned with optical transport solutions in TWAREN [23]. It uses a monolithic infrastructure to create virtual networks for supporting different purposes. The light-paths are configured with SDH SNCP protection, preventing single point failure occurred. The devices in this layer are the fundamental hardware of TWAREN infrastructure.
- **Logical Layer:** The logical layer is the middle layer for integrating the other two layers. It consists of numerous layer 2 devices and enabled VLAN to separate virtual networks. For building site-to-site connection among TWEAREN testbed sites, each connection is assigned with a unique VLAN ID. By doing this, the network traffic of each connection is isolated, operating as a virtual links for deploying testbed network.
- **Access Layer:** The access layer is the one appearing to the testbed users. The computing devices (e.g., server and storage) are located here, and layer 3 devices are deployed to establish the network connection among the resources and testbed users. There is also a resource control software in this layer provides the front-end GUI to testbed users. It is the interface bridge for connecting the testbed system with users. Testbed users can request resources (e.g., virtual machines and virtual networks) at the front-end interface first. After that, the resource control software allocates sliced resources to build testing environments. When the experiments are finished, testbed users can notify the testbed system to free the resources and make them re-useable.

B. Network Resource Control

The optical infrastructure of TWAREN is shared by testbed network and production network. Therefore, to avoid the interference, these two networks must be separated logically. There is a management mechanism [24] built on TWAREN for light-path control. It supports circuit and equipment protection. Therefore, we use existing light-paths to create multiple VLANs. By enabling QinQ [25] tunnel, each site-to-site link can be divided into as many slices as needed, and the slices are restructuring as virtual paths for traffic delivery. The packet switching is made by a SDN controller. By using VLAN tag-translation [26], the controller is able to manage the site-to-site flows in transmission.

C. Computing Resource Control

In anticipation, the institutes participating in TWAREN testbed would share their computing resources for the others, and a control software would be used to take control. For unifying computing resources, currently, the virtual machine is representing the smallest unit in computing resource. Currently, the XenServer [27] is used to manage virtual machines. The received instructions of the XenServer will be converted to create virtual machine. By doing this, the control software sends instruction to each resource site to setup sufficient virtual machines for serving testbed users. With the integration of network and computing resources,

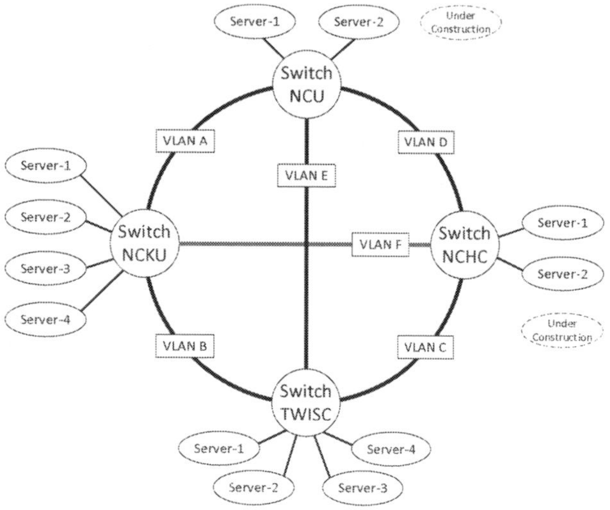

Figure 2. The virtual link among TWAREN testbed sites.

the TWAREN testbed is able to provide a private space for testbed users to conduct their experiments.

D. *Testbed Site Deployment*

In the initial phase, we establish four resource sites in the TWAREN testbed. The TWAREN facility provides 6 VLANs to setup virtual links between two sites. These links are constructed as a mesh topology for connecting testbed sites, which is shown as Fig 2. Each resource site is deployed with an OpenFlow switch, and there is a shared controller (with out-of-band connection) used to manage all the switches.

IV. INITIAL EVALUATION

The implementation of the testbed is still work in progress, while the four testbed sites are ready for initial evaluation. Currently, four available sites in TWAREN testbed are located at NCU, NCKU, NCHC and TWISC, and more sites are anticipated to join in the near future. For verification, we limit the site-to-site bandwidth to 1Gbps initially. By using the iperf [28], the result shows that each link is able to reach the line rate speed. The ping [29] availability test also shows a good response time. Furthermore, for long-term monitoring, we use a Cacti [30] system to collect and present traffic statistics.

For the initial evaluation, an experiment scenario with video broadcasting in 4K resolution is conducted [31]. The streaming VMs are allocated at NCU, NCKU and TWISC sites. By using video player, the receiver is able to get the streaming from broadcasting VMs, which is shown as Fig 3. In our observation, the video traffic for serving one receiver is about 20-24 Mbps. To conduct the stress-test on broadcasting VMs, we use flazr [32] to simulate numerous receivers for acquiring large traffic. Furthermore, due to the fact that each site-to-site connection is limited to 1Gbps, for processing oversubscribed traffic without conjunction, we let the SDN controller select available paths in mesh topology.

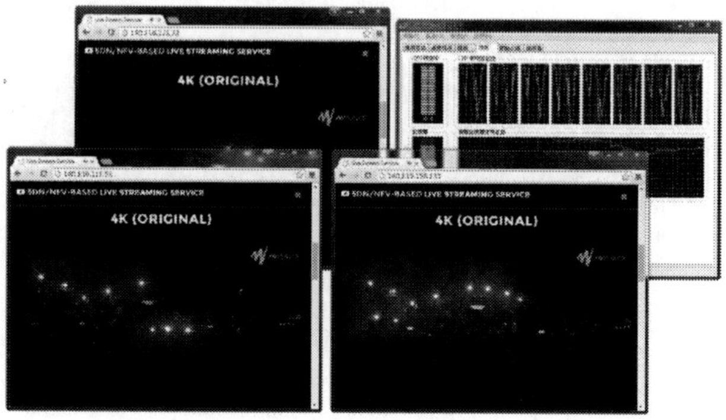

Figure 3. The received 4K streaming on PC.

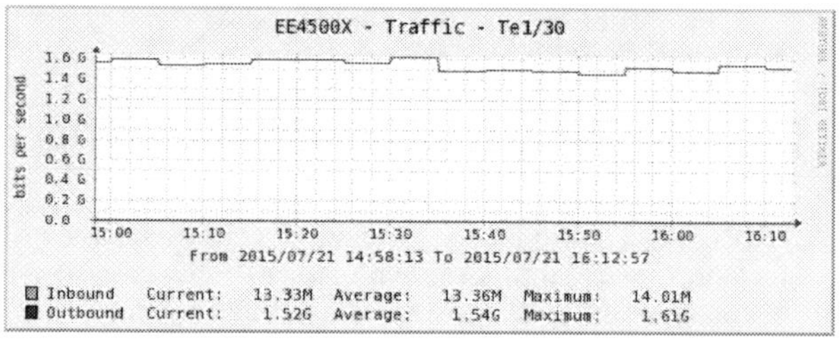

Figure 4. The monitoring result made by MRTG [33] tool.

For example, the traffic flow from NCU to NCKU can be divided in two available routes: NCU → NCKU and NCU → TWISC → NCKU. As a result, the monitoring traffic from NCU to NCKU site has a merged throughput, which is shown in Fig 4. The result of the initial evaluation shows that the testbed system is able to conduct simple network experiments, and the SDN controller is able to manage OpenFlow switches in the testbed for controlling network traffic.

V. CONCLUSIONS AND FUTURE WORK

This paper describes the experience of designing and implementing a network testbed to support innovative research in Taiwan. The design principle of this testbed system includes several concepts for achieving virtualization. The network of this testbed fully supports the OpenFlow protocol. For managing various resources in the testbed, a resource control software is implemented to allocate resources among different resource sites. The whole implementation of the testbed is still in progress, while the prototype has been verified. When fully completed, the testbed is expected to orchestrate and aggregate the various resources of domestic academic institutes in support of large-scale network researches.

Since testbed users may need various kinds of networking environments within which they can emulate the actual environment. Therefore, making network functions to be a service on the testbed is essential. The following works are expected to enhance the emulation functionality of TWAREN testbed:

- **Enhancement of Programmability in Underlay Network:** Owing to one of the characteristics in SDN is to enhance the programmability on the network, how to extend the controllability to underlay network becomes an important issue. For example, Belter et al. [34] introduced their experience on building GEYSERS, a multi-domain testbed for testing and validating cloud-oriented technologies. The extended controllability is expected to have more flexibility and adaptation on physical network. More testbed operations, such as optical route switching and light-path protection, can be controlled by softwarized methods for supporting advanced network research.
- **Resource Aggregation:** Because many testbed collaborators may have their own cloud solutions, for managing variety resources, making collaboration on these resource is a rapid way for extend the testbed scale. Currently, the TWAREN testbed only supports Xen-based virtual machine. If there is a standard protocol for integrated resources with control software of TWAREN testbed, it would be possible to serve more users to conduct large-scale experiments that are geographically distributed.
- **High-speed Network Infrastructure:** Nowadays, many scientific research projects on TWAREN generate massive amounts of traffic. As a consequence, at present, the TWAREN backbone has reached its limited bandwidth capacity, and the transmission performance of OpenFlow research network may be affected by the available capacity of TWAREN backbone. There is an ongoing plan for deploying 100G infrastructure of TWAREN. The capacity promotion is expected to achieve the ability of traffic engineering on delivering large traffic generated by possible killer applications on the testbed.

ACKNOWLEDGMENT

This research is financially supported by the MOST (under grants No.105-2218-E-194-002 and 104-2218-E-001-002) for which authors are grateful. Authors also appreciate to the Mobile Broadband Network Laboratory of National Central University and TWAREN Network Operation Center for their support.

REFERENCES

[1] E. G. Gran, T. Dreibholz, and A. Kvalbein, "Nornet core-a multi-homed research testbed," Computer Networks, vol. 61, pp. 75-87, 2014.

[2] J. Aug´e et al., "Tools to foster a global federation of testbeds," Computer Networks, vol. 63, pp. 205-220, 2014.

[3] "Global environment for network innovations." [Online]. Available: http://www.geni.net/ 2016.08.30

[4] "National institute of information and communications technology." [Online]. Available: https://www.nict.go.jp/ 2016.08.30

[5] "Fire testbeds." [Online]. Available: http://www.ict-fire.eu/home/fire-testbeds.html 2016.08.30

[6] D. Kreutz et al., "Software-defined networking: A comprehensive survey," Proceedings of the IEEE, vol. 103, no. 1, pp. 14-76, 2015.

[7] M. Berman, C. Elliott, and L. Landweber, "Geni: Large-scale distributed infrastructure for networking and distributed systems research," in Communications and Electronics (ICCE), 2014 IEEE Fifth International Conference on. IEEE, pp. 156-161, 2014.

[8] Y. Kanaumi et al., "Rise: A wide-area hybrid openflow network testbed," IEICE transactions on communications, vol. 96, no. 1, pp. 108-118, 2013.

[9] "Ofelia testbed." [Online]. Available: http://www.fp7-ofelia.eu/ 2016.08.30

[10] J. Kim et al., "Of@ tein: An openflow-enabled sdn testbed over international smartx rack sites," Proceedings of the Asia-Pacific Advanced Network, vol. 36, pp. 17-22, 2013.

[11] "Taiwan advanced research and education network." [Online]. Available: http://http://www.twaren.net/english/ 2016.08.30

[12] "National center for high-performance computing." [Online]. Available: https://www.nchc.org.tw/en/ 2016.08.30

[13] N. McKeown et al., "Openflow: enabling innovation in campus networks," ACM SIGCOMM Computer Communication Review, vol. 38, no. 2, pp. 69-74, 2008.

[14] J. Mambretti, D. Lillethun, J. Lange, and J. Weinberger, "Optical dynamic intelligent network services (odin): an experimental controlplane architecture for high-performance distributed environments based on dynamic lightpath provisioning," IEEE Communications Magazine, vol. 44, no. 3, pp. 92-99, 2006.

[15] M. Filer et al., "Elastic optical networking in the microsoft cloud," Journal of Optical Communications and Networking, vol. 8, no. 7, pp. A45-A54, 2016.

[16] M. Channegowda et al., "Experimental demonstration of an openflow based software-defined optical network employing packet, fixed and flexible dwdm grid technologies on an international multi-domain testbed," Optics express, vol. 21, no. 5, pp. 5487-5498, 2013.

[17] D. Larrabeiti et al., "Integrating a next-generation optical access network testbed into a large-scale virtual research testbed," in 2015 17th International Conference on Transparent Optical Networks (ICTON). IEEE, pp. 1-6, 2015.

[18] "Internet2." [Online]. Available: http://www.internet2.edu/ 2016.08.30

[19] "Protogeni." [Online]. Available: http://www.protogeni.net/ 2016.08.30

[20] "Exogeni." [Online]. Available: http://www.exogeni.net/ 2016.08.30

[21] "Jgn-x." [Online]. Available: http://www.jgn.nict.go.jp/ 2016.08.30

[22] "Trans-eurasia information network." [Online]. Available: http://www.teincc.org/ 2016.08.30

[23] T.-L. Liu and C. E. Yeh, "Planning and design of twaren: Advanced national research and education network in taiwan," in Advanced Information Networking and Applications Workshops, 2007, AINAW'07. 21st International Conference on, vol. 1. IEEE, pp. 918-922, 2007.

[24] S.-C. Lin et al., "Twaren optical network laboratory and lightpath control system," in Advanced Information Networking and Applications- Workshops, 2008. AINAW 2008. 22nd International Conference on. IEEE, pp. 1492-1498, 2008.

[25] L. Katzri and O. Yaron, "Apparatus for and method for supporting 802.1 q vlan tagging with independent vlan

learning in lan emulation networks," US Patent 6,639,901, Oct. 28 2003.

[26] P.-W. Tsai, P.-W. Cheng, C.-S. Yang, M.-Y. Luo, and J. Chen, "Supporting extensions of vlan-tagged traffic across openflow networks," in Research and Educational Experiment Workshop (GREE), 2013 Second GENI. IEEE, pp. 61-65, 2013.

[27] D. E. Williams, Virtualization with Xen (tm): Including XenEnterprise, XenServer, and XenExpress. Syngress, 2007.

[28] A. Tirumala, F. Qin, J. Dugan, J. Ferguson, and K. Gibbs, "Iperf: The tcp/udp bandwidth measurement tool," http://dast. nlanr. net/Projects, 2005.

[29] S. M. Bellovin, M. Leech, and T. Taylor, "Icmp traceback messages," IETF Internet Draft, 2003.

[30] "Cacti - the complete rrdtool-based graphing solution." [Online]. Available: http://www.cacti.net/ 2016.08.30

[31] C.-T. Lin (2014), SDN/NFV-based Resource Orchestrator for VNF Deployment and High Availability - A Case Study of Live Streaming Service (Master's thesis). Retrieved from http://handle.ncl.edu.tw/11296/ndltd/09173940899962258539 2016.08.30

[32] "Flazr" [Online]. Available: http://flazr.com/ 2016.08.30

[33] T. Oetiker and D. Rand, "Mrtg: The multi router traffic grapher." in LISA, vol. 98, pp. 141-148, 1998.

[34] B. Belter et al., "The geysers optical testbed: A platform for the integration, validation and demonstration of cloud-based infrastructure services," Computer Networks, vol. 61, pp. 197-216, 2014.

Cooperative Computing for Mobile Platforms

Jing Chen*, Jian-Hong Liu, Tin-Yen Lin#,

Institute of Computer and Communication Engineering
Department of Electrical Engineering, National Cheng Kung University
1 University Road, Tainan City 70101
Taiwan, R.O.C.
e-mail: jchen@mail.ncku.edu.tw*, {liuken, q36001169#}@rtpc06.ee.ncku.edu.tw

***Abstract*— While mobile platforms with increasing computing power nowadays have become popular, applications running on mobile platforms, however, still suffer from the limitations of resource availability and architecture variety imposed by mobile platforms. Offloading mobile application to a virtual machine deployed on a server or cloud computing environment is effective only for the cases of running stand-alone applications and is not able to achieve cooperative computing across platform boundary. In attempting to address the issue, this paper considers cross-platform Inter-Process Communication (IPC) to be an essential capability towards achieving cooperative computing at application level and, as a demonstrative example, expands the IPC mechanism of Android system to be the foundation of building a collaborative and cooperative working environment. This expanded IPC mechanism is called XBinder. The main contribution of this work is providing a way for mobile applications to cooperate with local or remote services without developing complicate network transmission mechanism. Mobile applications are able to effectively and efficiently communicate with services which execute either on local node or remote node.**

Keywords- Cooperative Computing; Mobile Computing; IPC; Resource sharing; Remote Service.

I. INTRODUCTION

With advances in hardware and software technologies, consumer embedded system products, in particular mobile platforms, are everywhere around our daily life. It has been envisioned that the next generation of computing systems would be mobile while embedded, in a virtually unbounded number, and dynamically connected [6]. This is getting true especially for mobile platforms such as smart phones and pad platforms which not only have become very popular embedded system products but also serve as personal mobile multifunctional platforms. It is also observed that desktop applications are being moved to run on mobile platforms. For example, accessing Internet services by using browser software or apps running on mobile platforms is now very common. However, a long existent issue is that most mobile platforms impose limitation on available resources such as computing capability, memory, storage, power supply (due to battery life), etc. In general, when application on mobile platforms is running in stand-alone manner, there would be some restrictions limiting its benefit or advantage.

Mobile applications which are executed on cloud server can overcome the limitations mentioned above [9]. Building a virtual mobile platform in cloud computing environment is another solution for resource limitation [12]. When a mobile application is offloaded to run on a server deployed on cloud side, the server pushes the screen display of execution results directly to the user side [18][21]. The disadvantage is that in general a lot of image data transmission is required. Another effective approach is developing, in a case-by-case manner, mobile application with specific constructs [8]. However, it usually needs to establish some protocols between server and mobile applications for the purposes of exchanging data or cooperating. This approach appears comparatively not only quite complicated but also generally error-prone. In general, resources can be shared and processes can be cooperative. When the capability of cooperative computing, which is one type of distributed computing model and in which resources are shared among processes running on different connected platforms (called nodes), is taken into consideration, the approaches mentioned above do not fit.

In this paper we consider that, in supporting cooperative computing at application level, cross-platform Inter-Process Communication (IPC) is essential, and present XBinder as an example of cross-platform IPC mechanism in attempting to address the issue of cooperative computing on networked mobile platforms. Fig. 1 illustrates an application scenario of XBinder, in which a number of services are shared among applications running on different networked platforms.

XBinder expands the IPC mechanism of Android system to help set up the foundation of building a collaborative and cooperative working environment. Its development shows the following desirable features:

- Remote process communication: A local process can communicate and cooperate with a remote process.
- Easy application development with remote objects: Remote services can be built without developing new complicate network transmission mechanism.
- Peer-to-peer communication: Every mobile platform with XBinder installed is a peer node. A peer node is able to directly transmit network packet to other ones, which may provide and apply remote service.
- Multiple concurrent connections: XBinder supports concurrent operations for multiple connected nodes. The IPC of a connection will not be interfered when there are other connections working concurrently.

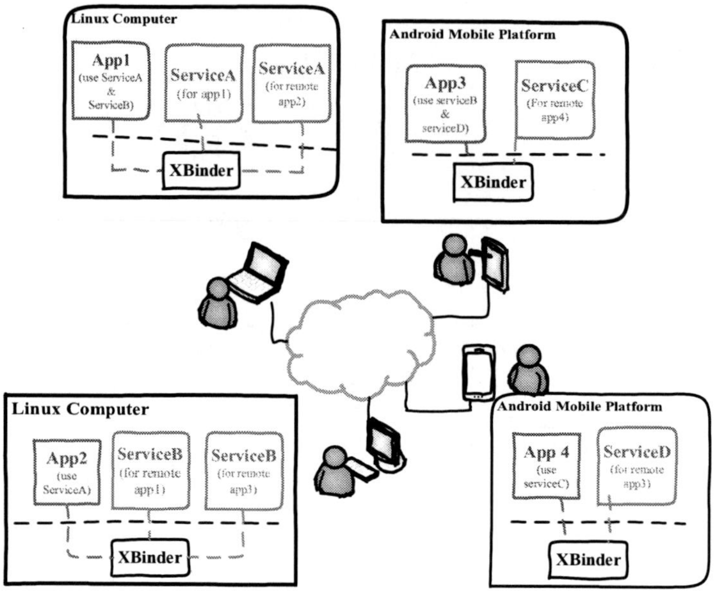

Figure 1. Cooperative computing with XBinder

The rest of this paper is organized as follows. Section II gives a brief discussion on related works. Section III presents the development of XBinder which serves as an example for demonstrating the fundamental capability to help achieve co-operative computing. Section IV describes the evaluation of XBinder. Finally, Section V concludes this paper.

II. Related Works

This section briefly discusses some works related to solving the issues of resource limitation and cooperative computing on embedded systems or mobile platforms.

Android as a Server Platform (AASP) [13] proposed to deploy Android applications on servers which work in cloud computing environment. The approach effectively addressed the issues, as described above, of resource constraint, power consumption and battery life through achieving a server of Android system. However, AASP did not take into account the operation requirements of data sharing, nor cooperation in either client-server or distributed computing styles.

Reference [17] presented Distributed IPC using Virtual Device Driver in Monolithic Kernel (DIPC) to realize an IPC mechanism for distributed computing systems and achieved communication among processes in different systems. DIPC was implemented in kernel space and showed advantages of high priority and reducing extra copying or movement in data sharing. The disadvantage, nevertheless, comes from its operating in kernel space because it can use only kernel level function library. In addition, security becomes another issue.

Borcea [6] and Iftode [11] both presented a distributed computing model for programming large networks which are composed of embedded systems and implemented prototypes for two applications on sensor networks. Their distributed computing model and the proposed architecture showed the main features of cooperative computing. In their works, co-operative computing applications are composed of migratory execution units (including both code and data), called Smart Messages, working together to accomplish a distributed task. Their model showed generality and worked based on the IPC through message passing. The work described in this paper is mainly motivated by their contributions.

Android system is developed based on Linux operating system [20]. It has its own IPC mechanism, called Android Binder, which demonstrates many desirable features such as stability, efficiency, security, and good resource management [3][19]. However, Android Binder adopts an object-oriented communication approach which put burdens on application developers by requiring case-by-case defined details. Nevertheless, this is considered quite suitable for remote process communication [10] and Android has shown its potential of being popular in the world of mobile platforms. Therefore, it is adopted in this work.

III. The Development of XBinder

The development of XBinder adopts the IPC mechanism of Android system as its base. The reasons are mainly that many software components of Android system, including the Binder driver and its associated software components, are open source software and freely available, and that Android has a large, and still growing, share in the arena of mobile platforms. XBinder has as its components XBinder Manager and XBinder Driver. Its architecture is depicted in Fig. 2 in which the dotted squares indicate the components which are modified from Android Binder framework [7], and the other parts are the components that are developed in this work.

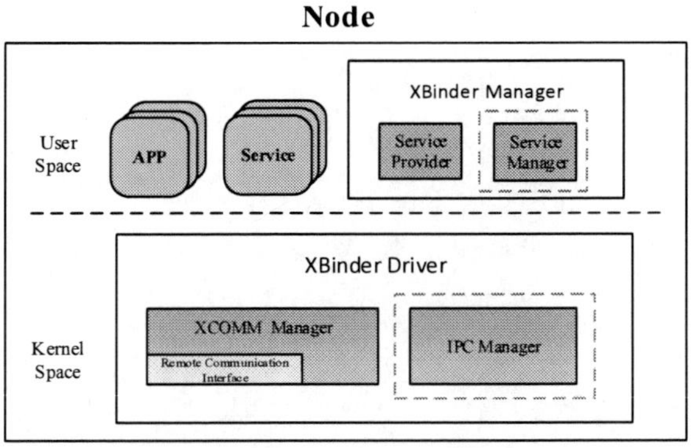

Figure 2. XBinder Architecture

A. XBinder Driver

- The IPC Manager manages all the communication between processes, such as applications and services, including allocating message space for processes, and helps transfer messages. Its functionality is achieved by modifying the mechanisms in Android for message delivery, process management, and space allocation.
- XCOMM Manager is responsible for setting up node-to-node connections and maintaining the connections. In addition to delivering services for those active connections, it handles the messages received from remote nodes.
- The Remote Communication Interface, which is part of XCOMM manager, allows the XCOMM Manager to establish connections with XBinder of other nodes and exchange messages through the connections.

XCOMM Manager is the core component in handling remote services. Its architecture is shown in Fig. 3. For each established connection, XCOMM Manager creates a Remote Request Handler and a corresponding Remote Node Object. There are two types of established connections: connecting the local node as requested by a remote node, and connecting a remote node requested by the local node. Remote Request Handler receives through Remote Communication Interface a message and processes that message. The Remote Request Handler puts the processed message into the corresponding Remote Node Object to be dispatched, by IPC Manager, to the destination process.

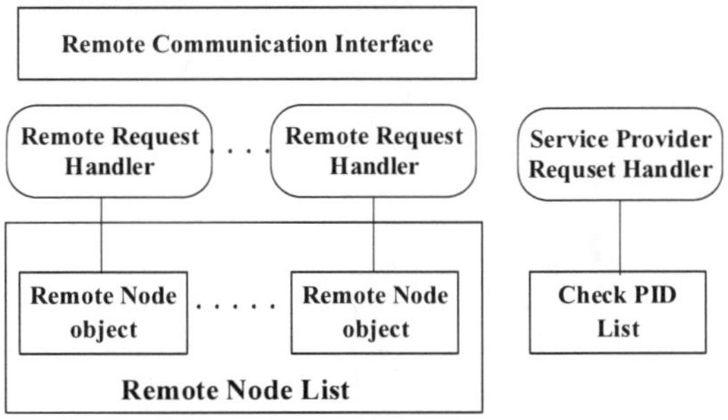

Figure 3. The Architecture of XCOMM

B. XBinder Manager

- The Service Manager manages all the services that are either executing on local node or provided by remote nodes. Its functions include acquiring, adding, and deleting services in order to serve processes.
- The Service Provider is responsible for servicing user demands by setting up and closing connection with remote nodes, allocating and releasing services.

Service Provider works internally with XCOMM Manger and IPC Manager in XBinder to achieve providing remote services. The main steps are depicted in Fig. 4. When user issues a request to access a remote service, Service Provider passes the connect command with the IP address of the remote node to local XCOMM Manager which attempts to establish the connection and returns the status of connection to Service Provider. At the time when the connection from a remote note is accepted, XCOMM Manager informs Service Provider in order to start the requested service by creating all needed processes to run the service and passes the identifiers of all these processes to XCOMM Manager for recording purpose. The IPC Manager is designed such that, for a launched service, there is no difference in serving requests from local node or remote nodes. An advantage of this is that existing services need not be modified in order to fit the operations with XBinder. When a connection of utilizing a service is to be closed, the local XCOMM Manager informs Service Provider to terminate all the processes associated with that service.

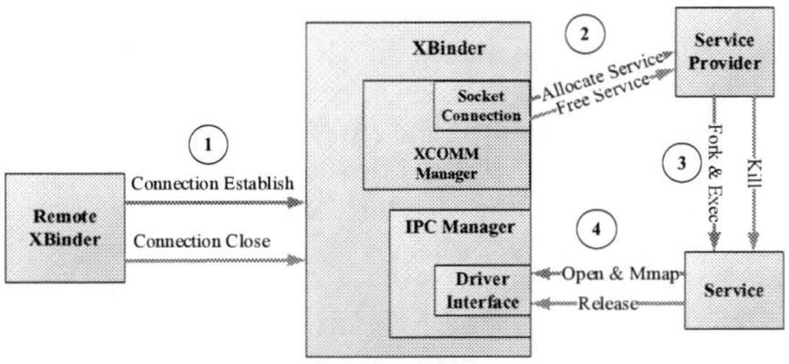

Figure 4. The steps in providing remote services

XBinder is implemented using C programming language with GNU library functions so that not only the required network operations can be realized using sockets without difficulty but also the implementation can be installed to work in both Linux and Android systems. The modification done to the components in Android is accomplished by using Android software development kit [1][2][4][5].

IV. EVALUATION

The evaluation of XBinder, including its functionality and performance, was conducted for the purpose of serving the proof of concept. A working environment of four nodes was set up, as shown in Fig. 5, in which two Wii sticks were connected to a desktop computer and serve as the controllers of user input devices [15]. In order to reduce the interference from possible yet unpredictable variation in the quality of network communication, wired Ethernet was adopted. The configuration of this environment is listed in Table I.

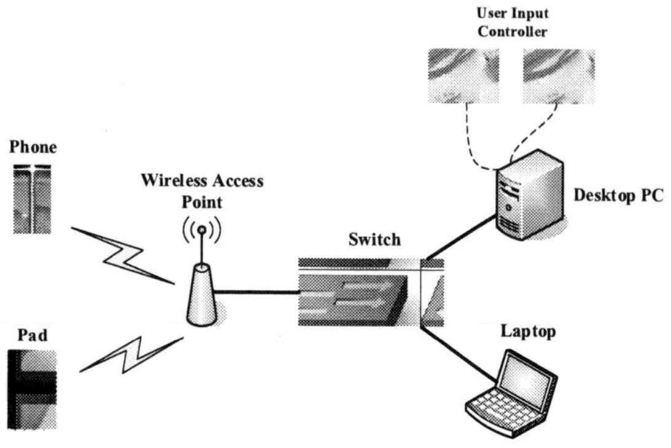

Figure 5. The environment for evaluating Xbinder

TABLE I. THE CONFIGURATION OF THE EVALUATION ENVIRONMENT

Node	Desktop PC	Laptop PC	Nexus 7	Nexus 5
CPU	Intel Core 2 Quad (2.5 GHz)	Intel Core i5-540M (2.5 GHz)	Nvidia Tegra 3 (1.3 GHz)	Qualcomm Snapdragon (1.5GHz)
Memory	4 GB	4 GB	1 GB	2 GB
O/S	Ubuntu 12.04	Ubuntu 11.10	Android 4.4	Android 4.4
Network	Wired	Wired	Wi-Fi	Wi-Fi
Devices	Wii stick	N/A	▪ Accelerator ▪ GPS	▪ Accelerator ▪ Vibrator ▪ GPS

In testing the functionality of XBinder, Fig. 6 shows the case in which multiple nodes were concurrently using remote services and Fig. 7 demonstrates the operations in the test. In Fig. 7, while the smart phone (Nexus 5) and the Smart Pad (Nexus7) were accessing concurrently the sensor service provided by the right Wii stick which was connected to the desktop PC [15], the Smart Pad is providing a remote service to the laptop computer [16]. The test conducted in this case verified the concurrent operations of multiple nodes (users), the IPC with Linux and Android systems, and the connection functions in peer-to-peer style.

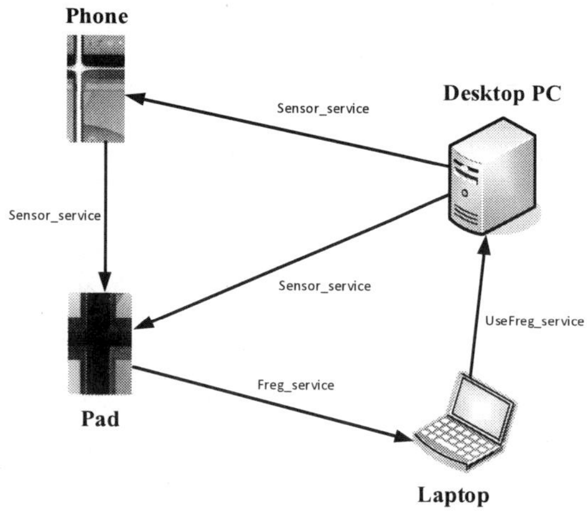

Figure 6. Multiple nodes concurrently access remote service

Figure 7. Applications concurrently access a remote service

The performance evaluation of this implementation was done by comparing the time of transmitting data blocks. Java RMI [14] was selected as the metric of comparison for the cases that involve remote communication, while the original Android Binder was the metric for the cases of local service. The transmission time measured starts from a data request is issued to the requested data is received, and for each selected data block size, 100 transmissions were separately measured. To avoid interference in measuring the transmission time, no file operations were involved. Table II lists the average time of transmitting data in different sizes, while Fig. 8 depicts the comparison of XBinder versus Java RMI. It can be observed that XBinder maintains similar performance compared with Android Binder and performs better than Java RMI in most test cases. When the data size grows larger, Java RMI shows better performance than XBinder. The reason is that XBinder needs two more copy operations during its operation in order to copy the data to the assigned address space.

TABLE II. COMPARING XBINDER WITH JAVA RMI

Data Size	Remote Communication		Local Communication	
	XBinder	*Java RMI*	*XBinder*	*Android Binder*
16 B	255	797	20	18
1 KB	555	995	21	19
64 KB	6095	6250	146	144
256 KB	23404	23132	531	516
1 MB	92788	90388	3669	3663
2 MB	185066	179943	N/A	N/A

Time Unit: micro-second (μs)

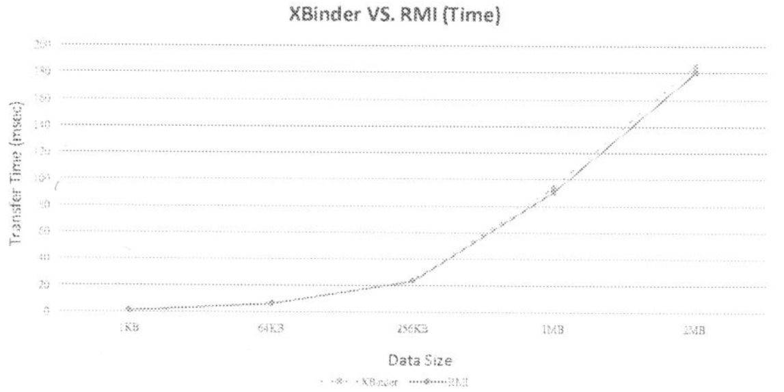

Figure 8. Performance comparison of XBinder with Java RMI

V. Conclusion and Future Work

Mobile platforms usually run applications with limitation on available resources. While sharing can be one solution for the issue of limited resources, cooperative computing across platform boundary is very beneficial for mobile platforms. In this paper, we consider cross-platform IPC to be the essential capability in achieving cooperative computing at application level and, as one demonstrative example, present XBinder to provide Android-based mobile platforms the functionality of IPC over network connections.

The design and implementation of XBinder are based on Android Binder which is the default IPC mechanism for processes running in Android-based platforms. XBinder extends the Binder Driver of Android to support network communication mechanism in order to form a multi-node working environment in which each node is an Android-based mobile platform. In addition, each node with XBinder installed can simultaneously function assuming both the roles of "client" and "server". The results of evaluating its implementation showed that a process can communicate with other process running on remote node over network connection effectively and efficiently.

An additional benefit of XBinder is that XBinder can be installed easily into any Linux-based platform to support cross-system IPC between Linux and Android systems. This is because Linux is the basis of Android and XBinder is built in the kernel space of Linux. Therefore, XBinder can run in Linux or Android system to provide a high-level abstraction of IPC mechanism and help programmers develop remote cooperative applications and services with ease.

Acknowledgment

This work is partially sponsored by Ministry of Science and Technology (MOST) of Republic of China (ROC) under the contract MOST105-3011-E-006-001.

References

[1] Android, "Android Interface Definition Language (AIDL)", https://developer.android.com/guide/components/aidl.html. [retrieved: July, 2016]

[2] Android Developers, https://developer.android.com, accessed on 2016-07-22.

[3] A. Gargenta, "Deep Dive into Android IPC/Binder Framework", Android Builders Summit, 2013. Available from: https://events.linuxfoundation.org/images/stories/slides/abs2013_gargentas.pdf.

[4] Android Studio, "Control the Emulator from Command Line", https://developer.android.com/studio/run/emulator-commandline.html, accessed on 2016-07-20.

[5] Android Studio, "Android Studio: The Official IDE for Android", https://developer.android.com/studio/index.html. [retrieved: July, 2016]

[6] C. Borcea, D. Iyer, P. Kang, A. Saxena, and L. Iftode, "Cooperative Computing for Distributed Embedded Systems", Proceedings of the 22nd International Conference on Distributed Computing Systems (ICDCS 2002), July 2002, pp. 227-236, doi: 10.1109/ICDCS.2002.1022260.

[7] D. K. Hackborn, "OpenBinder Documentation Version 1.0", http://www.angryredplanet.com/~hackbod/openbinder/docs/html/index.html. [retrieved: August, 2016]

[8] E. Kim, K. Yun, and J. Choi, "RSP: A Remote OSGi Service Sharing Scheme", Symposia and Workshops on Ubiquitous, Autonomic and Trusted Computing in conjunction with the UIC'09 and ATC'09 conferences, July 2009, pp. 318-323, E-ISBN: 978-0-7695-3737-5, Print ISBN: 978-1-4244-4902-6 doi: 10.1109/UIC-ATC.2009.79.

[9] K. Kumar and Y. Lu, "Cloud Computing for Mobile Users: Can Offloading Computation Save Energy?", IEEE Computer, Vol. 43, Issue 4, pp. 51-56, Apr. 2010, doi: 10.1109/MC.2010.98.

[10] K. Nakao and Y. Nakamoto, "Toward Remote Service Invocation in Android", Proc. of the 2012 9th International Conference on Ubiquitous Intelligence and Computing and the 9th International Conference on Autonomic and Trusted Computing (UIC-ATC'12), Sept. 2012, pp. 612-617, ISBN: 978-1-4673-3084-8, doi: 10.1109/UIC-ATC.2012.22.

[11] L. Iftode, C. Borcea, and P. Kang, "Cooperative Computing in Sensor Networks", in Handbook of Sensor Networks: Compact Wireless and Wired Sensing Systems, M. Ilyas and I. Mahgoub, Eds. Boca Raton: CRC Press, pp. 26-1--26-19, 2005, ISBN: 0849319684.

[12] M. Satyanarayanan, P. Bahl, R. Caceres, and N. Davies, "The Case for VM-Based Cloudlets in Mobile Computing", IEEE Pervasive Computing, Vol. 8, Issue 4, pp. 14-23, Oct. 2009, doi: 10.1109/MPRV.2009.82.

[13] M. Toyama, S. Kurumatani, J. Heo, K. Terada, and E. Y. Chen, "Android as a Server Platform", the 8th Annual IEEE Consumer Communications and Network Conference, Jan. 2011, pp. 1181-1185, ISBN: 978-1-4244-8789-9.

[14] Oracle Inc., "An Overview of RMI Applications", https://docs.oracle.com/javase/tutorial/rmi/overview.html. [retrieved: August, 2016]

[15] P. L. Wang, "The Design and Implementation of a Unified Hardware Abstraction Layer for Lunix Operating System", Master Thesis, National Cheng Kung University, Taiwan, ROC, 2014.

[16] R. Stones and N. Matthew, "Beginning Linux Programming", Wrox – Wiley Publishing Inc., 4th edition, 2007, ISBN: 0470147628.

[17] S. Bagchi, "Distributed IPC using Virtual Device Driver in Monolithic Kernel", The 18th IEEE International Conference on Embedded and Real-Time Computing Systems and Applications (RTCSA 2012), Aug. 2012, pp. 51-57, ISSN: 2325-1271, E-ISBN: 978-0-7695-4824-1, Print ISBN: 978-1-4673-3017-6.

[18] S. Ghorpade, N. Chavan, A. Gokhale, and D. Sapkal, "A Framework for Executing Android Applications on the Cloud", The 2nd International Conference on Advances in Computing, Communication and Informatics (ICACCI 2013), Aug. 2013, pp. 230-235, ISBN: 978-1-4799-2432-5.

[19] T. Schreiber, "Android Binder: Android Interprocess Communication", Seminar-thesis, Buhr University, 2011. [Online]. Available from: https://www.nds.rub.de/media/attachments/files/2012/03/binder.pdf.

[20] Wikipedia, "Android (operating system)", https://en.wikipedia.org/wiki/Android_(operating_system). [retrieved: July, 2016]

[21] Wikipedia, "Thin_client", http://en.wikipedia.org/wiki/Thin_client. [retrieved: July, 2016]

Sentiment Analysis using KNIME: a Systematic Literature Review of Big Data Logistics

Gary Graham
Leeds University Business School
University of Leeds
Leeds, UK
e-mail: g.graham@leeds.ac.uk

Roy Meriton
Leeds University Business School
University of Leeds
Leeds, UK
e-mail: cen5rfm@leeds.ac.uk

Abstract— **Text analytics and sentiment analysis can help researchers to derive potentially valuable thematic and narrative insights from text-based content, such as industry reviews, leading operations management (OM) and operations research (OR) journal articles and government reports. The classification system described here analyses the aggregated opinions of the performance of various public and private, medical, manufacturing, service and retail organizations in integrating big data into their logistics. Although our results show a promising high level of model accuracy, we also suggest caution that the performance of the solution should be compared in terms of the performance of other solutions. This work explains methods of data collection and the sentiment analysis process for classifying big data logistics literature using KNIME (Konstanz Information Miner). Finally, it explores the potential of text mining to build more rigorous and unbiased models of operations management.**

Keywords-Big data; logistics; sentiment analysis; KNIME; text analytics.

I. INTRODUCTION

Big data logistics can be defined as the modelling and analysis of (urban) transport and distribution systems through large data sets created by global positioning systems (GPS), cell phone and transactional data of company operations, combined with human generated activity (i.e., social media, public transport) [1][3]. The demands and requirements are literally changing on a daily basis with the innovation in technologies with smart computing and big data. All types of organization whose logistics operation functions in a big data environment will have to adapt to changing customer demands. At the same time, they will need to exploit the availability of big data technology to improve their process and operational capabilities [3]. Big data requires firms to have more technical and technological supports to handle the five V's of Big Data and analytics that is "*Volume*", "*Variety*", *Veracity*", "*Value*" and "*Velocity*" [2].

However, with the growth of big data there is privacy surveillance and data misuse challenges [3]. Organizations also face challenges around quality, comprehensiveness, collection and the analysis of data from various sources. Furthermore, big data also needs to be robust, accessible, and interpretable if it is to provide organizations with meaningful opportunities and solutions [2].

The purpose of this paper therefore is to explore the risks and challenges of organizations implementing "*big data logistics*" into their operations. Secondly, to investigate the opportunities that big data provides organizations with, to improve their logistics performance. This will be achieved through the text processing of 552 records containing industry reviews, leading OM and OR journal articles and government reports [4][7]. We will analyse the opinions of the performance of various public and private, manufacturing, medical, service and retail organizations in integrating big data (analytics) into their logistics.

In Section 2, the KNIME method of text processing is presented including dictionary building, term and inter-document frequency calculations and pre-processing procedures for sentiment analysis. Section 3 reports the results including tag clouds and graphical representation of aggregated sentiments. Then Section 4 presents the key findings from a classification experiment conducted using decision tree analysis on ten of the most occurring positive and negative sentiment words towards big data logistics. Finally, in Section 5, our key conclusions and potential scientific contribution are outlined.

II. KNIME METHOD

The KNIME text processing feature was designed and developed to read and process textual data [4][5], and transform it into numerical data (document and term vectors) in order to apply regular KNIME data mining nodes (for classification and clustering). This feature allows for the parsing of texts available in various formats (here we used .csv) as KNIME data cells stored in a data table. It is then possible to recognize and tag different kinds of named entities such as with positive and negative sentiment, thus enrichening the documents semantically. Furthermore, documents can be filtered (e.g., by the stop word or named entity filters), stemmed by stemmers for various languages pre-processed in many other ways. Frequencies of words can be computed, keywords extracted and documents can be visualized (e.g., tag clouds). To apply regular KNIME nodes to cluster or classify documents according to their sentiment, they can be transformed into numerical vectors.

Web of Science (WOS) and Scopus are powerful databases which provide different searching and browsing options [9]. The search options in both databases are the Standard Basic and Advanced. There are different searchable fields and several document types that permit the user to easily narrow their searching. Both databases sort the results by parameters such as: first author, cites, relevance, etc. The Refine Results section in both databases allows the user to quickly limit or exclude results by author, source, year, subject area, document type, institutions, countries, funding agencies and languages. The resulting documents provide a citation, abstract, and references at a minimum. Results may be printed, e-mailed, or exported to a citation manager. The results may also be reorganized according to the needs of the researcher by simply clicking on the headings of each column. Our search of "big data logistics" documents resulted in 552 records being retrieved from a ten year period from 2006 to 2016.

The described data was then loaded into KNIME with the File Reader node and processed. In this phase, only records in English language were collected. Language of the text is set to English and all texts that have different language values are filtered out, because English dictionary applied on reviews and posts written in other languages would not give results. Dictionary built for sentiment analysis of the phrase "*big data*" as it is used with respect to the term "*logistics*" was graded only as positive or negative. Scoring or sentiment analysis of the phrase "*big data logistics*" is done on the positive-negative level, therefore the phrase was analysed on the word level, giving each word associated with it a positive or negative polarity. For instance, efficiency would be scored positive whilst risks would be scored negatively.

For this task, a publicly available MPQA (multi-perspective answering) subjectivity lexicon was used as a starting point for recognizing contextual polarity [7], this was expanded with a big data vocabulary built from the authors previous papers [3]. The existing dictionary containing of approximately 8000 words is expanded to fit the needs for sentiment analysis in a way that initial portion of sentences are collected, which are separated into single words with Bag of Words processing. Unnecessary words, such as symbols or web URLs are filtered out and all useful, big data specific words are graded and added to the dictionary. For instance, "*veracity*", "*value*", "*volume*", "*variety*" and "*velocity*".

The records were analysed on the word level giving a positive or negative grade for a term connected to each phrase. Whilst text analytics of documents is usually accomplished simply with phrases counters and mean calculations, our analytics is frequency-driven. Two separate work flows were therefore built, one for calculating frequency based on a grade and category, and other one for positive-negative (sentiment) grading. These results are presented in Table 1.

TABLE 1 BIG DATA LOGISTICS SENTIMENTS

Table "default" - Rows: 110 | Spec - Columns: 6 | Properties | Flow Variables

Row ID	Term	Document	SENTIM...	IDF	TF rel	TF abs
Row1	value[POSITIVE[SENTIMEN...	"value sustaina...	+1	1.243	0.5	2
Row2	sustainable[POSITIVE[SEN...	"value sustaina...	+1	1.826	0.5	2
Row3	smart[POSITIVE[SENTIMEN...	"smart analytics"	+1	1.531	0.5	2
Row4	analytics[POSITIVE[SENTI...	"smart analytics"	+1	0.437	0.5	2
Row5	smart[POSITIVE[SENTIMEN...	"smart"	+1	1.531	1	2
Row6	analytics[POSITIVE[SENTI...	"analytics"	+1	0.437	1	2
Row7	moving[POSITIVE[SENTIME...	"moving"	+1	1.826	1	2
Row8	analytics[POSITIVE[SENTI...	"analytics"	+1	0.437	1	2
Row9	analytics[POSITIVE[SENTI...	"analytics"	+1	0.437	1	2
Row10	learning[POSITIVE[SENTIM...	"learning"	+1	1.079	1	2
Row11	learning[POSITIVE[SENTIM...	"learning against"	+1	1.079	0.5	2
Row12	against[NEGATIVE[SENTIM...	"learning against"	-1	1.531	0.5	2
Row13	large[POSITIVE[SENTIMENT]]	"large dynamic ...	+1	1.826	0.333	2
Row14	dynamic[POSITIVE[SENTIM...	"large dynamic ...	+1	1.362	0.333	2
Row15	volume[NEGATIVE[SENTIM...	"large dynamic ...	-1	1.531	0.333	2
Row16	analytics[POSITIVE[SENTI...	"analytics value"	+1	0.437	0.5	2
Row17	value[POSITIVE[SENTIMEN...	"analytics value"	+1	1.243	0.5	2
Row18	analytics[POSITIVE[SENTI...	"analytics dyna...	+1	0.437	0.333	2
Row19	dynamic[POSITIVE[SENTIM...	"analytics dyna...	+1	1.362	0.333	2
Row20	advanced[POSITIVE[SENTI...	"analytics dyna...	+1	1.826	0.333	2
Row21	support[POSITIVE[SENTIM...	"support"	+1	1.826	1	2
Row22	innovation[POSITIVE[SENT...	"innovation"	+1	1.362	1	2
Row23	analytics[POSITIVE[SENTI...	"analytics intelli...	+1	0.437	0.5	2
Row24	intelligence[POSITIVE[SEN...	"analytics intelli...	+1	1.826	0.5	2
Row25	open[POSITIVE[SENTIMENT]]	"open open risk"	+1	1.826	0.667	4
Row26	risk[NEGATIVE[SENTIMENT]]	"open open risk"	-1	1.826	0.333	2
Row27	analytics[POSITIVE[SENTI...	"analytics learni...	+1	0.437	0.5	2
Row28	learning[POSITIVE[SENTIM...	"analytics learni...	+1	1.079	0.5	2
Row29	analytics[POSITIVE[SENTI...	"analytics tradit...	+1	0.437	0.5	4
Row30	traditional[POSITIVE[SENTI...	"analytics tradit...	+1	1.531	0.25	2
Row31	success[POSITIVE[SENTIM...	"analytics tradit...	+1	1.826	0.25	2
Row32	analytics[POSITIVE[SENTI...	"analyticsconcer...	+1	0.437	0.5	2
Row33	concerns[NEGATIVE[SENTI...	"analyticsconcer...	-1	1.826	0.5	2
Row34	analytics[POSITIVE[SENTI...	"analytics"	+1	0.437	1	2
Row35	analytics[POSITIVE[SENTI...	"analytics"	+1	0.437	1	2
Row36	enable[POSITIVE[SENTIME...	"enable threats"	+1	1.826	0.5	2
Row37	threats[NEGATIVE[SENTIM...	"enable threats"	-1	1.826	0.5	2
Row38	benefits[POSITIVE[SENTIM...	"benefits"	+1	1.826	1	2
Row39	analytics[POSITIVE[SENTI...	"analytics"	+1	0.437	1	2
Row40	analytics[POSITIVE[SENTI...	"analytics"	+1	0.437	1	2

TF*IDF (Term Frequency*Inverse Document Frequency) [7] method assigns non-binary weights related on a number of occurrences of a word. Weighting exploits counts from a background corpus, which is a large collection of documents; the background corpus serves as indication of how often a word may be expected to appear in an arbitrary text. TF*IDF calculation determines how relevant a given word is in a particular document.

Besides term frequency fw,d which equals the number of times word w appears in a document, size of the corpus D is also needed. Given a document collection, a word w and an individual document $d \in D$, TF*IDF value can be calculated:

$$TF * IDFw = fw,d * \log \frac{D}{fwd} \quad (1)$$

Total score for each word is given by multiplying TF*IDF value with attitude of a term (Table 2). Attitude can have one of three values depending on the word polarity; -1 for word with negative polarity, +1 for word with positive polarity and 0 for neutral words. Final weights, which now represent attitude of each document, are grouped on the level of document and binned into three bins to give one of three final results for each term; positive, negative or neutral

TABLE 2. TF-IDF PROCESSING

Table "default" - Rows: 110 | Spec - Columns: 6 | Properties | Flow Variables

Row ID	Term	Document	SENTIM...	IDF	TF rel	TF abs
Row1	value[POSITIVE(SENTIMEN...	"value sustaina...	+1	1.243	0.5	2
Row2	sustainable[POSITIVE(SEN...	"value sustaina...	+1	1.826	0.5	2
Row3	smart[POSITIVE(SENTIMEN...	"smart analytics"	+1	1.531	0.5	2
Row4	analytics[POSITIVE(SENTI...	"smart analytics"	+1	0.437	0.5	2
Row5	smart[POSITIVE(SENTIMEN...	"smart"	+1	1.531	1	2
Row6	analytics[POSITIVE(SENTI...	"analytics"	+1	0.437	1	2
Row7	moving[POSITIVE(SENTIME...	"moving"	+1	1.826	1	2
Row8	analytics[POSITIVE(SENTI...	"analytics"	+1	0.437	1	2
Row9	analytics[POSITIVE(SENTI...	"analytics"	+1	0.437	1	2
Row10	learning[POSITIVE(SENTIM...	"learning"	+1	1.079	1	2
Row11	learning[POSITIVE(SENTIM...	"learning against"	+1	1.079	0.5	2
Row12	against[NEGATIVE(SENTIM...	"learning against"	-1	1.531	0.5	2
Row13	large[POSITIVE(SENTIMENT)]	"large dynamic ...	+1	1.826	0.333	2
Row14	dynamic[POSITIVE(SENTIM...	"large dynamic ...	+1	1.362	0.333	2
Row15	volume[NEGATIVE(SENTIM...	"large dynamic ...	-1	1.531	0.333	2
Row16	analytics[POSITIVE(SENTI...	"analytics value"	+1	0.437	0.5	2
Row17	value[POSITIVE(SENTIMEN...	"analytics value"	+1	1.243	0.5	2
Row18	analytics[POSITIVE(SENTI...	"analytics dyna...	+1	0.437	0.333	2
Row19	dynamic[POSITIVE(SENTIM...	"analytics dyna...	+1	1.362	0.333	2
Row20	advanced[POSITIVE(SENTI...	"analytics dyna...	+1	1.826	0.333	2
Row21	support[POSITIVE(SENTIM...	"support"	+1	1.826	1	2
Row22	innovation[POSITIVE(SENT...	"innovation"	+1	1.362	1	2
Row23	analytics[POSITIVE(SENTI...	"analytics intelli...	+1	0.437	0.5	2
Row24	intelligence[POSITIVE(SEN...	"analytics intelli...	+1	1.826	0.5	2
Row25	open[POSITIVE(SENTIMENT)]	"open open risk"	+1	1.826	0.667	4
Row26	risk[NEGATIVE(SENTIMENT)]	"open open risk"	-1	1.826	0.333	2
Row27	analytics[POSITIVE(SENTI...	"analytics learni...	+1	0.437	0.5	2
Row28	learning[POSITIVE(SENTIM...	"analytics learni...	+1	1.079	0.5	2
Row29	analytics[POSITIVE(SENTI...	"analytics tradit...	+1	0.437	0.5	4
Row30	traditional[POSITIVE(SENTI...	"analytics tradit...	+1	1.531	0.25	2
Row31	success[POSITIVE(SENTIM...	"analytics tradit...	+1	1.826	0.25	2
Row32	analytics[POSITIVE(SENTI...	"analyticsconcer...	+1	0.437	0.5	2
Row33	concerns[NEGATIVE(SENTI...	"analyticsconcer...	-1	1.826	0.5	2
Row34	analytics[POSITIVE(SENTI...	"analytics"	+1	0.437	1	2
Row35	analytics[POSITIVE(SENTI...	"analytics"	+1	0.437	1	2
Row36	enable[POSITIVE(SENTIME...	"enable threats"	+1	1.826	0.5	2
Row37	threats[NEGATIVE(SENTIM...	"enable threats"	-1	1.826	0.5	2
Row38	benefits[POSITIVE(SENTIM...	"benefits"	+1	1.826	1	2
Row39	analytics[POSITIVE(SENTI...	"analytics"	+1	0.437	1	2
Row40	analytics[POSITIVE(SENTI...	"analytics"	+1	0.437	1	2

In Table 2, the sentiment polarity, IDF, TF relative and TF absolute are each presented.

III. RESULTS

Tag clouds were initially used to visualise our initial findings. A simple tag cloud presented in Fig. 1 gives the most used words in the positive (left hand cloud) and negative used words (right hand cloud).

Figure 1. Tag clouds of sentiment

The attitudes towards big data were classified as "positive", "neutral" and "negative". Neutral grades can be avoided, and we accomplished this by removing grade bins and removing a bin for neutral grade. The results of the sentiment analysis are presented in Fig. 2.

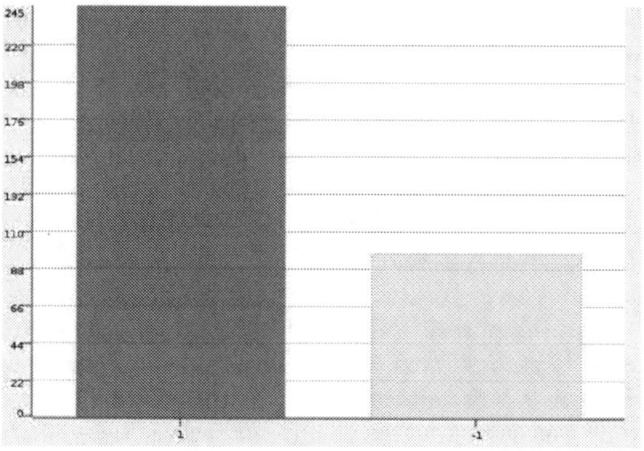

Figure 2. Aggregated sentiments

The positive and negative grades were aggregated for all terms associated with big data. In Fig. 2, it can be seen that sentiments are far more positive (245) than negative (95).

IV. CLASSIFICATION EXPERIMENT

In order to test the validity of the TF*IDF classification model, we ran a prototype experiment with the ten most common words extracted (i.e., those with the highest TF*IDF scores) (see Table 3 below).

TABLE 3. MOST OCCURRING WORDS

Positive	Negative
Agile	Security
Asset	Inefficient
Capability	Confusing
Competitive	Dark
Effective	Challenges
Enrichment	Failures
Optimization	Culture
Flexible	Liability
Intelligence	Complex
Sustainable	Waste

Then, using the TF*IDF decision tree learner/predictor approach, we tested the accuracy of the classification system (that we had adopted in differentiating the big data logistics sentiments). Our tests are presented in Table 4.

TABLE 4. CLASSIFICTION ACCURACY

Classification	TruePo	FalsePo	TrueNe	FalseNe	False No	Recall	Precision	Sensitivity	Specificity	F Measure	Accuracy	Cohen Kappa
Analytics	13	31	12	0		1	0.295	1	0.279	0.456		
Unspecified errors	2	10	44	0		1	0.167	1	0.815	0.286		
											0.268	0.096
	Mean	SD	Skew	Kourtsis								
FalsePo	0.9318	4.871	5.9587	35.7322								
TruePo	0.3409	1.9759	6.4517	41.8415								
TrueNeg	0.7955	6.708	-5.9538	37.1936								
FalseNeg	0.9138	0.8436	0.6156	-0.8109								
Recall	0.0645	0.2497	3.7281	12.717								
Precision	0.2311	0.0911										
Sensitivity	0.0645	0.2479	3.7281	12.717								
Specificity	0.9794	0.1116	-6.0956	38.4034								
F Measure	0.3709	0.1205										
Accuracy	0.8779	0										
Cohen's Kappa	0.0961	0										

Our model shows a predictive accuracy of 88% in classifying the textual data. We then tested using the hierarchical classification function in Knime the ability of the classification model to deal with the addition of features. From Fig. 3, we can see by feature 4 that the model peaked at 100% accuracy and then maintained this level of accuracy as features kept being added to it.

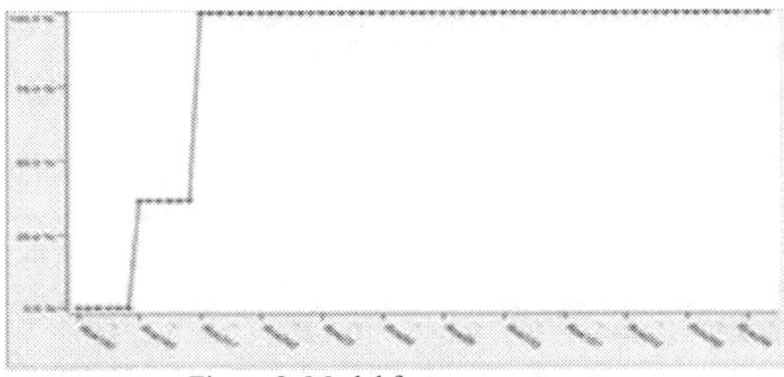

Figure 3. Model features accuracy

So, this initial test prototype of the model seems to have a high degree of accuracy and validity in dealing with sentiment classification. However, this is only a prototype of the decision model, so more robust testing will be needed in the future. Specifically, this will provide more stringent MPLA testing for variance.

V. CONCLUSIONS

In this paper, we have presented a novel approach to extracting key words and predicting "positive" and "negative" sentiments. We proved the validity of our approach by examining different classifiers that utilized twenty features extracted from the TF*IDF processing [7].

This model is only a prototype to highlight the text processing potential of KNIME [6][8]. In the future, we intend to build comparisons between a range of industrial and retail sectors. We see the role of KNIME potentially as an important mediating step in the framing and building of theoretical frameworks. Furthermore, it could be adopted to build much more grounded and unbiased coding systems of qualitative data.

Our work confirms that of Foss Wamba et al. [2] and Mehmood et al. [3], that is, we can confirm there is a growth in opinion on big data, not only at strategic and policy levels, but also with respect to its operational implementation. Thematic patterns and framework categories need building from our extracted key terms. Then, linkages and co-occurrences need exploring to establish a grounded approach for building theory from KNIME and other data mining tools [4[10]. As well as positive sentiments theoreticians need to factor in more negative and risk constructs to enable more robust and accurate model development. More in-depth analysis and more discrete modelling are clearly needed to assist in the implementation of big data initiatives [2].

REFERENCES

[1] E. E. Blanco, and J. C. Fransoo, "Reaching 50 million nanostores: retail distribution in emerging megacities," TUE Working Paper Series 4, pp. 1-18, January 2013.

[2] S. Fosso Wamba, S. Akter, A. Edwards, G. Chopin, and D. Gnanzou, "How 'big data' can make big impact: Findings from a systematic review and a longitudinal case study," International Journal of Production Economics, vol. 34, no. 2, pp. 77-84, 2015.

[3] R. Mehmood, R. Meriton, G. Graham, P. Hennelly, and M. Kumar, "Exploring the influence of big data on city transport operations: a Markovian approach," International Journal of Operations and Production Management. Forthcoming, 2016.

[4] M. Hofmann, and R. Klinkenberg, R, "RapidMiner: Data Mining Use Cases and Business Analytics Applications," Boca Raton: CRC Press, 2013.

[5] M. Hall, E. Frank, G. Holmes, B. Pfahringer, P. Reutemann, and I. H. Witten, "The WEKA data mining software: an update," SIGKDD Explorations, vol. 11, no. 1, pp. 10–18, 2013.

[6] J. Demšar, J. T.Curk, and A. Erjavec, "Orange: data mining toolbox in Python," Journal of Machine Learning Research, vol. 14, pp. 2349–2353, 2013.

[7] M. R. Berthold, N. Cebron, F. Dill, T. R. Gabriel, T. Kötter, and T. Meinl, KNIME: the Konstanz information miner, in data analysis, machine learning and applications (studies in classification, data analysis, and knowledge organization), Berlin: Springer, 2008.

[8] E. Archambault, D. Campbell, and Y. Gingras, "Comparing bibliometric statistics obtained from the Web of Science and Scopus," Journal of the American Society for Information Science and Technology, vol. 60, no. 7, pp. 1320-1326, 2009..

[9] K-N. Lau, L. Kam-Hon, and Y. Ho, "Text mining for the hotel industry," Cornell Hotel and Restaurant Administration Quarterly, vol. 46, no. 3, pp. 344-362, 2005..

[10] B. G. Glaser, and A. L. Strauss, The Discovery of Grounded Theory: Strategies for Qualitative Research,. New Jersey: Transaction Publishers. 2008.

Relative Importance of Key Requirements of Business Analytics 3.0. : An Empirical Study

Fosso Wamba Samuel
Department of Information, Operations and Management Sciences
Toulouse Business School, University of Toulouse
Toulouse, France
e-mail: s.fosso-wamba@tbs-education.fr

Abstract— **The main objective of this study is to assess the relative importance of the ten key requirements proposed by Thomas H. Davenport that will help a firm capitalize on business analytics 3.0. Drawing on data collected from 34 experts in the field through an online survey, the study assesses the relative importance of each requirement and proposes a set of new complementary requirements. Finally, implications for business analytics research, theory and practice are discussed.**

Keywords- big data; business analytics; analytics 3.0; requirements; empirical study.

I. INTRODUCTION

Big data analytics (BDA) and related topics have attracted a huge interest from both scholarly and business literatures [1] [2] [3], mainly due to their high operational and strategic potentials. For example, the BDA market that includes sales of related hardware, software and services was estimated to about $18.6 billion in 2013, representing an approximate growth rate of almost 58% over 2012 [4]. The worldwide market of BDA is expected to reach $125 billion in 2015 [5].

Recently, Thomas H. Davenport [1] pointed out that we were moving into the 'Analytics 3.0' era, an era in which 'big data will power consumer products and services'. Even if business analytics 3.0 holds the capability of transforming competition and thus competitive advantage, many managers are still struggling to capture its business value. In order to help a firm capitalize on business analytics (BA) 3.0, Thomas H. Davenport proposed 10 requirements. However, we know from the information technology (IT) innovation history that the acceptance of any given IT innovation within the business ecosystem depends on the change of the perceived benefits or risks related to the said innovation. Therefore, it is critical to assess the importance of the proposed 10 requirements as enablers of competitive advantage though the adoption and use of 'Analytics 3.0'. More specifically, the main objective of this study is to answer the following questions:

- What is the relative importance of the 10 requirements proposed by Thomas H. Davenport [1]?
- Are we missing some important requirements?

The paper is organized as follows. After the introduction in Section 1, we discuss some of the relevant papers for the study, with an emphasis on business analytics requirements, as well as a discussion on the 10 requirements proposed by Thomas H. Davenport [1] in Section 2. In Section 3, we present the methodology used in the study. In Section 4, our results and discussion are presented. Finally, we conclude the study and propose some future research directions in Section 5.

II. LITERATURE REVIEW

IT has been recognized as an important tool for firm optimization for high level competitive advantage achievement and realization. However, we know from the IT innovation history that the acceptance of any given IT innovation within the business ecosystem depends on the change of the perceived benefits or risks related to the said innovation. The Internet is the classic example. Indeed, developed in the early 1970s, Internet acceptance by the business ecosystem only happened in the late 1990s mainly because of the "change in the business perceptions of value based on the advent of fast, reliable and low cost hypertext markup language applications" [6]. Radio frequency identification, another IT innovation that is considered to be at the core of the so called 'Internet of Things' was expected to transform how firms conduct their operations [7]. However, recent studies on the topic showed that the adoption and use of RFID is slower that predicted mainly because of technological, data management, security and privacy, organisational and financing issues [7] [8].

In [9], the author suggests not starting a big data project unless a firm has a clear business objective to achieve with the adoption and use of big data. He further proposes to make sure that any firm that is planning to access internal and external data sources needs to secure this access (e.g., using Application programming interface, pricing in case of external data sources), and develop mechanisms that ensure of the data quality.

According to [10] : "big data isn't just data growth, nor is it a single technology; rather, it's a set of processes and technologies that can crunch through substantial data sets quickly to make complex, often real-time decisions". She argued that big data analytics will require an "infrastructure that spreads storage and compute power over many nodes, in order to deliver near-instantaneous results to complex queries".

In [11], the authors suggest that the realization of the high operational and strategic potential of big data in the healthcare context requires: a clear understanding of user needs and requirements of the various stakeholders of healthcare (e.g., patients, clinicians and physicians, healthcare provider, payers, pharmaceutical industry, medical product suppliers and government), followed by the alignment of this objective with big data technologies.

In [12], the author proposes the top 5 requirements that make big data work for all stakeholders involve in an adoption project, namely: (1) the necessity of having a good big data infrastructure, (2) no need to pre-plan, pre-think, or pre-limit your analysis, (3) the ability to analyze the data universe, (4) pre-built analytics to do analysis faster, and (5) easy to use with familiar, excel-like interface.

In [13], a scholar from the firm SAS highlights a seven steps strategy necessary for realizing the full potential of big data : (1) data collection from various data sources that are distributed across multiple nodes (e.g., a grid which processes a subset of data in parallel), (2) process that analyses the data, (3) management of data (e.g. data needs to be understood, defined, annotated, cleansed and audited for security purposes), (4) measure (e.g., measure the rate at which data can be integrated with other customer behaviors or records, and whether the rate of integration or correction is increasing over time). She argued that "business requirements should determine the type of measurement and the ongoing tracking", (5) consume. Here, Dyche [13] argues that we need to make sure that "the resulting use of the data should fit in with the original requirement for the processing", (6) store: for storage, Dyche states that "whether the data is stored for short-term batch processing or longer-term retention, storage solutions should be deliberately addressed", (7) data governance that includes the policies and oversight of data from a business perspective. For Dyche, "data governance applies to each of the six preceding stages of big data delivery. By establishing processes and guiding principles, governance sanctions behaviors around data. And big data needs to be governed according to its intended consumption. Otherwise, the risk is disaffection of constituents, not to mention overinvestment".

In [2], the authors defined BDA as a holistic approach to manage, process and analyze the "5 Vs" data-related dimensions (i.e., volume, variety, velocity, veracity and value) in order to create actionable insights for sustained value delivery, measuring performance and establishing competitive advantages. Therefore, it is critical to look at each requirement related to the BDA "5 Vs" to achieve expected business value.

III. METHODOLOGY

Given the exploratory nature of the adoption and use of big data and analytics for improved decision making and competitive advantage, as well as the scarcity of prior studies on these topics, a web-based survey was used to collect data among big data and analytics experts. The survey was designed using the 10 requirements proposed by Thomas H. Davenport [1]. Each requirement was measured using a seven-point Likert scale with anchors ranging from strongly disagree (1) to strongly agree (7). Also, all respondents were asked to specify any new requirement they believed is very important in achieving the expected business value from big data and analytics. The data collection started on the February 11, 2014 and ended on March 13, 2014. A personalized invitation was sent to 37 big data and analytics experts identified via LinkedIn specialized groups on big data and analytics. Of the 37 invited experts, 35 agreed to participate in the study. After a careful analysis of all responses, we found that 34 questionnaires were correctly filled out and appropriate for further analysis.

IV. RESULTS AND DISCUSSION

TABLE I presents the analysis of respondents by age, gender, and the level of education. From the table, we can see that the vast majority of the respondents are aged more that 50+ (18 (51%)), followed by 10 (29%) who are aged between 34-41 years old. Also, we have 6 respondents (17%) that are aged between 42-49 years. Only 1 respondent is aged between 26-33 years. The same table shows that 86% of respondents are males and 14% are females. Regarding the level of education, 97% of the respondents hold a postgraduate degree (Masters or Ph.D.), and only one respondent (3%) has an undergraduate degree, and thus showing that the panel of experts is clearly dominated by very highly educated people. Finally, the sample is composed of respondents with a range of profile and responsibilities' including: President or CEO (2), Assistant Professor (2), Professors (Marketing, MIS, Operations and Information Systems) (10), Assistant Commissioner (1), Director (e.g., Operations and practice lead, Purchasing) (4), Consultants (2), Associate Professor (4), Partner (1), Doctoral Researcher (1). It should be noted that not all respondents provided their title and responsibilities.

TABLE I. ANALYSIS OF RESPONDENTS BY AGE, GENDER AND EDUCATION

Age	
26-33	1 (3%)
34-41	10 (29%)
42-49	6 (17%)
50+	18 (51%)
Total	35 (100%)
Gender	
Male	30 (86%)
Female	5 (14%)
Total	35 (100%)
Education	
Undergraduate degree	1 (3%)
Postgraduate degree (Master/Ph.D.)	33 (97%)
Total	34 (100%)

TABLE II displays the analysis of respondents by business association. The vast majority of respondents are from the education sector (67%), followed by 9% from the professional, scientific, and technical activities, 6% from both 'Information and communication' and 'Other service activities'. Finally, the 'Administrative and support service activities', 'Electricity, gas, steam and air conditioning supply', 'Human health and social work activities' and 'Manufacturing' each represent 1% of respondents.

TABLE II. ANALYSIS OF RESPONDENTS BY BUSINESS ASSOCIATION

Administrative and support service activities	1 (3%)
Education	22 (67%)
Electricity, gas, steam and air conditioning supply	1 (3%)
Human health and social work activities	1 (3%)
Information and communication	2 (6%)
Manufacturing	1 (3%)
Professional, scientific and technical activities	3 (9%)
Other service activities	2 (6%)
Total	33 (100%)

TABLE III presents a summary of the important points related to the assessment of the 10 proposed BA requirements.

From the table, we can observe that all respondents, by and large, agree with all proposed requirements by [1]. All the requirements have an average rating higher than 5 and 8 out of 10 of the requirements have an average rating higher than 6. This suggests that the panels not only validate the proposed 10 requirements but also agree with their relative importance in capturing the business value from BA. Based on the rating, the top 4 requirements are as follow: "R1: Multiple types of data often combined" (1st), "R10: New ways of deciding and managing" (2nd), "R2: A new set of data management options" and "R6: Cross-disciplinary data teams" both in the 3rd place.

From the answers of the respondents regarding new important requirements that are missing from Thomas H. Davenport [1], we generated a consolidated list of four (4) high level requirements namely: 1. Corporate culture and capability, 2. Social issues (e.g., ethic, privacy, legal), 3. Analytics tools capability (e.g., data and results presentation, visualization) and 4.Talent management (e.g., training, skills). These are the four important requirements suggested by our panel members (TABLE IV.).

TABLE III. RESPONSES SUMMARY (NUMBER OF RESPONDENTS (%))

Requirements	Strongly Disagree(1)	Moderately Disagree (2)	Slightly Disagree (3)	Undecided (4)	Slightly Agree (5)	Moderately Agree (6)	Strongly Agree (7)	Total	Average rating
R1: Multiple types of data often combined	0 (0%)	0 (0%)	1 (3%)	0 (0%)	4 (12%)	7 (21%)	22 (65%)	34 (100%)	6.44
R2: A new set of data management options	0 (0%)	0 (0%)	1 (3%)	1 (3%)	5 (15%)	12 (35%)	15 (44%)	34 (100%)	6.15
R3: Faster technologies and methods of analysis	0 (0%)	0 (0%)	1 (3%)	1 (3%)	7 (21%)	10 (29%)	15 (44%)	34 (100%)	6.09
R4: Embedded analytics	0 (0%)	1 (3%)	1 (3%)	3 (9%)	4 (12%)	6 (18%)	19 (56%)	34 (100%)	6.06
R5: Data discovery	0 (0%)	0 (0%)	2 (6%)	1 (3%)	5 (15%)	10 (29%)	16 (47%)	34 (100%)	6.09
R6: Cross-disciplinary data teams	0 (0%)	1 (3%)	2 (6%)	1 (3%)	3 (9%)	7 (21%)	20 (59%)	34 (100%)	6.15
R7: Chief analytics officers	1 (3%)	0 (0%)	5 (15%)	4 (12%)	5 (15%)	12 (36%)	7 (21%)	33 (100%)	5.24
R8: Prescriptive analytics	1 (3%)	0 (0%)	0 (0%)	1 (3%)	9 (27%)	7 (21%)	16 (48%)	33 (100%)	6.00
R9: Analytics on an industrial scale	0 (0%)	0 (0%)	3 (9%)	0 (0%)	10 (29%)	12 (35%)	9 (26%)	34 (100%)	5.71
R10: New ways of deciding and managing	0 (0%)	0 (0%)	0 (0%)	3 (9%)	1 (3%)	14 (41%)	16 (47%)	34 (100%)	6.26

TABLE IV PROPOSED COMPLEMENTARY REQUIREMENTS

1. Corporate culture and capability	1.1. Ability to analyse situations instead of making decisions mostly on positional power 1.2. Ability to distinguish between issues that require qualitative vs. quantitative analysis 1.3. General ability to evaluate and analyse information (e.g., widespread numeracy in corporations) 1.4. Corporate culture must view analytics as a BUSINESS decision instead of a Technology issue 1.5. Corporate should couple data science with business judgment in order to leverage investment in analytics 1.6. Corporate success in deploying analytics should be to answer contemporary business questions with strategic impact
2. Social issues (e.g., ethic, privacy, legal)	2.1. Ethic is an important issue in data gathering and use for big data 2.2. Requirement to consider legal and social ramifications (e.g., privacy and ethic) of new analytic techniques and results when applied to big data (e.g., social media)
3. Analytics tools (e.g., data and results presentation, visualization,)	3.1. Requirement for good analytic tools with improved data and results presentation 3.2. Need to develop integrated analytic frameworks that allow dynamic evolution of problems solutions as problem spaces morph 3.3. Need for effective interchange standard for importing and exporting data 3.4. Advanced analytics means using and providing open data 3.5. Need for the integration of analytics tools with a knowledge management systems and strategy 3.6. Need for the presentation of the results in various formats that are understandable to senior decision-makers who are not numerate 3.6.1. Visualization is not enough, as they are also not comfortable with graphs: verbal, logical 'translations' are needed. 3.6.2. Need for improved analytics visualization tools (e.g., dynamic Visualization) 3.6.2.1. Requirement to have our data and plots constantly updated in real-time 3.7. Need to combine analytics tools with techniques for risk assessment and design of risk responses
4. Talent management (e.g., training, skills)	4.1. Need to define the concept of an "Analytic Scientist" or "Data Scientist" and how to educate him/her 4.2. Need for human skills development to need new challenges created by analytics

Regarding the corporate culture and capability, for example, our respondents believe that corporations should develop their ability to analyse situations rather than making decisions mostly on positional power, distinguish between issues that require qualitative vs. quantitative analysis, and evaluate and analyse information (e.g., widespread numeracy in corporations). Also, corporate culture must view analytics as a business decision instead of a technology issue and should couple data science with business judgment in order to leverage investment in analytics. Furthermore, corporate success in deploying analytics should be to answer contemporary business questions with strategic impact.

Regarding social issues (e.g., ethics, privacy, legal), our respondents believe that firms should start paying attention to these important issues. They estimate that ethics is an important issue in data gathering and use for big data. Also, firms should consider legal and social ramifications (e.g., privacy and ethic) of new analytics techniques and results when applied to big data (e.g., social media).

V. CONCLUSION AND FUTURE RESEARCH DIRECTIONS

In this study, we were interested by the assessment of the 10 requirements proposed by Thomas H. Davenport [1] in order to capture the business value from Analytics 3.0, followed by the exploration and the identification of complementary requirements. First, the study confirms the importance of all the 10 requirements proposed by Thomas H. Davenport [1] in capturing the business value from Analytics 3.0.

Also, a set of four complementary requirements was identified namely: 1. Corporate culture and capability, 2. Social issues, 3. Analytics tools capability and 4. Talent management. These requirements can be used by managers to direct their effort when exploring the potential of analytics 3.0.

While this list of requirements represents a starting point for future studies, the list may not reflect a majority of analytics 3.0 users across industries. In addition, the study only focuses on key requirements of business analytics 3.0. proposed by Thomas H. Davenport [1]. Future research needs conduct a robust literature review to identify an improved list of key requirements of business analytics 3.0. Also, it would be interesting to validate our final list of requirements using a case study or a Delphi study. Also, it will be fascinating to explore the importance of these requirements across various industries, cultures, and countries.

REFERENCES

[1] T. H. Davenport, "Analytics 3.0," Harvard Business Review, vol. 91, pp. 64-72, 2013.

[2] S. Fosso Wamba, S. Akter, A. Edwards, G. Chopin, and D. Gnanzou, "How 'big data' can make big impact: Findings from a systematic review and a longitudinal case study," International Journal of Production Economics, vol. 165, pp. 234-246, 2015.

[3] W. Samuel Fosso, A. Shahriar, K. Hyunjin, B. Mithu, and U. Mohammed, "The Primer of Social Media Analytics," Journal of Organizational and End User Computing (JOEUC), vol. 28, pp. 1-12, 2016.

[4] J. Kelly. (2014, 8 April). Big Data Vendor Revenue and Market Forecast 2013-2017 Available: http://wikibon.org/wiki/v/Big_Data_Vendor_Revenue_and_Market_Forecast_2013-2017, [retrieved: July, 2016].

[5] IDC. (2014, 8 April). Worldwide Big Data and Analytics Predictions for 2015. Available:

http://www.idc.com/getdoc.jsp?containerId=prUS25329114, [retrieved: August, 2016].

[6] G. Piatetsky. (2014, 7 April). Wikibon: Big Data market to reach $50 Billion by 2018. Available: http://www.kdnuggets.com/2014/02/wikibon-big-data-market-to-reach-50-billion-by-2018.html, [retrieved: July, 2016].

[7] B. W. Keating, T. R. Coltman, S. Fosso-Wamba, and V. Baker, "Unpacking the RFID Investment Decision," Proceedings of the IEEE, vol. 98, pp. 1672-1680, 2010.

[8] S. Fosso Wamba, A. Gunasekaran, M. Bhattacharya, and R. Dubey, "Determinants of RFID adoption intention by SMEs: an empirical investigation," Production Planning & Control, pp. 1-12, 2016.

[9] S. Fosso Wamba and E. W. T. Ngai, "Importance of issues related to RFID-enabled healthcare transformation projects: results from a Delphi study," Production Planning & Control, pp. 1-15, 2013.

[10] S. Saitta. (2013, 11 April). Big data requirements. Available: http://www.dataminingblog.com/big-data-requirements/, [retrieved: July, 2016].

[11] B. Pariseau. (2013, 10 April). Big data projects require big changes in hardware and software. . Available: http://searchdatacenter.techtarget.com/feature/Big-data-projects-require-big-changes-in-hardware-and-software, [retrieved: July, 2016].

[12] S. Zillner, N. Lasierra, W. Faix, and S. Neururer, "User Needs and Requirements Analysis for Big Data Healthcare Applications," Studies in Health Technology and Informatics, vol. 205, pp. 657 - 661, 2014.

[13] S. Norris. (2015, 10 April). Top 5 Requirements to Make Big Data Work for You and Me. . Available: http://www.datameer.com/company/datameer-blog/top-5-requirements-to-make-big-data-work-for-you-and-me/, [retrieved: July, 2016].

[14] J. Dyche. (2015, 9 April). The seven steps of big data delivery. . Available: http://www.sas.com/en_us/news/sascom/2012q4/big-data-delivery.html, [retrieved: July, 2016].

What is the Feasible Business Model in the Age of Big Data? Case Studies on the Business Models of Two Chinese Mobile Applications

Liang Guo, Mingtao Fu, Ruchi Sharma
NEOMA Business School
Mont Saint Aignan,France
email: Liang.guo@neoma-bs.fr;
fu.mingtao.14@neoma-bs.com
Lei Yin
Institut Superieur de Management et Communication Paris
email:l.yin@ismac.fr

Ruodan Lu
Cambridge University, UK
email: Rl508@cam.ac.uk
Sebastien Tran
ISC Paris, France

***Abstract*—The present day mobile application's pick-and-shovel business is not thriving, as the vast majority of developers make very little revenue. In order to gain insights into mobile application business model, we conduct longitudinal case studies on two Chinese high profile health-fitness applications. The results of our study show both applications have experienced three significant business model innovations, from the initial freemium, hardware-application hybrid, and open source-based coopetition. We discuss the impact of these business models on value creation and appropriation. We thereby advocate that in the age of Web 3.0, embracing open source movement in an application's business model is a smart move to turn competitors into collaborators and hence achieve a positive sum game. Our study contributes to the technology management literature by integrating the business model perspective with an analysis of open source. This also adds to the existing business ecosystem conceptualizations, which do not explicitly take competitors into account.**

Keywords- Mobile Application; Business Model; Coopetition; Open Source; Web 3.0.

I. INTRODUCTION

The mobile computing technology has opened up new frontiers to do business that was inconceivable years ago [1]. The recent trend of falling device prices, easy accessibility and usability of mobile phone has also spurred the higher adoption of the smartphone. From being a device that was previously being used for voice or text based communication, a smart phone now offers a wide collection of functions and utilities including social connectedness, business agility and personal well-being. Thus these devices now keep users connected, organized, and amused through a range of multi utility applications.

The great "anything, anytime, anywhere" mobile gold rush is on with an unprecedented number of firms engaged in methods to best monetize the high-value touch points between their applications and users. However, the mobile application's pick-and-shovel business is not thriving. Although a few savvy mobile application companies are like the golden eggs, the vast majority of developers find themselves with little revenue. There is a pressing need to understand how the business model of a mobile application creates value. In this study, we intend to fill in the abovementioned research gap by suggesting a new business model that may help a mobile application to create and appropriate enhanced value. We broadly define the business model as the one that describes the rationale of how an organization creates, delivers, and captures value, and how market players in a business ecosystem are linked through business model components [2, 3]. Unlike the previous studies in this field that have mainly focused on Web 1.0 and some on Web 2.0 technologies, we focus on the emerging Web 3.0 technologies highlighting how these technologies have triggered the business model innovation in mobile application business. We have conducted longitudinal case studies of two Chinese mobile application start-ups. Our study reflects the business model innovation of these firms from a freemium (free premium) to an open-source-based coopetition (collaborative competition) model over the period of 2011-2014. We found that the consumer mobile application market at present has been flooded with too many players hence making business extremely competitive. The traditional freemium business model creates a zero-sum, red ocean market in which most mobile applications struggle to survive. By nurturing an open source IoT hardware ecosystem, mobile applications can create a blue ocean market [4], enhance value creation by involving collaborators and even competitors in their business model, capture greater value from the expanded market horizon and achieve efficiency in resource utilization. We combine these insights with a theoretical development, resulting in propositions on business model's impact on value appropriation in mobile application business.

The results contribute theoretically to the technology management literature by integrating the business model perspective with the analysis of new technology trends. Our study also adds to the existing business model and business ecosystem theories, which we believe so far, have not included the open source movement and strategic alliances with competitors within their conceptual framework. We also advance prior coopetition studies [5, 6] by analyzing how the emerging open source IoT hardware ecosystem, that is a brand new governance mechanism, can benefit from the new features of Web 3.0. The remainder of this study is organized as follows. First, we review major theories in the field of business model, followed by the presentation of two longitudinal case studies. Thereafter, we discuss a set of propositions. Finally, we present our conclusions and suggestions for further research.

Two case studies will be presented in the second section. We will provide three propositions and conclude this paper in the third section.

II. EMPIRICAL STUDY

We conducted two longitudinal, qualitative case studies. A lack of prior theorizing about mobile application business model makes this kind of inductive case study approach an appropriate choice for a holistic analysis of previously unexplored phenomena, theory development and study of business network-related issues. Hence, to gain a deeper understanding in mobile application business model, we have conducted in-depth analyses of Gudong and Maikai, two leading health and fitness mobile application start-ups in China and elicited the sources of value creation from these descriptive case studies to explain the phenomenon and the real-life context of occurrence.

The cases are based on a variety of secondary data sources, which have been accessed, analyzed, and synthesized in order to gain an accurate understanding of the diverse facets of the evolution of these firms' business model over the period of 2011-2014. The main data sources include: 1) the venture capital investment reports of these firms, 2) historical web pages of the firms' websites; 3) news releases, 4) expert reviews and 5) user comments on major App Stores. To ensure the quality of the secondary data, we mainly rely on more or less direct interview data of the CEOs and co-founders of these two firms and subjective reports written by industry experts. The limitations of the secondary data should be acknowledged. These limitations include the difficulty of assessing the reliability of the data, as well as a lack of relevant data access. We intend to tackle (at least some of) these limitations through the actions outlined above and through data triangulation by gathering additional primary data. In this way, the validity of our understanding of the business model of these firms will be enhanced. The primary data includes four semi-structured interviews (30 minutes each) with one chief engineer, one project manager and two senior developers regarding revamping the firms' existing business models. The insights gained from these primary data sources complemented with secondary data have assisted us in interpreting the business models of these firms.

This multi-sourced case study approach is chosen as we believe that current research on mobile application business model innovation is still sparse. We treat a series of information sources like a series of experiments. Each source serves to test the theoretical insights gained from the examination of previous sources, and we thereby modify or refine them. Prior studies prove that this replication logic can foster the development of a new theory with less researcher bias and allows for a close correspondence between theory and data. Such a grounding of the emerging theory in the data is especially useful in the early stages of research in which it is difficult to develop a proper research question based on existing theories.

A. *Case Study 1*

Gudong Sport, incorporated by five running enthusiasts, started its humble beginning in 2009 in a south-west city of China with 1.53 million USD funded by a high-profit venture capital firm dealing in IT and mobile business. The first version of the application, released in August 2011, was a mobile pedometer to count the user's footstep based on the user's hip movement measured by the iPhone's inertial measurement unit. It was the first GPS-based running tracker in China. Just like millions of other mobile applications, irrespective of its rich collection of service offers the business model of Gudong could not go beyond the widely-adopted advertising-supported freemium model. As our interviewees pointed out, "the freemium version was so gimmicky that Gudong could not convert its free user base to its subscription model". Thus Gudong failed to solicit the desired customer loyalty and lost its customer base to other free applications in the extremely price sensitive mobile application business. In 2013, Gudong completely abandoned the freemium business model and embraced the centuries-long asset-sales business model.

But Gudong could not sustain its first move advantage in the wearables market for too long. The high profit margin of wearable devices attracted many new entrants. In a business characterized by fierce competition and lack of proper intellectual property rights regime, the application market is ruled more by players focusing merely on "imitation" than on "innovation". By late 2013, around 400 small and big manufacturers launched similar devices such as smart scale, wristband and portable activity trackers on Taobao.com (China's largest online store) creating a fierce price war. According to our interviewees, the average price of a smart wristband dropped to less than 20 USD from its initial price of 66 USD by spring 2014. The market share of Gudong shrunk quickly, which forced the firm to integrate and support several third-party devices in its application. Its business model was adjusted from "free App + devices sales" to a "sports social network" platform that could collect sport data from the devices made by different producers, integrate social elements and create an incentive mechanism.

The sports social platform of Gudong depended on one crucial hypothesis—a large amount of mobile phone users use Gudong application to manage their workout activities even though they may not necessarily use Gudong wearables gadgets. This hypothesis, as our interviewees stated, was flawed, "on one hand, the sport application market is highly fragmented with hundreds of producers who provide virtually the same application and closely similar wearable devices. There is no obvious advantage for most users to connect their non-Gudong devices with the Gudong application and on the other hand, the price of wearable fitness devices continues to decline". By mid2014, the market for wearables and mobile application turned into a red ocean with numerous players in a highly competitive market. Some business trends are clearly visible, including huge price drop in the wearable gadgets segment and hundreds of homogeneous mobile applications.

Gudong noticed a new business opportunity with most fitness and wearable devices not sharing their data with third party applications. Gudong has decided to create a new business model by opening its hardware framework to public access. It provides a variety of micro-sized modules that are highly customizable, for example a battery charger module, acceleration sensor module, heart rate sensing module, OLED display module and so on. The modular-design enables any third-party producer to create various wristbands based on the user's requirements by easily assembling the relevant modules together and slipping them onto a wearable rubber ring. This open source design offers far better options of customization to end-users. Gudong also provides its Software Development Kit (SDK) and APIs to third-party application developers. By opening the door to its competitors, Gudong intends to develop a collaborative wearable gear ecosystem that co-creates China's wristband market with its low-cost open source product. Gudong's business model has evolved from an asset sales based to a more open and ecosystem based business model. In 2014, Gudong partnered with Kangtai, one of China's largest life insurance companies to jointly develop mobile health metrics. Now, data collected by millions of wristbands will empower Gudong and Kangtai joint-venture to unleash some innovation into the connected health-fitness market. More importantly, Gudong's open source hardware becomes a social hub to support the growing community of third party developers. The collective intelligence co-creates continuous modifications along with new health-fitness algorithms that would have never been developed by traditional business models. As our interviewees state, Gudong expects that its new open-source-based coopetition business model can "unite wristband and fitness gear producers and fitness mobile application developers to build a strong ecosystem that will be able to co-develop highly intelligent applications to be built on top of the sensor data and thus make big data health metrics affordable and actionable". Also thanks to its new business model, Gudong has managed to substantially reduce the cost and development time in the rapidly evolving mobile IoT market. Thus by anchoring a collaborative ecosystem Gudong's open-source-based coopetition model creates valuable competitive advantage.

B. Case Study 2: Maikai Ltd.

Beginning with its humble origin in 2011 by three young entrepreneurs it was not until 2012 that Maikai launched its sports and fitness mobile application on China's leading mobile App Stores. The mobile application allowed users to share sport/fitness experiences on the social network, helped in community building (through online friends feature) and also offered an e-commerce platform dealing with the sale of fitness gears such as activity trackers and Bluetooth scales. Following the crunch of being a late entrant in the health-fitness application market, Maikai failed to differentiate itself from its competitors, and finally could not provide any appealing value to end customers. In late 2012 and early 2013, Maikai decided to follow Gudong to launch its own branded activity tracker and Bluetooth scale. Maikai successfully raised about 20 000 USD through a crowdsourcing website for its R&D projects. According to our interviewees, these low-cost products (about 10 USD) turned out to be quite successful and generated sufficient cash flow (about 1.4 million USD) to support the firm to expand. In the middle of 2013, the CEO decided to launch Maikai's own wristband but soon realized the market for wearable gears was turning red. With too many hardly differentiable products, the fierce price war made the CEO believed that Maikai could not compete with hundreds of wristband producers. Hence the firm had to stop the venture.

The firm made a strategic shift to a related but unexploited IoT segment called the "smart mug". After months of R&D in June 2014, the firm launched a wired mug "CupTime" that was meant to automatically log the hydration habits of its users throughout the day. The benefits of this 53USD device included not just to remind the user to drink water but also to eliminate the need to manually update the water intake in Maikai's mobile application "CupTime App". This smart mug used thermoelectric semiconductor material to convert the heat of the beverage to electricity. Evidently Maikai smart mug was an innovation in the market of health and fitness. As a result, Maikai received huge media coverage and its sales surged. With this new product, Maikai was able to leap over competitor pressure by expanding its own market horizon. However, Maikai was aware that the blue ocean for smart mugs would soon turn red because its product and application may not be able to lock in customers for too long. Also our interviewees stated, "CupTime's novelty could be easily imitated by its competitors as the innovation is incremental but not radical". For start-ups like Maikai, it is important to engage partners in order to enhance the value of its smart mug with partners' additional offers and to appropriate value from the locked-in customers through its smart mug ecosystem in which third-party applications provide complementarities. Hence Maikai started building its "health data ecosystem" by providing its smart mug SDK and APIs to other health and fitness gear producers and mobile applications that could automatically baseline the fluid intake according to the physical activity. Maikai also partnered with weather and pollution data providers to synchronize weather information and enrich the user experience according to different external environment condition. Through data sharing, Maikai's latest mobile application is able to offer complementarities in value by combining the core product in novel ways with partners' offerings, thus eventually resulting in customer lock-in.

Our interviewees predicted that the smart mug market became a red ocean in just a few months. Maikai decided to use open source hardware as a weapon against future competitors. They are designing a Smart Mug Kit (SMK) that provides the 'building block' components and free ROM source code to third-party mug producers and application developers or even consumers who need to build a connected mug with minimum skills and tools. The design will be based on the GNU Lesser General Public License (LGPL), so that anybody can integrate Maikai's SMK into their own products without being required by the terms of a strong copyleft license to release the source code of their own development-parts. As a modular platform, SMK will also allow third-party companies to easily create, alter, customize and fabricate their own-branded mugs with additional sensors and mobile applications. Maikai expects that its open source SMK will lower the price and help it gain a major market share so that it can become the hub of water intake and lifestyle data in an ecosystem around its open hardware kit. Maikai is building a brand-new open source hardware ecosystem in which it provides the hardware framework for developing advanced projects and kernel algorithms that might be beyond the available resource of any single start-up and involves many developers who might not collaborate otherwise. In addition, Maikai hopes its ecosystem will bring network effects and open new revenue streams through beverage sales and advertisements. Maikai's latest business model seems to be promising and it has received its very first round 0.8 million USD venture capital investment in 2014.

III. DISCUSSION

These two cases vividly present the visible trend of business model innovation resulting from different business models created in response to changing competitive environments. Having started from the famous "freemium" model, both mobile application start-ups evolved into a hybrid business model manufacturing IoT products and finally ended up embracing open source-based cooperation model.

There are two significant takeaways from these cases. First, being that continuous business model innovation as a business strategy can provide firms with the much desired momentum to success and stay in business. The second and the more prominent trend is the emergence of "open source based coopetition" as a successful business model. This can present newer and diverse ways of engagement through "cooperation over competition" and allow mobile application start-ups to generate value in ways that would not have been previously possible with conventional competitive strategies. The direct implication of this business model is to unearth unexplored blue oceans (i.e. new business opportunities) from the red ocean (i.e. over-exploited market).

In the following section, we formulate distinct propositions based on the insights of the two case studies. In particular, we take into account the characteristics of Web 3.0 to understand how the open source-based coopetition business model creates and appropriates value. We hope to enrich the fundamental business model theories through these propositions that answer our research questions on how a mobile application business model increases value creation by collaborating with competitors while allowing collaborative market players to appropriate value for themselves.

1. Freemium is no longer a lucrative business model for mobile application business.

Acknowledging well that free aspect of freemium applications are online traffic aggregators, yet there is hardly any scope for customer lock in with the freemium model. This was the cause of failure of Gudong's freemium business model. When it comes to the freemium model, even though mobile-specific ads are designed to be less obtrusive, with the screen space they occupy the ads only create major visibility issues to users. As every pixel counts on a 3~5-inch screen, users do not prefer viewing ad-banners which obstruct the screen space and distract them. Thus the free part of this business model usually results in compromising both user experience and potential opportunities to appropriate value from customers. In addition, the urgency to reach out to the customer segment and to improve bottom-line is seen as the primary requirement for most startup developers. Focusing too much on monetization through regular pop ups further jeopardizes user experience and reduces traffic to the application. This also affected the sustainability of Gudong's business model.

The premium part of Gudong's business model also could not materialize owing to a weak value proposition. The explosive rate of mobile application development has resulted in far too many nearly similar applications in the market. With increasing competition, it becomes extremely difficult for any market player to retain its customers because most users may prefer to switch over to a competing application that offers consumers the free option. With several free applications in the market, even the novelty of differentiated applications available in premium versions gets tarnished and it becomes difficult for developers to convert free users to a subscription model. As the two cases suggest, due to the lack of proper intellectual property rights regime in the software industry, novel features are prone to quick imitation by competitors. A part credit of this phenomenon goes to the open source movement revolution and technological upgradations like open APIs and mashups with which communication between applications has been rendered easy to allow developers integrate various functionalities with other applications to produce much richer applications. The unique features of open APIs and mashups are more eminent with the open boundaries principle that lowered the entry barriers of application development. Thus, open API and mashups are double-edged swords for mobile application start-ups. On the one hand, businesses have benefitted immensely from open resources by effectively expanding the business horizons and leveraging free technical upgradations through novel business propositions. But on the other hand, the freely available open knowledge stand the chance to hamper the ability of any novel mobile application to fully capitalize its innovation effort, as open source makes imitation so easy that innovation is no longer cost-effective in a crowded market. As the resource based theory states that "a firm's resources and capabilities are valuable if, they reduce a firm's costs or increase its revenues compared to what would have been the case if the firm did not possess those resources", it becomes critical for application developers to ascertain the choice of resources (i.e. innovation or imitation) to attain a novelty. For the extremely price sensitive mobile application consumers and in a market filled with free substitutable offers, imitation may work better for reasons of cost effectiveness. Given that mobile application business is ruled by players focusing merely on "imitation" than "innovation", it is not easy for any mobile application to achieve adequate returns on innovation through its novel, value-added features. In short, freemium business model may slacken the value creation potential of an application.

Proposition 1: Freemium business model does not appropriate value for a mobile application.

2. IoT products are indispensable for mobile applications.

Our cases illustrate that both Gudong and Maikai abandoned the freemium business model while adopting the new model that associates mobile application and IoT products. This "App+IoT" hybrid business model not only creates new revenue streams for an application but also serves as an effective mechanism to create greater value for customers. This business model is a successful way to harvest the monopoly rents derived from innovation. IoT products contain advanced circuitry, possess independent processing capability, and add mobility as these can be worn by the user or placed close to the body for an extended period of time. Significantly enhancing the user's experience, IoT products play a crucial role in the age of Web 3.0 because IoT technologies permit access of information from disparate sources and machines/sensors to make the Web technologies more valuable to its users. The advancement in IoT also allows machine to machine content sharing resulting in superior applications by adding the context variable to the content generated on the Web. The ability to closely link IoT products to a wide variety of services has emerged as an opportunity of success for any mobile application. The two companies in this study are good examples of this continuously evolving relationship between "smart things" and mobile applications as a fertile ground for innovation. Both the hardware and software of these two firms were interwoven and mutually supportive, and increasingly, these firms effectively utilized the combined potential in a networked context. IoT products and mobile applications designed for their own unique "efficiently connected" destiny create a novel business model that helps firms in redefining industry boundaries, avoiding cut throat competition and moving into a blue ocean in which demand for health-fitness gears is created so that there is ample opportunity for growth that is both profitable and rapid.

The case of Gudong shows that as an extension of smartphone, wearable gears become the dominant gateways to complementary business opportunity for a mobile application. The beauty of a smart gear is that it is sleek, easy to interact with, more socially acceptable in certain situations, and less cumbersome to carry, adding novelty in business model re-design. Wearable gears also extend the boundary of mobile applications by providing complementary functionalities about physical activities which could otherwise not be possible through mobile applications alone. Also wearable gears offer aesthetic benefits to users without obstructing their physical activity regime. Thus enhanced complementarities are offered by the combination of hardware and mobile application services. In addition, IoT products such as Maikai's smart mug can provide new, unique data collection methods supported with powerful processing capabilities of the mobile applications. This uniqueness turns out to be an efficient mechanism to lock in mobile application users. In short, embracing IoT products alters the boundaries of the over-crowded mobile application business and therefore,

Proposition 2: IoT products create and appropriate value for a mobile application.

3. Open source-based coopetition business model is a win-win choice in the age of Web 3.0

Beyond the "App+IoT" business model, our case studies show that both Gudong and Maikai chose the open source-based coopetition and are trying to develop an ecosystem in which they serve as focal firms while third-party IoT product manufacturers as well as application developers are engaged as coopetitors. There are several reasons that they adopt the open source-based coopetition business model.

Firstly, for both the firms IoT products alone could not guarantee a competitive position, making value appropriation difficult. Our cases show that, as more and more manufacturers are entering the growing consumer IoT business, what looks like a blue ocean will soon turn red with far too many players. Open source hardware can improve the firms' competitive position. By encouraging open source hardware innovation, Gudong has been able to offer stiff competition to the existing giants like Fitbit and Jawbone in the fitness activity tracking market, as it allows third-party developers to developer new algorithms for Gudong's open wristband. It is not only the sale of wristbands, but also Gudong's latest mobile application that seamlessly integrates with any third-party developed complementary functionalities that steer the monetary and strategic wheel of success.

Thus, through open source-based coopetition, focal firms like Gudong and Maikai can weave an ecosystem in which they enjoy a hub position. The collaborative ecosystem anchored on open innovation can help the focal firm to gain the valuable and intangible collective creativity added by the vast ecosystem participants that engages with the focal firm to create their own innovations and refurbish the same to the larger developer ecosystem. This novel business model helps the focal firm to accrue knowledge repositories, lower cost of innovation, reduce development time and thus achieve resource efficiencies. In addition, open innovation allows reuse of IoT data by third-party developers in other applications. Increasing returns from the same data service can be achieved at a lower cost of same knowledge creation or acquisition by a single firm.

Secondly, the ubiquitous connectivity of Web 3.0 makes it clear that the key resource in a Web 3.0-based business model is not the product (i.e. wearable gear or application) but the way in which the data services are implemented. With its power of context awareness, semantic Web technologies and superior business analytics, Web 3.0 has rendered immense strength to mobile services with free linking of disparate data sources, adding personalization through extensive social computing, and allowing businesses to better organize collective knowledge systems. There is an increasing need to access both structured and unstructured data, and derive better knowledge lessons from it by the enhanced data-mining and artificial intelligence technologies. Essentially, value is created by the fast acquisition of rich information and the generation of wisdom through business analytics. Therefore, the business model of any mobile application should focus on how to better deliver more open and intelligent web services with the capacity of enhanced data analysis and crunching.

The open-source-based coopetition business model enables mobile application to collect and aggregate information from different sources, making the same data exponentially valuable. Gudong represents a good example. Releasing its wristband hardware design, ROM and SDK to the ecosystem for free largely facilitated the production of wearables by third party manufacturers and stimulated the consumer adoption. As more and more wristbands were worn by users, huge amount of user behaviour data was collected and transferred back to Gudong, enabling the firm to develop value-added intelligent algorithms.

Thirdly, a big challenge to nurture big data services is that most IoT products work in silos with an IoT device (for instance, a property wearable gear) locked in with its own supporting mobile application. The open-source-based coopetition business model can overcome the "information silo" issue by encouraging open collaborative networks based on both insourcing and outsourcing of knowledge and expertise. Both Maikai's and Gudong's open source products are compatible with all smartphone equipped with Bluetooth and their APIs allow any third-party mobile applications to receive data from their devices. The firms gain value as their hardware platforms gain novelty of usability through new applications developed by the developer ecosystem. The platforms of these firms also become richer and they are able to counter competition and foster novelty from new entrants.

IV. CONCLUSION

To sum up, it is definitely not be easy for any mobile application start-up to enjoy the market leader position though traditional generic strategies and freemium business model. The open-source-based coopetition business model offers an out-of-the-box solution to substantially increase the size and the total value of the pie in collaboration with other market players rather than fighting for a larger share of a small pie.

Proposition 3: The open source-based coopetition business model creates and appropriates value for a mobile application.

Our study proposes several important managerial implications for mobile application practitioners. Firstly, open-source-based coopetition business model creates a collaborative ecosystem which differs from today's supply chain networks. This ecosystem is the coalition of self-motivated, proactive market participants that pursue a common goal and provide common network benefits. Open source eliminates the potential conflict that usually happens in the traditional supplier/OEM network and encourages participants to invest their resources. This non-conflicting business model increases customer intimacy, creates operational efficiencies, enables fast-paced innovation and allows all parties to reap rewards while pursuing individual interests. Secondly, the evolving nature of business model innovation driven by pervasive connectivity and open source movement has shifted the center of value creation from close ended, proprietary products / applications to more open and collaborative business ecosystems. Competitive advantage of a business model no longer lies in outperforming their rivals to grab a greater share of product or service demand usually through marginal changes in offering level and price, but in the creative use of big data resources and the real-time, intimate multi-sided interactions they make possible. This is because the open-source-based coopetition business model enables focal mobile applications to aggregate data from market collaborators and to provide the central processing power. These applications cannot be eliminated from the value-creation loop by competitors thanks to their possession of key data resources, which allow them to offer services more intelligently and create distinct barriers to competition. And finally, mobile application start-ups should not be wary of adopting the open-source-based coopetition business model for fear of diminishing value and differentiation. As revolutionary and far-reaching as the positive-sum business ecosystem is, the greater opportunity usually creates the greatest value for all ecosystem participants. No doubt, there are risks associated with open technology such as dilution of brand identity and loss of control of customer relationships. However, the risks of openness can be compensated by the value that the new, collaborative business model creates in a blue ocean environment with more connected products and intelligent applications. Indeed, the greatest risk is to be surpassed by risk takers who experiment with the business model innovation.

This study is a first step in attempting to understand the business model innovation issue faced by mobile application start-ups in a fast-changing digital market. We acknowledge the inherent limitations of our study. We are limited by our reliance on the information of only two start-ups. Our propositions may not be sufficiently universal and hence a larger sample is needed to re-examine their applicability as well as their boundary conditions. Further, as our study deals with the health-fitness category of mobile applications more inter-category comparisons on business model innovation are necessary to take the category idiosyncrasy into account. Finally, future large-scale survey and quantitative analyses on the impact of different business models on mobile application value should be implemented to test our propositions.

REFERENCES

[1] K. Ishii, "Internet use via mobile phone in Japan," Telecommun Policy, vol. 28, no. 1, pp. 3–58, 2004.

[2] A. Osterwalder and Y. Pigneur, "Business Model Generation," London John Wiley Sons, 2010.

[3] C. Zott and R. Amit, "The business model: a theoretically anchored robust construct for strategic analysis," Strateg. Organ., vol. 11, pp. 403 – 412, 2013.

[4] W. C. Kim and R. Mauborgne, "Value innovation: a leap into the blue ocean," J. Bus. Strategy, vol. 26, no. 4, pp. 22–28, 2005.

[5] D. R. Gnyawali and B. J. R. Park, "Co - opetition and technological innovation in small and medium - sized enterprises: a multilevel conceptual model," J. Small Bus. Manag., vol. 47, no. 3, pp. 308–330, 2009.

[6] A. Ritala, P., Golnam and A. Wegmann, "Coopetition-based business models: The case of Amazon. Com," Ind. Mark. Manag., vol. 43, no. 2, pp. 236–249, 2014.

AUTHOR INDEX

Alohali, Bashar 29
Badri, Sahar 23
Bazli, Behnam 17
Chalmers, Carl 34
Chen, Jing 91
Chen, Kai-Sheng 75, 81
Cheng, Jhe-Ren 11
Cheptsov, Alexey 63
Cho, Hyeisun 42
Choi, Jong-Woo 56
Choi, Seungjin 40
Dricot, Jean-Michel 45
Falchuk, Ben 50
Fergus, Paul 23, 34
Fu, Mingtao 69, 105
Graham, Gary 65, 96
Guo, Liang 69, 105
Hai-Han, Lu 6
Hennelly, Patrick 65
Hsu, Yu-Fang 1
Huang, Jen-Fa 11, 75, 81, 85
Hubain, Charles 45
Hurst, William 17, 23, 29, 34
Jeong, Youn-Kwae 56, 59
Kifayat, Kashif 29
Kim, Byungik 42
Kim, Jin-Tae 59
Kim, Jong-Won 56
Kim, Jungtaek 40
Kim, Tae-Hyung 56, 59
Lee, II-Woo 59
Lee, Il-Woo 56
Lee, Seulgi 42
Lee, Taejin 42
Lin, Tin-Yen 91
Lin, Wen Piao 1
Liu, Chun-Chieh 11
Liu, Jian-Hong 91
Liu, Te-Lung 85
Loeb, Shoshana 50
Lu, Ruodan 69, 105
MacKay, Michael 34
Meriton, Royston 65, 96
Mesterharm, Chris 50
Moon, KyungDuk 40
Nam, Hong-Soon 56, 59
Pagé, Jérémy 45
Panagos, Euthimios 50
Park, YunKyung 40
Sharma, Ruchi 105
Shi, Qi 17, 29
Shone, Nathan 17
Su, Ting-Ju 75
Tew, Bethany 65
Tran, Sebastien 105
Tsai, Pang-Wei 85
Wamba, Samuel Fosso 100
Wei-Hung, Chiu 6
Wen-Shing, Tsai 6
Yang, Chao-Ching 81
Yang, Chu-Sing 85
Yi-Lin, Chen 6
Yin, Lei 105